FORENSIC SCIENCE

for

Writers

A Reference Guide

PHILL JONES

ISBN: 1475267207
ISBN-13: 9781475267204

Table of Contents

About the Author

Phill Jones earned a PhD in physiology and pharmacology from the University of California at San Diego. After completing postdoctoral training at Stanford University School of Medicine, he joined the Department of Biochemistry at the University of Kentucky Medical Center as an assistant professor. Later, he earned a JD at the University of Kentucky College of Law and worked ten years as a patent attorney, specializing in biological, chemical, and medical inventions. After completing a Certificate in Forensics program at the University of Washington (Seattle, WA), he wrote articles on forensic science for *Forensic Magazine*, *Forensic Nurse Magazine*, *Law and Order Magazine*, *History Magazine*, *Today's Science*, and *All Points Bulletin* (newsletter of the Northwest chapter of the Mystery Writers of America). Phill also wrote four articles for the award-winning *Encyclopedia of Forensic Science* (Salem Press, 2008), and he wrote and taught the online course "Forensic Science for Writers" for about seven years. More than 350 articles of his appear in various publications with topics in the areas of science, medicine, history, law and business. For the education market, Phill wrote seven science books and two law books for Chelsea House. His science fiction/mystery novella, *Thin Ice* (2010), and numerous short stories have also seen publication.

Introduction

During February 2005, Education To Go launched my online course, "Demystifying Forensic Science: A Writer's Guide" (later renamed "Forensic Science for Writers"). For seven years, Education To Go offered the course through schools and organizations across the globe. The students included schoolteachers, law enforcement personnel (based in the United States and abroad), retired federal agents, attorneys, a professional tracker, and of course, many writers—both published and pre-published.

Why were these students interested in a survey course about forensic science and criminal investigation procedures? Many were simply curious. Writers often said that they wanted to acquire a foundation in the subject so that they could offer their readers realistic depictions of forensic science technology. A basic understanding about forensic science is helpful for a writer who plans to revise forensic science procedures to suit a plot. If a writer drifts too far or too often from reality, the storyteller may disrupt the suspension of disbelief for a knowledgeable reader. With a foundation in forensic science, a writer can decide how far he or she needs to wander from real-life forensic analysis and can evaluate reasons for doing so. Knowledge about the scientific and legal principles of forensic science also can provide a framework for a plot. When you need to construct a world for your story, it can help to have some prefabricated structure to build upon. Finally, the capabilities and limitations of forensic analysis can inspire plot twists and ideas for stories.

As we progress, we'll look at various techniques for analyzing physical evidence and survey numerous types of forensic specialists. From the code-breaking tricks of the cyber-sleuth to the traditional procedures of the autopsy room, we'll take a look at the strengths and weaknesses of forensic technology. Along the way, I'll point out historically significant investigators and technique invention dates for those who contemplate writing historical mysteries. We'll also explore fictional works that illustrate how authors successfully blended aspects of forensic science into their stories. And we'll cover common misconceptions about forensic analysis found in films and novels, errors that you'll want to avoid in your own writing.

CHAPTER 1

Laying the Groundwork

An objective of a criminal investigation is to reconstruct a crime, a pursuit that requires a combination of logic, observation of the crime scene, and an analysis of physical evidence. Forensic science is often defined as the analysis and interpretation of physical evidence for use in a court of law. Although forensic evidence can aid an ongoing investigation, it's important to keep in mind that forensic evidence may find its ultimate use in court. Practitioners of forensic analysis provide scientific information to the legal community. Consequently, a forensic scientist must perform his or her duties not only according to accepted scientific practices, but also in a manner consistent with legal standards.

The CSI Effect

CSI: Crime Scene Investigation seems to irritate genuine practitioners of forensic science. In Tampa, Florida, the Department of Law Enforcement's crime lab analysts passed around a list of the top 10 reasons why *CSI* is unreal. The complaints included:

- You can't get DNA results in an hour.

- It's unlikely that a Hummer H2 will be used as a crime scene vehicle.

- DNA data and drug data are not produced by the same instrument.

- It can take 40 people six months to do the work that one crime scene technician accomplishes in one hour on *CSI*.

- Lab facilities have bright, buzzing fluorescent lights, not moody blue lighting.

- Proper crime scene attire is Tyvek® gowns and latex gloves, not leather pants and high heels.

- You can't get DNA results in an hour!

Forensic pathologist Cyril H. Wecht wrote an article in *The Patriot-News* about forensic science myths concocted by popular TV shows.

Here's a sample:

- Laboratory personnel can examine the evidence as soon as it arrives in the lab. (Actually, months may pass before technicians have the opportunity to examine evidence.)

- One person can examine all types of evidence. (Forensic scientists specialize in a field, which is how a person becomes an expert.)

- A crime scene always yields fingerprints susceptible to testing and identification. (The recovery of sufficient fingerprint traces to run an automated search tends to be the exception, not the rule.)

- Testing for drugs and chemicals in blood is quick and easy. (Chemical testing can take weeks or months in a busy forensic science lab.)

Like Frankenstein's monster, misconceptions about forensic science have taken on a life of their own. Judges, prosecutors, and defense attorneys call it "the *CSI* effect." Nobody's happy about it. District attorneys worry that shows like *CSI* taint potential jurors with impossibly high expectations about how forensic science technology can be applied to solve a case in an irrefutable and easily comprehensible manner. It's more difficult to win convictions in cases that lack forensic evidence, prosecutors complain, thanks to the heightened reality of forensic science programs. Forensic evidence often does not come into play during a real trial, because the evidence was irrelevant to issues in the case or evidence was not available. A prosecutor may decide to present negative evidence witnesses, who assure jurors that it is not unusual for investigators to fail to find DNA, fingerprints, and other evidence at crime scenes. Some defense lawyers complain that jurors who watch *CSI* and similar shows place too much faith on scientific results, and may not consider that human or technical error could have compromised forensic analyses. Police investigators grumble that a skyrocketing demand by juries to see DNA evidence has increased the amount of evidence submitted to labs already facing substantial backlogs for DNA analysis.

The *CSI* effect also impacts writers. In his 2004 *Mystery Scene* article, Lee Goldberg dubbed it the *CSI*-ification of cop shows. Goldberg, whose TV writing credits include *Spenser: For Hire, Nero Wolfe,* and *Monk,* asserted that *CSI* is real to the people who develop TV shows. Consequently, if you want to write about crime on TV, then you must incorporate the *CSI* world into the story. He called *CSI* the new fictional reality by which network executives measure all other fictional realities for fictional authenticity.

Uses of Forensic Evidence During an Investigation

Forensic evidence can help investigators to decide whether a crime was committed and to establish the elements of a crime. This is sometimes called corpus delicti (body of the crime) evidence. For example, one of the definitions of burglary under Iowa state law requires that a person breaks into an occupied structure with the intent to commit a felony, assault, or theft. To establish that a burglary occurred, an Iowa prosecutor has three requirements, or "elements," that he or she must show: (1) someone broke into a structure, (2) that structure was occupied, and (3) the person who broke into the structure had the intent to commit a felony, assault, or theft. If investigators find toolmarks on a door that someone forced open, then this evidence indicates that a crime was committed and supports the "breaking in" element of the crime.

Forensic evidence can also help to establish a criminal's characteristic way of committing a crime. This signature of the criminal is known as the modus operandi. A serial killer, for example, might prefer a particular poison.

A vital role of forensic evidence is to establish an association between a crime scene, a victim, a perpetrator of the crime, and certain devices, such as a weapon. Most evidence uncovered in criminal investigations is used to establish these associations. As an illustration, suppose that police arrest a murder suspect and find a gun in his coat pocket. Ballistic analysis reveals that the gun had been used to shoot the murder victim. The gun links the murder victim and the suspect.

Forensic evidence can also support other evidence to establish an issue in a criminal investigation. Let's take the burglary case. Suppose that the owner of the house says that she was in her upstairs bedroom when she heard a stranger moving around the first floor. The toolmarks on the forced door are a type of physical evidence that corroborates the house owner's statement. Of course, forensic evidence may also disprove a witness's statement.

Forensic evidence can provide investigative leads. For example, ballistic analysis may reveal that a bullet was fired from an uncommon model of a gun. DNA evidence, fingerprints, and dental evidence may identify a prime suspect for a crime.

Investigators also use forensic evidence to elicit a confession from a suspect. According to one school of thought, confronting a suspect with incriminating evidence provokes an inner turmoil of self-generating guilt. The suspect relieves the turmoil by confessing. When confronted with incriminating evidence, a suspect may also decide to confess to obtain more favorable terms in a plea bargain. This use of incriminating evidence raises an important point. Forensic evidence can incriminate or exonerate. Incriminating (or inculpatory) evidence tends to establish the guilt of a person. In contrast, exonerating (or exculpatory) evidence can clear a person of blame. Although criminal investigations tend to focus on discovering incriminating evidence, that evidence can also clear a suspect.

Uses of Forensic Evidence in Court

Prosecuting attorneys can use four types of evidence to prove facts during a trial. Physical evidence (or "real" evidence) is an object associated with the investigation, such as forensic evidence. Examples of physical evidence include a murder weapon, a fingerprint, and blood.

Demonstrative evidence is a representation of facts. Examples of demonstrative evidence include photos and sketches of a crime scene.

Testimonial evidence is evidence given orally by a witness. Trials typically include testimony from people who are either lay witnesses or expert witnesses. A lay witness is a person who usually limits testimony to facts that the person observed. For example, a lay witness may testify that she saw a certain car speed through a red light. An expert witness, such as a forensic scientist, has special knowledge about a particular issue in the case. Expert witnesses can provide facts and also express an opinion in their area of expertise.

Documentary evidence can be used to show that a particular item of evidence exists, or to show the appearance of an item of evidence at a particular time. Types of documentary evidence include lab reports, photos, video pictures, and investigative reports.

A prosecutor can use these forms of evidence in one of two ways: as direct or indirect evidence. Direct evidence is evidence that proves or disproves a fact at issue in the case. Indirect evidence (circumstantial evidence) does not directly prove a fact at issue, but may establish a strong inference about the truth of that fact.

Suppose that a prosecutor wants to prove that John Widget shot a murder victim. If investigators found Widget's gun at the crime scene, then the gun is circumstantial evidence that John Widget had been present at the scene. It's only circumstantial, because someone might have taken Widget's gun and left it at the scene. But suppose that a witness testifies that she saw Widget shoot the victim. The witness's statement—testimonial evidence—is direct evidence: A judge or juror does not have to infer anything about the witness's statement to conclude that Widget shot the murder victim.

A criminal investigation can uncover physical evidence in a variety of locations, including the criminal's dwelling and the criminal's person. But it is the crime scene that often provides the richest source of evidence— from a discarded weapon to the fading aroma of cigar smoke. In the next chapter, we'll meet the people who mine the crime scene for clues.

A Few FAQ from the Course

In movies and on TV shows, a lawyer will try to prevent the other side from introducing evidence by shouting "I object." How does anyone know why that lawyer is objecting?

In real life, the lawyer had better give a reason for the objection. A U.S. judge can exclude evidence from a trial if the evidence fails to meet three tests: competency, relevancy, and materiality. *Competent evidence* possesses qualities that render it trustworthy or reliable. The competency of evidence can be determined by considering the evidence itself or by considering the person who is offering the evidence in court. *Relevant evidence* is evidence that has a tendency to make the existence of any fact that is of consequence to the trial more or less probable than it would without the evidence. In other words, relevant evidence relates to the issue at hand. *Material evidence* is evidence that is reasonably likely to influence the jury in making a determination that must be made. If it seems difficult to distinguish between relevancy and materiality tests, it's because the tests are very similar. Usually, a lawyer will raise an objection based on the grounds of relevancy, not materiality.

When is a photograph considered to be demonstrative evidence or documentary evidence? Is this distinction important?

The difference between demonstrative and documentary evidence lies in the purpose for presenting the evidence in court. For example, a photo showing an image from a crime scene reconstruction program demonstrates one party's view of the crime. A photo of blood spatter at the scene of the crime can be used to document the pattern of bloodstains. The distinction is important for the attorney who wants to get the photo before the jury. A crime scene photo should be supported by the photographer who can testify that the photo shows what the photographer saw at that time. The photo of a reconstruction may have to be supported by testimony about the validity of the program used to reconstruct the crime scene.

CHAPTER 2

From the Crime Scene to the Crime Lab

Before we cover specific techniques for analyzing physical evidence, we'll look at the professionals who uncover that evidence, and take a brief tour along the path from the crime scene to the crime lab. So, shrug on those protective lab coats and prepare to walk the grid.

First Responders and Lead Investigators

A criminal investigation can be divided into three phases. During the preliminary investigation, the criminal offense is determined, the crime scene is protected and processed, statements are taken, and witnesses and victims are identified. During the in-depth investigation, a crime scene may be processed further, new witnesses (or victims) may be located, and facts and evidence are gathered. In the last phase, an investigation can be concluded and prepared for prosecution, or a case can be suspended (a cold case).

The first responder to a crime scene will probably be a uniformed officer. This person has duties vital to the success of the investigation, such as detaining any victims and witnesses, attending to injured victims, and detaining suspects found at the scene. The first responder also must separate victims and witnesses so that they cannot discuss their observations. Furthermore, the first responder may discover facts, such as descriptions of vehicles or people, which must be transmitted to the police department for follow-up. Yet the first responder's most significant duty, at least from the forensic scientist's viewpoint, is to isolate the crime scene and protect the area until the arrival of the official responsible for the investigation.

When the detective who is the lead investigator of the case arrives at the scene, he or she will probably review the first responder's observations. The lead investigator also will want to know whether the first responder altered the scene, for example, by opening doors or windows, or switching lights on or off. The lead investigator shoulders a heavy burden. Responsibilities include determining whether a crime has been committed, deciding if the crime was committed within the investigator's jurisdiction, discovering all facts pertinent to the crime, identifying the perpetrator, locating and apprehending the perpetrator, aiding the prosecution of the offender by providing evidence of guilt that is admissible in court, and testifying effectively as a witness in court.

At the crime scene, the lead investigator may establish the boundaries of the protected area and perform an initial walk-through of the scene to develop a strategy for detailed examination. During the walk-through, the investigator can observe physical evidence and note locations and objects that require processing, such as areas to dust for fingerprints.

A variety of lead investigators thrive in mystery and crime novels. For example, consider Lynda LaPlante's Detective Chief Inspector Jane Tennison, Michael Connelly's Detective Harry Bosch, Donna Leon's Commissario Guido Brunetti, P.D. James' Commander Adam Dalgliesh, Martin Cruz Smith's Chief Investigator Arkady Renko, and Nora Robert's Lieutenant Eve Dallas. On TV, take a look at Detectives Robert Goren and Alexandra Eames (*Law and Order: Criminal Intent*), Joe Friday (*Dragnet*), Detectives Olivia Benson and Elliot Stabler (*Law and Order: SVU*), or agent Teresa Lisbon (*The Mentalist*).

Have you noticed how detectives in films can't wait to rearrange a corpse to search for clues or to find victim identification? A real detective will probably let a crime scene technician or a medical examiner inspect the body first. Moving the corpse disturbs evidence. For example, fibers from the perpetrator's clothing might be trapped within the folds of the victim's clothes. By the way, those folds in the victim's clothing may indicate not only that the killer dragged the body but also the direction of movement.

Crime Scene Specialists

So far, we've looked at the first responder and the lead investigator. Now it's time to consider the crime scene team who gathers the evidence. The size of the local police department can determine the composition of the team. In a small police department, the responsibility for collecting evidence may fall to the lead investigator. Large departments often have full-time forensic specialists who gather and analyze evidence.

The structure of a crime scene processing team varies considerably by location. In Washington State, for example, local authorities can request a Washington State Patrol Crime Scene Response Team (CSRT) after securing the crime scene. Available 24 hours a day, the CSRT includes crime laboratory personnel and detectives from the Washington State Patrol Criminal Investigation Division. Team members help local law enforcement personnel to recognize, handle, preserve, and store physical evidence, such as biological specimens, firearms, explosive residues, and shoeprints. Team members also record the crime scene and reconstruct the events that occurred at the scene. The Morristown, Tennessee police department's Forensic Unit is composed of a police detective who manages a team of 17 crime scene technicians. The forensic specialists collect evidence, photograph crime scenes, obtain fingerprints, and preserve evidence. In Miami, the Crime Scene Investigation Unit, which the police department calls "the real Miami CSI," has civilian Crime Scene Investigators who support criminal investigation activities throughout Miami. After securing a crime scene, police officers or investigators can request the services of CSIs. Members of the Crime Scene Investigation Unit arrive in vans or in a Mobile Crime Scene Laboratory, rather than Humvees as often depicted on TV. The CSIs record crime scenes with photos and sketches, collect and preserve evidence, and later, provide testimony during criminal court proceedings.

Writers should note these variations. If you plan to write a story set in a real location, and you're aiming for authenticity, then you'll want to study the local police department's organization. The Internet is a good place to start this research. On the other hand, if you don't care about authenticity, or you're setting your story in a fictional location, then the variety of organizational types offers many models to choose from.

Finding Evidence

"Lincoln Rhyme had always searched scenes alone. He let the Latents people do the print work and Photo do the snap-shooting and videoing. But he always walked the grid by himself."

—Jeffrey Deaver, *The Bone Collector* (1997).

We've assembled a team of experts who search the crime scene for physical evidence. Now your crime scene team is ready to burst into action. What do they do? This section will provide ideas about how your evidence experts can examine a crime scene. But first, let's consider Locard's Exchange Principle, which controls the approach to examining a crime scene.

Edmond Locard, a Frenchman born in 1877, provided criminology with one of its essential doctrines: Every contact leaves a trace. An encounter between two people may result in the transfer of hair or clothes fibers from one to the other. A criminal may leave a crime scene with traces of the victim and location, while the victim and the crime scene may contain traces of the criminal. The search for this trace evidence is an essential pursuit of the crime scene technician.

Here's another important point about the Exchange Principle: It dictates that crime scene technicians must wear clean protective garments to prevent contamination of the scene. Many fiction writers appreciate this fact. Take a look at Linda Fairstein's *The Bone Vault* (2003), for example. Notice how Detective Mike Chapman insists that assistant district attorney Alexandra Cooper cover herself with a lab gown, plastic gloves, and gauze booties before she can approach the crime scene.

We can divide crime scene processing into three stages: an initial search for evidence and possible hazards, documentation of the scene, and collection of evidence. The particular actions of crime scene specialists will depend upon the nature of the crime. Regardless of the crime, however, your crime scene personnel should perform certain basic duties.

An essential activity is to record the conditions of the site and locations of physical evidence. A mixture of photographs, video, sketches, and notes can achieve this objective. Typically, crime scene photos are shot in a series. Overview photos of the scene and surrounding area are taken from various angles, and physical evidence is photographed to show its location and position. After the overviews, evidence is photographed close-up. When taking pictures of small items, a photographer may want to include a measurement marker, such as a ruler. Typically, a crime scene photographer will snap pictures of the evidence as found, and then add a ruler for additional pictures. Why does this matter? A photo of an altered crime scene may not be admissible in court.

In addition to notes and photos, crime scene personnel may draft rough sketches that illustrate the essential information and measurements of the crime scene. Is your team high-tech? Some police departments use a computer-aided design program at the crime scene, which enables an investigator to diagram the site directly on a computer. Later, the investigator can use the information to measure distances and view the scene from different perspectives. High-definition laser scanning offers another recent advance for thoroughly documenting details of a crime scene.

A crime scene team might also perform on-site testing to decide whether to collect material for lab analysis. For example, the team may perform presumptive tests (tests that indicate that a fact is likely) for blood, semen, or chemicals, such as gasoline in a suspected arson. If firearms were discharged at the scene, then evidence experts will study the paths of bullets. Bloodstain patterns are also photographed and assessed on the site.

Crime scene personnel use a number of approaches in their systematic search for physical evidence. In the line-search method, a common procedure for an indoor investigation, the searcher starts at one end of the crime scene and walks directly across until reaching the opposite end. The searcher turns and walks back to the original end, looking left or right of the original path, and then moves to one side and repeats the walk. Sound familiar? Think about mowing a lawn. A spiral search method is used both indoors and outdoors. Here the searcher begins from the outer perimeter of the scene and moves inward in a circular path. On the other hand, a large room or an outdoor area may be searched by dividing the zone into sections (sector method). A grid method may also be used in large crime scenes or when searching for small items. In this approach, one or more investigators crisscross the scene. In this way, they search all areas several times. These types of standardized searches are what Jeffrey Deaver calls "walking the grid."

Collecting and Processing Evidence

After the location and position of physical evidence have been recorded, the evidence must be collected and preserved for examination in the lab and, possibly, for presentation in court. Preservation must meet the requirements of scientists and lawyers. From a scientific perspective, the evidence must be preserved to minimize changes, such as degradation of biological material. In addition, the evidence must be collected, stored, and handled in a way that prevents contamination, especially any intermingling of evidence from different sources.

One important legal requirement is certainty of identification. To be admissible in court, evidence presented during trial must be identical to the evidence collected at the crime scene. To thwart a successful challenge by a defense attorney about identification, an investigator who collects the evidence can mark it at the time of collection. This identifying mark connects the evidence to the investigator and the crime scene. For example, a murder weapon can be identified with a tamper-proof tag that provides the investigator's name as well as the date and place that the investigator acquired the evidence.

Another legal requirement is that evidence must be continuously accounted for from the time of discovery until it is presented in court. Anyone who possessed the evidence, even momentarily, may have to testify about when, where, and from whom they received the evidence, what they did to the evidence, and to whom and when they surrendered the evidence. A disruption in this chain of custody may provoke a judge to declare the evidence to be inadmissible.

Procedures for marking, transporting, and storing evidence vary among police departments. Here are a few basic principles.

- Evidence that can be hand-carried should be packaged in sealable bags or boxes to prevent contamination. The packaging also aids in the recovery of trace particles that the object may shed during transport.
- Particular trace evidence can be collected with a piece of tape, a forceps, or by brushing into a vial. What if trace evidence cannot be seen but is suspected of residing, for example, in a rug? Trace

evidence can be collected from the rug with a vacuum. Note that this will reveal what was there but not where it was located.

- Impressions, such as shoeprints, can also be collected. A material like plaster of paris can be poured into the impression mold to produce a replica of the item that made the impression.

- After harvesting the evidence, the crime scene team should seal containers to prevent contamination. Evidence seals or tape can prevent access to the evidence, and evidence can be stored in a place available only to those with proper authority.

Useful details about collecting and preserving evidence can be found in the FBI's *Handbook of Forensic Services* (2007), which is available at the FBI website. The handbook also offers suggestions for ensuring the safety of investigators who handle hazardous evidence. When crime scene investigators need to collect biological material, the possibility of AIDS is a genuine concern.

Crime Labs

In 1910, Edmund Locard opened a small lab in Lyon, France, and established the first police crime laboratory. Three men inspired Locard's innovation: Alexandre Lacassagne, Hans Gross, and Arthur Conan Doyle. Locard had studied with Lacassagne, a forensic medicine professor at the University of Lyon. Lacassagne promoted the application of science to the investigation of crime. German criminologist Hans Gross advocated scientific analysis to reconstruct a crime and advised police to carefully examine crime scenes for traces of blood and fingerprints. Arthur Conan Doyle inspired Locard by writing the stories of Sherlock Holmes. Many years later, in a 1929 article in *Revue Internationale de Criminalistique*, Locard credited Arthur Conan Doyle as second only to Hans Gross for influencing techniques of trace evidence analysis. Conan Doyle influenced Locard in another way: Holmes' Baker Street residence, which Holmes had equipped with scientific instruments, suggested a design for a crime lab. Locard pestered the Lyon police force until they granted the use of two attic rooms perched at the top of a steep winding staircase in the attic of the Palais de Justice, the Lyon Law Courts building. Although Locard had to buy his own equipment, the police did supply two assistants from the Sûreté Nationale, the plainclothes undercover unit. Locard's humble crime lab transformed criminal investigation.

The idea of scientific investigation of crime gained acceptance in North America. In 1909, Dr. Wilfred Derome, Director of Laboratories at Notre Dame Hospital in Montréal, studied with Professor Victor Balthazard in France. A professor of forensic medicine at the Sorbonne, Balthazard pioneered hair comparison analysis, forensic firearm examination, and other aspects of forensics. When he returned to Canada, Derome urged the premier of Quebec to supply funds for a scientific laboratory in Montréal. The Laboratoire de Recherches Medico-Legales was established in 1914. The first forensic lab in North America was a small room above the city morgue.

At the same time, Luke S. May, one of the earliest successful practitioners of scientific criminal investigation in the United States, founded the Revelare International Secret Service in Salt Lake City. Inspired by Conan Doyle's detective, Luke May combined methods of traditional investigation with emerging forensic science techniques. His agency assisted law enforcement officials, state prosecutors, and the general public. In 1919, Luke May—"America's Sherlock Holmes"—relocated his organization to Seattle, Washington. During the same year, chemist Edward Oscar Heinrich established a private practice as a forensic scientist by opening a lab on the ground floor of his home in the Berkeley Hills, overlooking San Francisco Bay. Like Luke May, Heinrich taught himself the necessary skills to reconstruct a crime, including examination of spent ammunition, hair, blood, and documents. Heinrich assisted the local police and members of the public, while promoting the adoption of scientific methods by law enforcement. Berkeley police chief August Vollmer, who has been called "the father of American policing," also believed in the importance of science to police work. He set up a small lab for the Berkeley police department and, eventually, he collaborated with Heinrich in criminal cases.

The first large-scale U.S. crime lab arose from a Chicago gang carnage. On February 14, 1929, Al Capone gang members entered a garage used by the Bugs Moran mob, lined up seven men against a brick wall and opened fire with shotguns, machine guns, and automatic pistols. A special coroner's jury investigated the St. Valentine's Day Massacre, and requested the assistance of Colonel Calvin H. Goddard, who worked with three other experts in a New York forensic science consulting firm, The Bureau of Forensic Ballistics. After analyzing the spent ammunition recovered from the Chicago crime scene, Goddard wrote a detailed description of the shooting. Impressed with Goddard's expertise, the Chicago law enforcement community asked Goddard to move to their city. A financier donated $125,000 to help Goddard set up a forensic lab at the Northwestern University Law School. Chicago's Scientific Crime Detection Laboratory opened in 1930, and boasted a small, but highly skilled, permanent staff: Director Goddard analyzed evidence from crimes committed with firearms, an assistant director specialized in chemistry and toxicology, and a second assistant director had expertise in fingerprints, typewriting, handwriting, and casts of toolmarks and shoeprints. Consulting staff included a fire expert, a forensic anthropologist, a pathologist, and a microbiologist.

National public crime labs became established in North America during the 1930s. As soon as the Chicago lab offered a scientific crime detection training program, FBI Agent Charles Appel signed up. In 1932, Appel proposed that the FBI establish a criminological research laboratory. That same year, the FBI's lab opened in room 802 of the Old Southern Railway Building in Washington, D.C., a room that had once served as a break-room for Identification Division personnel. Appel worked as the FBI's sole criminology laboratory scientist. In 1937, the Royal Canadian Mounted Police's Regina Crime Detection Laboratory opened its doors. Dr. Maurice Powers ran the one-man operation in cramped temporary quarters in the Regina Officers' Mess.

Public Crime Labs in England

For decades, Scotland Yard's Criminal Investigation Department relied on the assistance of independent forensic science advisors, such as pathologist Bernard Spilsbury and gunsmith Robert Churchill. During the 1920s, Scotland Yard gained an in-house specialist: forensic science enthusiast Sergeant Cyril Cuthbert, who used a second-hand microscope

---

and simple equipment to perform basic services, such as bloodstain analysis. In 1935, Scotland Yard's Division Laboratory opened at Hendon Police College with a pathologist, a chemist, Cuthbert as police liaison officer, a technician, a clerk and a cleaner. During the late 1930s, local police forces set up their own forensic laboratories. Eventually, the Home Office brought regional labs under its control, and established the Forensic Science Service. The organization changed radically in the 1990s. The Forensic Science Service became an executive agency of the Home Office and then transformed into a business organization legally separate from the government. For years, the Forensic Science Service® was the trading name of Forensic Science Service Ltd., a UK government-owned company, which operated independently from police services. With more than ten facilities in England and Wales, the organization served clients in both criminal and civil matters within the United Kingdom and abroad. However, in December 2010, the BBC announced that cost reductions would force closure of the Forensic Science Service. During early 2012, the Forensic Science Service ceased its evidence analysis services. Commercial labs are expected to fill the gap left by the demise of the world-class organization.

Today, U.S. public crime labs operate at many levels of government: federal, state, county, and municipal. Lab sizes range from facilities with a staff of several to over 100. Most crime labs function as part of a police department, but others are placed under the direction of the district attorney's office. A crime lab may have its functions combined with labs of the medical examiner or coroner. Some states have developed a system of regional labs that operate under the direction of a central facility. Take a look at Alabama's Department of Forensic Sciences, and you'll find a system consisting of a headquarters and district labs dedicated to specific forensic science disciplines. Virginia and Washington State have similar forensic laboratory systems. In contrast, Montana has one crime lab in Missoula that supports the state's law enforcement efforts.

In his book *Criminalistics* (2004), Richard Saferstein described a full-service crime laboratory. Basic services would include a Physical Science Unit to perform chemical tests and trace evidence analyses; a Biology Unit to examine DNA, blood and other bodily fluids, hair, and plant material; a Firearms Unit to analyze ammunition, firearm discharge residues, and toolmarks; a Document Examination Unit to examine handwriting and to perform paper and ink analyses; and a Photography Unit to examine and record physical evidence using specialized techniques, such as infrared, ultraviolet, and X-ray photography. Optional services provided by a full-service lab would include a Toxicology Unit, a Latent Fingerprint Unit, a Polygraph Unit, a Voiceprint Analysis Unit, and an Evidence Collection Unit.

Quite an outfit! Of course, not every state government can afford to build and maintain such a facility or to provide all of these functions among regional facilities. Consider this reality of budgetary limitations when you are describing a crime lab in your story. In real life, a police department may have to send physical evidence to the FBI crime lab for analysis. Many private companies also offer forensic science services to law enforcement.

Does your story's hero work in the private sector? If so, then your private detective might want to take advantage of forensic analysis services provided by commercial labs. Orchid Cellmark, for instance, offers a variety of testing services, such as DNA analysis. A private investigator might use a commercial service to establish a familial relationship, for example, in a paternity suit. This issue of relationship also arises in inheritance cases, in which a client attempts to prove a family connection with an individual to gain entitlement to an estate or other benefits.

The decision by local law enforcement to send evidence to an off-site crime lab has a significant consequence: The investigator must wait for the results. It's not only the shipping time that causes a delay; forensic tests take time to perform. Consider DNA analysis—a standard test in modern fiction. Orchid Cellmark offers a DNA Express service for law enforcement agencies. How long do you have to wait for this rush service? Based upon TV crime shows, you might guess that an investigator would have just enough time to gulp down a short latte before getting the results. The reality is that a five-day wait is considered an extremely rushed job; the standard turnaround time can run two to four weeks.

Summary

In this chapter, you've briefly met the professionals who process clues at a crime scene, and you've seen how investigators face delays in obtaining the results of forensic analysis from a crime lab. In a 2010 Office of Legislative Research Report for the Connecticut government, Jeanne Hayes summarized a survey of 34 state labs located across the country. Here are some of the results for turnaround times:

- Non-DNA tests of biological evidence rushed for a homicide case: 1 day to 115 days,
- Expedited DNA testing with an identified suspect: 2 days to 240 days,
- DNA testing in a property crime case: 20 days to 2 years,
- Trace evidence analysis: 15 days to 1 year,
- Fingerprint analysis: 1 day to 1 year, and
- Toolmark analysis: 2 days to 1 year.

If you plan to write a story featuring a fictional criminal investigator, do you really want your hero to deal with these delays in obtaining news about forensic analyses? You bet. Delayed information creates plot twists. Any investigation requires the investigator to make deductions based on assumptions and facts. Certain of these assumptions may be preliminary ideas about the nature of physical evidence. Forensic analysis may prove these assumptions false. So if you carefully trickle forensic test results into your story, you can force your investigator to change his or her perspective about the case.

A classic example of the delayed forensic results tactic is a case in which a drowning victim is discovered on an ocean beach. Was this an accidental death or a murder? The investigator searches for clues in the vicinity but only finds a red herring or two. Later, an autopsy shows that the corpse had fresh water, not salt water, in the lungs. The investigator now knows that somebody had transported the body to the beach.

The movie *Chinatown* (1974) provides a variation on this idea. Private detective J.J. Gittes learns that the drowned victim found in a freshwater riverbed has saltwater in his lungs. This revelation sets the detective on a new path of investigation. And, of course, audiences must rethink their ideas about the villain's identity. You too can keep your protagonist—and your readers—off-balance with these shifting kaleidoscopic patterns of evidence.

By the way, have you considered the character of your protagonist? Your story's hero may be a crime scene specialist or the lead investigator of the case. If so, you may want to make your character look brilliant. There are two ways to achieve this: dumb down surrounding characters, or make an impression on your readers by having your hero take unusual approaches to the investigation. The second option is clearly the high road and the preferred choice.

As an illustration, your investigator may look for evidence in odd places or search for evidence in unusual ways. Consider Jeffery Deaver's novel, *The Bone Collector* (1997). Here, Lincoln Rhyme advises Amanda Sachs to look up when she examines a crime scene; Lincoln once cracked a case by analyzing a hair that he found on a ceiling. On the TV show *CSI*, Zen-like Gil Grissom advised his assistants to acquaint themselves with the crime scene before making inferences about what they think that they see. Like Sherlock Holmes, Detective Robert Goren of *Law and Order: Criminal Intent* frequently used his sense of smell when he explored a crime scene. Think about fashioning your crime scene specialist or lead investigator as someone who inspects the scene in a distinctive (or even idiosyncratic) manner.

In the next chapter, we'll look at the clues that forensic investigators glean from bloodstains. We'll also consider a few cases—in fact and in fiction—solved with blood evidence.

A Few FAQ from the Course

Are federal crime labs mainly used by field offices for the FBI or do local law enforcement agencies rely on the labs as well?

The FBI does offer lab services to local and state law enforcement agencies. You can learn more about the FBI's crime lab at: www.fbi.gov/hq/lab/labhome.htm.

I plan to write a detective story set in the late 1800s or early 1900s, and I want to get ideas about the writing styles of this time. Is Sherlock Holmes the only example of a fictional scientific detective from this era?

Sherlock Holmes had company. Starting in 1907, Dr. R. Austin Freeman wrote short stories and novels featuring Dr. John Evelyn Thorndyke, whom some consider to be literature's first real scientific investigator. Freeman is also credited with creating the inverted detective story, in which the reader first learns the details of the crime and then follows the investigation. Around the same time that Thorndyke appeared in England, Arthur B. Reeve's scientific detective, Craig Kennedy, solved crimes in the United States. Kennedy, a chemistry professor, used scientific techniques and psychoanalysis to solve crimes.

CHAPTER 3

Blood Work

"Classification, identification, differentiation, individuation ... that's criminalistics in a nutshell."

—Jeffrey Deaver, *The Stone Monkey* (2002).

The concepts of classification, identification, differentiation, and individuation relate to potential links between the victim, the crime scene, and the perpetrator. *Classification* is the process of placing evidence into a group. For instance, an investigator finds a fiber in a safe that someone broke into. If that fiber is a hair—not a strand of rope or other type of fiber—then it belongs to the group of naturally-occurring filaments. Or, perhaps, a paint chip is found on a hit-and-run victim, leading investigators to search for a car painted cerulean blue. Although class evidence doesn't point a finger at a particular person, an accumulation of class evidence can link a person to a crime. Consider the case of Wayne Williams, a suspect in 28 killings, who was convicted for two murders. Georgia prosecutors linked Williams to 12 murders using microscopic examinations of 62 fibers, including dog hair and carpet fibers. In the fictional world, Jeffery Deaver's book, *The Broken Window* (2008), shows how an accumulation of class evidence can lead to a conviction.

Identification is a process of determining the physical or chemical identity of physical evidence. White powder is found in a suspect's pocket. Is it heroin, cocaine, or does the suspect stash powdered donuts in his pocket? Identification tests provide results characteristic of specific materials and exclude other substances. Basically, identification is a process in which material is placed in a restricted class.

Differentiation refers to the ability to distinguish among similar objects or sources. For example, a shoe impression is found at a crime scene. An investigator examines the heel and sole design and concludes that the impression had been made by someone wearing a shoe produced by Swifty Shoes and not another manufacturer.

Individualization extends the classification process to the point in which the material is in a class by itself. Individual characteristics are properties that can be linked to a common source with a high degree of certainty. Certain types of evidence provide an extremely high degree of certainty in identity: ridge patterns of fingerprints or a DNA profile, for instance.

Let's go back to the shoe impression example. Suppose that close examination of the impression reveals gouges and other wear marks that correspond to imperfections on the sole of the suspect's shoe. Arguably, these wear marks are individual characteristics that point to the suspect's shoe. Note that the presence of the wear marks doesn't prove identity, but they are persuasive. There's still room for error. And any possibility for error is an opportunity for a writer to mislead the reader.

The concepts of classification, identification, differentiation, and individualization (or individuation) are particularly significant in forensic blood analysis. In *More Chemistry and Crime* (1997), Richard C. Shaler described the historical progression of the forensic analysis of the chemical properties of blood. During the mid-1800s, investigators developed the ability to categorize a stain as blood—classification. Around 1900, advancements in medical science provided investigators with tools to determine whether a bloodstain was human blood (identification) and to tell the difference between blood samples of unrelated sources (differentiation). The 1960s saw progress in individualization—the ability to link a bloodstain with the person who shed the blood. These efforts to define a "blood fingerprint" became moot when DNA analysis appeared in the 1980s. Today, DNA profiling is considered to be one of the ultimate methods to link evidence to an individual.

The history of blood analysis can be summarized as three questions that investigators ask: Is the stain found at a crime scene blood? Is the blood-stain human blood? Whose blood is it? These questions can be answered by examining chemical properties of a blood sample. The physical properties of blood can tell a story, as well. We'll look at how forensic investigators examine these physical properties found in blood spatter.

A Primer on Blood Evidence Collection

At a crime scene, investigators may search for the presence of blood with a high-intensity light. An investigator who uses a high-intensity light source can detect blood in areas that have been cleaned. Diluted blood often leaves a brownish stain. Blood also can evade someone who tries to eradicate it by flowing into floorboard cracks, carpet padding, behind baseboards, and by residing inside drains. Blood is tough to get rid of.

Investigators may decide to use luminol, which reacts with blood to produce a faint blue luminescence that varies according to the amount of blood present. This sensitive test can detect bloodstains diluted up to 300,000 times, reproducing original bloodstain patterns on walls, clothing, and furniture that the perpetrator attempted to clean. You've probably seen this test in movies or on TV shows. As cool-looking as the luminol test is, high-intensity light is the first choice for detecting blood. A luminol solution can destroy chemical properties of blood and prevent conventional blood analysis.

At a crime scene, investigators can recover blood samples as fresh blood, spatters, smears, or flakes of blood. Fluid blood can be collected with a clean medicine dropper and transferred to a small vial or tube that is sealed to prevent contamination. Samples should be delivered to a laboratory promptly because liquid blood decomposes rapidly. Bloodstains can be scraped from the surface onto a clean piece of paper with a knife, scalpel, or spatula. Clothing that contains wet blood should be allowed to air dry. This type of evidence should not be placed in a plastic or air-tight container, because retained moisture promotes the growth of microorganisms that can destroy or alter blood evidence.

Crime scene investigators, police, and technicians know that blood and other bodily fluids carry the risk of infectious diseases, such as AIDS, hepatitis B, and hepatitis C. Your fictional investigators should be aware of these risks as well. Here are a few precautions that you may wish to keep in mind:

- consider any blood or bodily fluid infectious,
- place any needles or sharp instruments in puncture-resistant containers,

- keep any wound bandaged while on duty,
- wear double latex gloves, surgical masks, and protective eye wear when collecting and handling biological material or a corpse,
- always be on the alert for sharp objects,
- do not place your hands in an area that you cannot see while conducting a search,
- nobody working the crime scene should eat or drink,
- wear latex gloves, eye coverings, surgical masks, and gowns when attending an autopsy,
- and, yes, that last point means that you should not have your pathologist eating lunch while performing an autopsy.

Now that we've covered a few basics about collecting blood evidence, let's look at the questions that investigators ask about a stain: from "What is it?" to "Who are you?"

Plight of Forensically Aware Criminals

An article in the September 9, 2005, issue of *New Scientist* described tricks that forensically aware criminals use to avoid DNA detection. You can try, say the experts.

> For one thing, it is extremely difficult not to contaminate a crime scene, even by wearing protective clothing. Police officers' DNA is automatically excluded from the inquiry to avoid the problem of falsely accusing them of a crime. [Guy Rutty, of the Forensic Pathology Unit at the University of Leicester, UK] tested just how easy contamination is by asking a volunteer to walk around a sterile room and repeat a phrase.

> Rutty was able to retrieve the subject's DNA even though the man had been in the room for only a few seconds. Contamination occurred even if the subject was wearing a face mask of the kind used by crime scene investigators.

The article closes with a challenge from Peter Bull, a forensic sedimentologist at the University of Oxford: "A forensically savvy criminal might set [investigators] on a false trail initially, but that's the best he can hope for, he says. 'If you want to commit the perfect murder there's one thing I'll ask you,' he says. 'Do you feel lucky, punk?'"

Blood Classification (Is It Blood?)

How can an investigator tell if a stain is blood? Color is a poor indicator. The appearance of blood changes as it dries and ages: Red transforms to brown and then to greenish-yellow colors. By the late 19th century, scientists had devised tests for blood with chemical indicators. The Dutch scientist J. Van Deen developed a blood test using guaiac, a resinous substance obtained from a West Indian shrub. The extract contains a phenol (alpha-guaiaconic acid) that is converted to a blue-colored compound in the presence of hemoglobin, the protein in red blood cells that transports oxygen. Christian Friedrich Schönbein, a German scientist, invented another approach when he discovered that hemoglobin oxidizes hydrogen peroxide to produce foam. Later-developed tests were also based upon the observation that hemoglobin can accelerate the oxidation of certain organic compounds.

These simple methods are considered to be presumptive tests because they are not specific for blood. That is, the tests can give a false positive result. For example, the Kastle-Meyer test uses phenolphthalein as a color indicator. When a bloodstain, phenolphthalein reagent, and hydrogen peroxide are mixed, hemoglobin will cause the formation of a pink or deep rose color. However, a similar reaction will be observed with constituents of potatoes or horseradish. As mentioned above, another blood test uses luminol. One limitation of the test is that luminol can give a false positive result, for example, if substances containing copper or certain vegetable materials are present. Investigators also use microcrystal tests to identify a stain as blood. Two popular microcrystalline tests are the Takayama and Teichmann tests. In these tests, a sample of the stain is mixed with chemicals that produce characteristic crystals of hemoglobin derivatives if blood is present. Rust and other contaminants may interfere with these tests.

Blood Identification (Is It Human Blood?)

During the early 1880s, Dr. John Watson met Sherlock Holmes in a chemical laboratory of a London teaching hospital. In Arthur Conan Doyle's *A Study in Scarlet* (1887), the great detective lectured the doctor on the problem of stains found on a criminal suspect. Are the stains mud, blood, rust, or fruit? This is a question, he said, that has puzzled many an expert because there was no reliable test. The detective dismissed the "old guaiacum test" as uncertain and inferior to the new Sherlock Holmes blood-detection method. "Had this test been invented," Holmes boasted, "there are hundreds of men now walking the earth who would long ago have paid the penalty of their crimes."

The characteristically immodest and enthusiastic Holmes overlooked a significant problem that his new test would not cure. Suspects found with fresh bloodstains on their persons could always maintain that the stains came from slaughtering an animal or handling meat. Police could not disprove these claims; scientists could not distinguish between animal and human blood. Early studies in the field of immunology provided a method for detecting *human* blood.

In 1900, Paul Uhlenhuth, assistant professor at the Institute of Hygiene at the University of Greifswald, performed experiments in which he injected hen's blood into rabbits. He found that the serum of injected rabbits precipitated proteins in hen's blood, but caused no reaction with blood from cows, horses, sheep, or pigs. Uhlenhuth concluded that the blood of different animals had one or more distinctive proteins. Eventually, he proved that he could use serums from various animals to distinguish human from animal blood. He soon applied his new "precipitin test" in a criminal investigation.

After two children were murdered on the Baltic Island of Rügen in 1901, the police arrested a journeyman carpenter named Ludwig Tessnow. An examination of the suspect's wardrobe revealed that some items contained barely dried spots. Tessnow claimed that these spots were cattle blood or a wood stain. The police sent Uhlenhuth two packages of Tessnow's clothing. After examining nearly 100 stains with presumptive blood tests, Uhlenhuth used his precipitin test and identified human bloodstains on Tessnow's jacket, pants, vest, hat, and shirt.

The modern precipitin test is still based on the reaction between human proteins in a blood sample and human antiserum. Human antiserum can be obtained by injecting rabbits with human blood. The rabbit reacts to the presence of foreign human proteins by producing antibodies that bind with these human blood proteins. Rabbit blood is then collected and serum is prepared that contains anti-human antibodies: "human antiserum." In one type of precipitin test, the forensic scientist layers an extract of the suspected stain on top of human antiserum in a thin test tube. The formation of a cloudy ring at the interface of the two layers indicates that the sample contains human proteins. The precipitin test can also be performed in a gel matrix instead of a test tube. In one such gel diffusion test, the extracted stain and human antiserum are placed in holes at opposite ends of a plate coated with a gelatinous substance. The two liquids diffuse toward each other, and a precipitate forms where they meet if the stain contained human blood. Human bloodstains dried for 10 years or more can still give a positive precipitin test.

Blood Differentiation (Blood Typing)

"'No less certain is the fact that human blood differs from the blood of animals, that in faint variations the blood of no two people is alike . . . .'"
—Craig Kennedy in Arthur B. Reeve's *The Film Mystery* (1921).

Around the same time that Paul Uhlenhuth was inventing his precipitin test, Karl Landsteiner, assistant professor at the Institute of Pathology and Anatomy in Vienna, discovered blood types. He took blood samples from six people, centrifuged the samples to separate serum from red blood cells, and then mixed red blood cells and serum samples from different people. In certain mixtures, the serum seemed to attract the red blood cells, causing the cells to clump together, whereas this reaction did not occur in other mixtures. He labeled the two blood types A and B. Soon, he found a third blood type that showed characteristics of both A and B, and he called this C (later renamed type O). A year later, an assistant discovered another type of blood that did not cause aggregation of either type A or type B blood. This one was called AB, the fourth major blood group.

We know now that, in the ABO system, blood type is determined by the presence or absence of A antigens and B antigens on red blood cells. An antigen is a molecule—typically a protein—that stimulates the production of antibodies. Antibodies are proteins that bind with the antigen. If an individual is type A, then that person has red blood cells that have A antigens located on the red blood cell surface. Similarly, a type B person has red blood cells with B antigens, whereas a type AB person has red blood cells with both A and B antigens. Type O persons have neither A nor B antigens on the red blood cells.

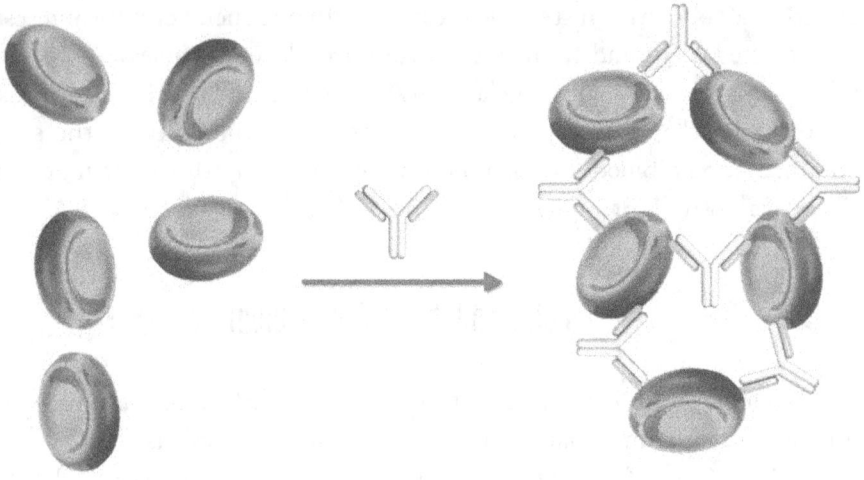

Figure 3.1. Antibodies cause agglutination of red blood cells. For example, anti-A antibodies bind with red blood cells bearing A antigens and force the blood cells to aggregate.

An anti-A antibody binds with red blood cells that carry A antigens. Since one antibody can bind at least two antigens, an anti-A antibody can bind with A antigens on two red blood cells. A collection of anti-A antibodies can create a network of cross-linked red blood cells; the red blood cells aggregate and form a clump of cells. Blood typing takes advantage of these antibody-antigen reactions. Anti-A antibodies cause clumping, or "agglutination," of type A red blood cells, anti-B antibodies agglutinate type B blood, both types of antibodies agglutinate AB blood, and neither type of antibody will agglutinate type O blood. By the way, A antigens and B antigens can be detected in very old tissues. Scientists have detected ABO antigens in tissue from 4000- to 5000-year-old mummies. Of course, if your story's villain is a mummy, then its blood type is probably the least of your hero's worries.

Table 3.1. Blood typing.

Determination of Blood Type		
Reaction with anti-A antibody	Reaction with anti-B antibody	Conclusion
Agglutination	No agglutination	Type A
No agglutination	Agglutination	Type B
Agglutination	Agglutination	Type AB
No agglutination	No agglutination	Type O

The frequency of these blood groups varies by race, ethnicity, and region. In the United States, the overall distribution of blood groups is approximately: O-43%, A-42%, B-12%, and AB-3%. Suppose that a bloodstain is found at the scene of a murder. Analysis reveals that the victim has type A blood, whereas the blood in the bloodstain was shed by someone with type B. This information suggests that the bloodstain came from the perpetrator and, if true, narrows the group of suspects to about 12% of the population. Although ABO analysis can exclude suspects or provide corroborating evidence against a suspect, blood type alone will not identify a perpetrator.

You don't always need a blood sample to determine blood type. In the mid-1920s, the Japanese scientist Saburo Sirai found that about 80% of the population secretes blood group-specific antigens into other bodily fluids. These people are known as secretors. Investigators can determine a secretor's blood type by examining saliva, teardrops, skin tissue, urine, or semen.

A blood sample can also reveal gender. Humans have 46 chromosomes in their body cells; 23 are derived from the mother's egg and 23 from the father's sperm. In a male, the body cells contain 44 autosomes, an X chromosome, and a Y chromosome. A female's body cells have 44 autosomes and two X chromosomes. During early embryonic development of a female, however, one of the X chromosomes of each X chromosome pair is inactivated, and becomes shortened and condensed. In 1949, two British scientists observed these condensed chromosomes in cell nuclei of female tissue. This chromosomal structure, termed the Barr body, is most noticeable in a female's white blood cells and is rare in males.

Blood Individualization (Whose Blood?)

"He's an AB secretor and belongs to group two in the PGM tests, so it narrows the field dramatically."

—Willy Chang explains test results to Detective Chief Inspector Jane Tennison in Lynda La Plante's *Prime Suspect* (1991).

Although scientists had identified many types of blood antigens by the end of the 1950s, blood characterization was still more useful to show who had *not* shed the blood rather than point out who had shed the blood. Then, in 1967, Brian Culliford of the British Metropolitan Police Laboratory found that he could detect the enzyme phosphoglucomutase (PGM) in dried bloodstains. This enzyme is polymorphic; that is, the enzyme is found in multiple, distinct forms. The PGM polymorphic forms are inherited and occur in the population in frequencies useful to investigators.

Here's how PGM characterization aids an investigation. Suppose that a bloodstain contains the PGM form PGM2-1 and is type A blood. In the United States, 42% of the population have type A blood. Regardless of blood type, PGM2-1 is found in 36% of the population. This means that PGM2-1 is present in type A blood in 15% (0.36 x 0.42) of the population. Although blood samples from different people might well have the same blood type or blood enzyme, it is less probable that two unrelated people have the same blood type *and* same form of blood enzyme.

By the 1980s, scientists had identified about 100 protein polymorphisms. Blood analysis had come a long way in the century since the famous meeting of Holmes and Watson. But the blood fingerprint remains elusive.

Blood Spatter Evidence

"It was common investigative knowledge in regard to blood spatter evidence that round drops are formed when blood drops directly down to a surface. Elliptical-shaped drops occur when blood is spattered in a trajectory or at an angle to the surface."

—Harry Bosch in Michael Connelly's *Lost Light* (2003).

Yes, you read that right. It's spatter, not splatter. "Spatter" means to scatter in droplets, and that's what blood does.

The term forensic serology typically covers the investigation of chemical aspects of blood, such as a determination of blood type or whether a bloodstain contains human blood. Blood spatter analysis is quite different. Here, we consider blood physics rather than blood chemistry. Blood spatter interpretation can provide information about:

- the distance between a surface and the origin of blood at the time of bloodshed,
- the point of origin of blood,
- the number of actions that caused the bloodshed or dispersal of blood,
- the type and direction of impact that produced the bloodshed,
- the position of the victim or an object during bloodshed,
- the movement of the victim or an object after bloodshed, and
- evidence of a struggle.

This information assists investigators to reconstruct a crime scene and can support or contradict statements given by a witness or a suspect.

A blood drop is held together by surface tension and falls as a sphere when it drips. Both the direction of travel and the surface on which the blood drop strikes affect the appearance of a blood spot. Suppose that a blood drop falls perpendicular to a horizontal surface. The drop will break apart and form a sunburst pattern if that surface is a rough porous surface, such as a concrete floor. If the blood drop hits a hard smooth surface, then the blood spot will appear round with few irregularities.

If a blood drop hits a surface at an angle, the leading edge will be round because the drop was still round at that point. The far side of the drop will be irregular. The narrow end of the bloodstain points in the direction of travel. The impact angle of blood on a flat surface can be determined by measuring the degree of circular distortion of the stain. After calculating the impact angle, the investigator can run a string from the bloodstain toward the direction of travel. When this is repeated for a number of blood spots, the strings will cross each other, establishing the point of origin for the blood. In this way, investigators can start to determine the positions of the victim and the assailant.

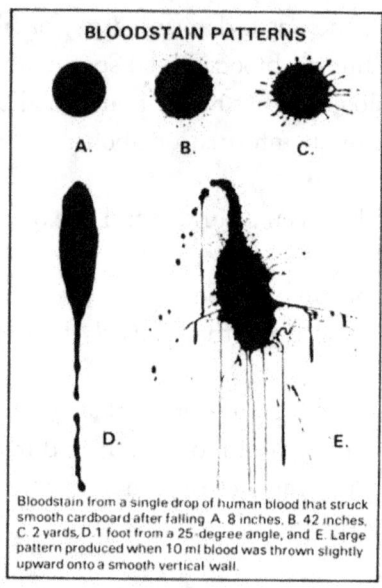

Figure 3.2. Bloodstains. Source: *Law Enforcement Investigations, U.S. Army Field Manual No. 19-20* (November 25, 1985).

The size of a blood spot indicates the blood drop's speed of travel; the smaller the spots, the faster the drops were moving. A low force event, such as a punch, creates a low-velocity impact bloodstain, which can range from four millimeters and larger. A medium-velocity impact spatter stain is caused by a medium-force event, such as a stabbing or beating. Medium velocity stains tend to range from one to four millimeters. A high-force event, such as a gunshot or a cough, creates a high-velocity impact spatter stain. These stains are quite small—one millimeter and below—and have the appearance of a mist.

Three general types of bloodstains are passive, impact, and transfer.

- Passive stains include clots, flows, drops, and pools.
- Impact stains include spatter, cast-off, splashes, and arterial spurts. Cast-off blood is a bloodstain pattern created when blood is thrown from a bloody moving object, such as a weapon. Think about what

that means. Cast-off spatters are typically associated with two blows. The first produces bloodshed and subsequent blows allow blood to adhere to the weapon. Blood present on the ceiling typically indicates cast-off spatter.

- Transfer stains are images left when a bloody object contacts a surface, such as pattern transfers, wipes, and swipes. A transfer bloodstain pattern can involve transfers of shoeprints, weapons, and palm prints, among other impressions. A wipe occurs when an object is moved through a bloodstain. A swipe is blood transferred from a moving source onto a clean surface.

The importance of blood spatter analysis is illustrated by a 1984 murder investigation in England, which is detailed in *Written in Blood* (2003) by Colin Wilson and Damon Wilson. On April 30 of that year, police entered the farm of Graham Backhouse and found him covered in blood with slashes across his face and chest. They also found a dead man lying in a hall at the bottom of a flight of stairs. Backhouse claimed that while he and a neighbor drank coffee in the kitchen, the neighbor went berserk, slashing his host with a knife. Wounded, Backhouse ran down his hall, grabbed a shotgun, and fired two shots into his attacker's chest.

Although the story seemed convincing, Dr. Geoff Robinson, the forensic biologist on the case, had doubts. The spots on the kitchen floor had the wrong shape; they were round, as if they had dripped to the floor from a person standing still. If there had been a struggle, then the blood drops would have been flung from Backhouse to produce an elliptical pattern. Robinson also could not find a trail of blood leading from the kitchen down the hall where Backhouse stored his shotgun. As it turns out, Backhouse had shot his neighbor and then used a knife to inflict his wounds and stage the attack.

A researcher might decide to investigate the significance of blood evidence by experimentally reproducing bloodstains. Testimony from the 1893 trial of Lizzie Borden reveals that one of the experts performed an experiment with dog blood to determine the drying time of blood on a particular carpet. In a more recent (and fictional) example, the *Law and Order* episode "DR1-102" (2002) concerned a victim who bled from a head wound onto a carpet. The CSU technician poured pig's blood on a sample of the carpet to match the bloodstain found at the scene. He explained to

Detectives Briscoe and Green that by replicating the crime scene conditions, he could give them an estimate for the time of the attack. Dexter Morgan of *Dexter* routinely reproduces bloodstains in his investigations—even if he had created the crime scene.

During a trial, the prosecution may present information gleaned from blood spatter by showing images in which strings are run from the blood drops at the proper angles or by using lasers instead of strings. An investigator may use computer-assisted design software to calculate angles and generate an image of the result.

Bloodstain analysis requires considerable training and experience. If you plan to feature a blood spatter expert in your story, consider mentioning that the expert is certified as a bloodstain pattern examiner. Keep in mind that your experts may not be faced with simple stain patterns. For example, there may be overlapping patterns from multiple wounds. Also, blood spatter can be destroyed by the perpetrator, the victim, or anyone who investigates the site. In the *Silent Witness* episode "Voids" (2010), for example, a young police officer unintentionally wreaks havoc in the case by altering a bloodstain to hide her blunder.

Summary

In this chapter, you've seen how forensic investigators determine whether a stain is blood and whether a human shed the blood. We've also surveyed blood analysis methods that provide information about identity and basic techniques for interpreting bloodstains.

Blood evidence offers opportunities for misdirection in a story. Blood spatter can be staged, and not everybody who claims to be an expert at interpreting bloodstains is one. As we've seen, presumptive tests for blood can give false positive results. In your story, did the precipitin test give a false positive result or a false negative result for human blood? Perhaps the company that supplies your crime lab with reagents made an error. This idea isn't far-fetched. During the mid-1950s, a German man was almost convicted of murder on the basis of blood evidence. Apparently, the anti-human antibody supplied by a large pharmaceutical company was defective and gave a false positive result. Mistakes in the crime lab can also lead to erroneous blood type results. Sometimes, blood groups can seem to change due to bacterial contaminants (such as *Proteus* and *Clostridium* bacteria). These bacteria reportedly produce substances that mimic B antigens and possibly A antigens.

John Mortimer put the changing blood type idea to good use in *Rumpole's Return* (1982), in which barrister Horace Rumpole had a client accused of murder. Part of the evidence against his client was a note that he had supposedly written soon after the murder using his victim's blood. The deceased's blood type was O, and blood analysis indicated that the message had been written with type O blood. But Horace showed that his client had written the note with his own type A blood months earlier. The type A antigens had "faded in strength," giving a negative—type O—result. Considering that current technology can reveal blood type from ancient mummy tissue, this scenario doesn't seem terribly realistic. But it's sufficiently plausible, especially for a reader who's willing to go along. After all, Rumpole has a reputation as a blood evidence expert in Mortimer's fictional world.

Let's take one more look at a true case. Here blood analysis, coupled with clever police work, led to the identity of an unknown killer. On October 24, 1983, workmen arrived at the Laitner home in a suburb of Sheffield, England, where they found the Laitner's 18-year-old daughter in a bloodstained nightgown. She told them that she had been raped and that her parents and brother had been murdered. Mr. Alfred Faragher, who was in charge of a local serology lab, found a small bloodstain that he believed had come from the killer. Faragher's team analyzed the bloodstain and found a combination of factors that should occur in one person in fifty thousand. Faragher had recently seen this combination in the blood of a rape suspect named Hutchinson.

Hutchinson had managed to escape police custody by leaping out of a second story window of the police station. He then climbed a 12-foot wall topped with barbed wire that wounded his leg. To flush out Hutchinson, the police spread reports that the barbed wire had been specially treated and would turn the suspect's leg gangrenous. The police captured Hutchinson as he made his way to a hospital.

The Hutchinson case is significant because blood analysis produced a sufficiently unique result that allowed one investigator to identify a likely suspect. In 1983, the case might have been seen as proof that the "blood fingerprint" was becoming a reality. But around the same time and in another part of England, Alec Jeffreys was inventing the DNA profiling method. DNA analysis has overcome detailed blood analysis as a means of identification. In fact, ABO typing for criminal investigation has become less common since the acceptance of DNA profiling during the mid-1990s. If you want blood typing to play a key role in your story—even if that role is a temporary misdirection—then consider setting your story before the mid-1980s or in a place where DNA analysis is not routinely performed. On the other hand, you could present your lead detective with ABO typing results while waiting for delayed DNA profiling analysis.

We'll explore DNA profiling in the next chapter. We'll also look at how criminal investigators use a national DNA database system to identify potential perpetrators by the DNA that they leave behind.

A Few FAQ from the Course

Sometimes, the term negative or positive is mentioned along with the blood type, such as AB negative. What does that mean?

"Positive" or "negative" refers to the presence or absence of the Rh factor. In 1940, scientists used immune serum from Rhesus monkeys and found that people sometimes have a blood protein, which they named the Rh factor.

How does a blood transfusion reaction occur?

The surfaces of red blood cells contain proteins that the immune system can identify as foreign antigens. Blood is classified according to the presence of these antigens. That is, red blood cells from people with Type A blood have A antigens, red blood cells from people with Type B blood have B antigens, red blood cells from people with Type AB blood have both A and B antigens, while red blood cells from people with Type O blood have neither A nor B antigens. A blood transfusion between incompatible groups (such as Type A blood given to a person with Type B blood) stimulates an immune response against the transfused blood cells carrying the antigen, causing the cells to burst. The burst red blood cells can cause serious problems, including kidney failure and shock.

Does the velocity one is moving when a blood drop falls affect its shape?

Yes, a bleeding person's movement does affect a blood drop's shape. If a person stands still and bleeds, blood drops create a round shape on a hard, smooth surface. If the bleeding person is moving, then the blood drops can take on an elongated shape.

CHAPTER 4

The Telltale Double Helix

"'Pardon my ignorance, but how did you get my DNA?'"
—Detective Andrew Berringer in April Smith's *Good Morning, Killer* (2003).

In 1986, the police discovered a rapist-killer's second victim in the village of Narborough, near Leicester, England. Semen analysis indicated that the killer was a secretor with type A blood and the enzyme marker PGM1, a combination that occurred in 10% of the adult male population. When a teenage boy fell under suspicion, the Leicestershire constabulary asked Dr. (now Sir) Alec Jeffreys to perform his new technique to compare DNA extracted from the suspect's blood sample with DNA from the killer-rapist's semen. Jeffreys confirmed that one man was responsible for both murders. But he also showed that the suspect was not that person.

The police devised another tactic to take advantage of DNA analysis: Flush out the killer. They collected blood samples for DNA testing from every local male between the ages of 16 and 34. The tactic worked. As chronicled in Joseph Wambaugh's book *The Blooding* (1989), a woman who worked at a Leicester bakery informed the police that a coworker had donated blood for a cake decorator named Colin Pitchfork. The police arrested Pitchfork, who confessed his crimes. Later, Jeffreys' analysis confirmed that Colin Pitchfork's DNA and the killer-rapist's DNA shared identical profiles. Colin Pitchfork was the 4,583rd male to be tested.

The Pitchfork case marked the first use of DNA testing in a criminal investigation. Since then, advancements in molecular biology and computer technology have forged DNA analysis into an essential tool of law enforcement. In this chapter, we'll look at the techniques that forensic scientists have used to analyze DNA—from Jeffreys' original method to cutting-edge tactics supported by extensive DNA databanks. Before considering these forensic techniques, let's take a quick overview of DNA.

A DNA molecule is a polymer made of linked nucleotides. Nucleotides are composed of a sugar molecule, a phosphorus-containing group, and a nitrogen-containing molecule called a base. The four types of bases—adenine, cytosine, guanine, and thymine—are usually designated by the first letter of their names. Do you recall the science fiction film *Gattaca*? The title represents the following stretch of DNA: guanine-adenine-thymine-thymine-adenine-cytosine-adenine. *Gattaca* is obviously the catchier title.

Two DNA molecules coil into a double helix. The steps of this spiral staircase are provided by bases from each DNA molecule that pair off: A pairs with T, whereas G pairs with C. Let's say that "~GATTACA~" represents a segment of a DNA molecule with the "~" symbol representing various other bases on either side of "GATTACA." If one strand of a double helix included this segment, then the other strand would have the segment "~CTAATGT~." We know this because the first G in GATTACA pairs with the first C in CTAATGT, the first A in GATTACA pairs with the first T in CTAATGT, and so on.

The average human chromosome has a double strand of DNA containing 100 million base pairs, and the 23 pairs of human chromosomes contain a total of about three billion base pairs. The chromosomes are located in the nucleus of a cell. An individual's chromosomes are identical in all cells and remain the same throughout an individual's lifetime, unless there is a mutation. Each person's DNA is unique, with the possible exception of a pair of identical twins. In recent years, scientists discovered that even identical twins can have differences in their genes due to the loss of segments of DNA and the gain of extra copies of DNA segments.

Only a small portion of nucleotide sequences code for the production of proteins. Within the noncoding regions reside nucleotide sequences that are repeated numerous times. These repetitive sequences vary from person

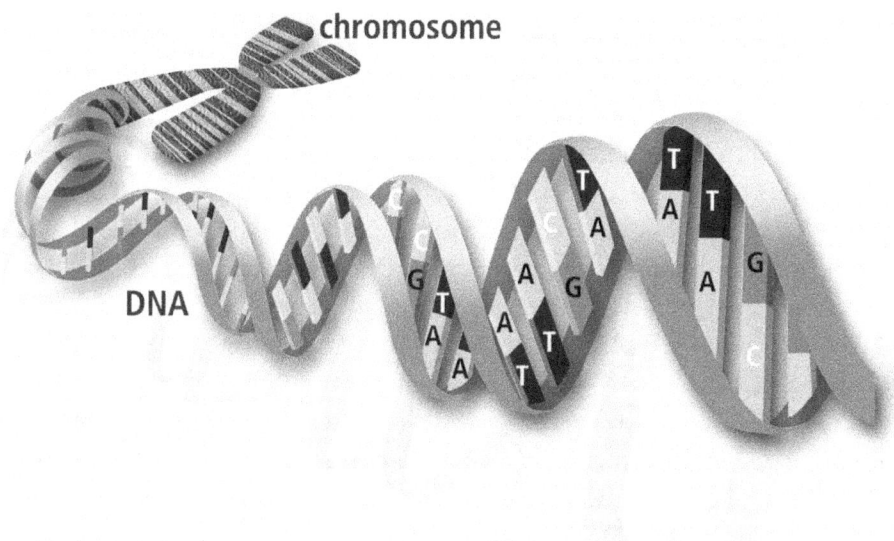

Figure 4.1. DNA with features. Source: Office of Biological and Environmental Research of the U.S. Department of Energy Office of Science. science.energy.gov/ber.

to person and can be used to identify an individual. And that's what Alec Jeffreys did when he analyzed Colin Pitchfork's DNA.

DNA Analysis: The Early Days

Six years before Jeffreys' involvement in the Pitchfork case, scientists discovered hypervariable regions of DNA. These regions consist of short tandem sequences repeated over and over again and show extreme variation between individuals. In their book *An Introduction to Forensic DNA Analysis* (2001), Norah Rudin and Keith Inman offer an analogy that may help you to visualize the structure of these tandem repeats in a DNA molecule. Imagine a train with boxcars in which each boxcar contains the same short nucleotide sequence. That is, each boxcar represents a tandem repeat. The distance between the engine and caboose varies from train to train according to the number of boxcars present.

Similarly, the distance between certain genetic markers varies from person to person according to the number of tandem repeats present between the genetic markers.

Alec Jeffreys found that certain tandem repeats contain core nucleotide sequences of 10 to 15 bases. He isolated several core sequences and used them as probes to detect variable regions in DNA samples that he obtained from members of a family. First, he treated DNA samples with restriction enzymes, which recognize certain nucleotide sequences and cut DNA to produce DNA fragments of various lengths. For example, the restriction enzyme *Hae*III recognizes the sequence "GGCC" and cleaves at the G-C junction. Jeffreys then placed cleaved DNA on a gel and applied a high-voltage electric current, drawing negatively charged DNA fragments through the gel and toward the positive electrode. The gel acts like a molecular sieve, sorting DNA fragments by size as the smaller pieces move farther through the gel.

Jeffreys then transferred the separated DNA fragments from the gel to nylon membranes and treated the membranes with a radioactive marker that binds with selected nucleotide sequences. After the nylon sheets were placed against X-ray sensitive film and the X-ray film was developed, the DNA fragments carrying the radioactive markers appeared in a series of bars that look like bar codes. When he compared X-ray film from parents and children, he found that these bar codes varied between individuals, indicating that he could use the technique to characterize a person's DNA. Jeffreys also found that the bar code patterns were inherited, which meant that DNA typing could provide information about family relationships.

Let's take another look at how Jeffreys' original DNA typing works. But this time, let's consider a weird analogy. Suppose that you're given four 8-foot wood planks. You must detect the two planks that have identical knothole patterns. The problem is that you can't see these particular knotholes (any more than anyone can see a nucleotide sequence in DNA), but you have an electric saw that can detect knotholes and will cut a plank at each knothole. You cut the four planks, sort the cut pieces, and you find the results shown in the table below. Planks 1 and 4 were cut into one 6-foot piece and two 1-foot pieces. According to this test, these two planks have identical knothole patterns.

Table 4.1. RFLP-type analysis of wood planks.

Fragment size (feet)	Plank 1	Plank 2	Plank 3	Plank 4
6	1	0	0	1
4	0	1	0	0
3	0	0	2	0
2	0	2	0	0
1	2	0	2	2

Jeffreys' DNA typing test is known as a Restriction Fragment Length Polymorphism test, or RFLP, because the test relies upon differences among individuals in DNA fragment lengths obtained after treatment with restriction enzymes. The use of DNA typing in the Colin Pitchfork case garnered international attention, and the technique was hailed as the most significant development in forensic science since fingerprinting. A modification of Jeffreys' RFLP test became the first accepted protocol in the United States for forensic characterization of DNA. The American public became aware of the RFLP technique after the Federal Bureau of Investigation used it to analyze stains on Monica Lewinsky's infamous blue dress.

Polymerase Chain Reaction—A Revolution in Forensic DNA Analysis

RFLP analysis has a drawback for forensic scientists: The technique requires large amounts of intact DNA. This requirement can exclude DNA samples from old evidence or thwart DNA analysis if a crime scene yields only minute amounts of biological material.

Today, most crime labs use a DNA typing system that takes advantage of the polymerase chain reaction, or PCR, a technique that duplicates short segments of DNA. Forensic scientists use PCR to make copies of a selected, small portion of DNA. An investigator can copy a DNA target sequence one million times or more, and as little as one-billionth of a gram of DNA may be required for analysis. Since PCR targets small segments of a cell's DNA, the technique can be used with partially degraded samples.

The PCR technique's impact on forensic DNA analysis is reflected by the revolution in biological evidence collection practice. Traditional biological samples for RFLP analysis included tissues and fluids, such as blood and semen. Now, PCR enables DNA analysis with minute biological samples acquired from dental molds, cigarette butts, eating utensils, chewing gum, postage stamps, ski masks, licked envelopes, toothbrushes, razor shavings, Band Aids, and clothing. Using PCR, forensic analysis can be performed with DNA extracted from a single cell. Even fingerprints can contain sufficient DNA for genetic profiling. The table below presents a sample of locations for DNA evidence. This information can be found in the e-booklet *DNA Evidence: What Law Enforcement Officers Should Know* (2003), which is available from the National Institute of Justice website (www.nij.gov). As the National Institute of Justice proclaims, DNA evidence can be collected from virtually anywhere.

Table 4.2. PCR enables DNA recovery from many sources.

Evidence	Possible Location of DNA on Evidence	Source of DNA
Bandana, hat or mask	Anywhere on item	Dandruff, hair, saliva, sweat
Bottle, can, glass	Mouthpiece, rim, sides	Saliva, sweat
Eyeglasses	Ear-or nosepiece, lens	Hair, skin, sweat
Fingernail fragment	Scrapings	Blood, sweat, tissue
"Through and through" bullet	Outside surface	Blood, tissue

Human DNA contains conserved regions and variable regions. In the conserved regions, nucleotide sequences are the same or similar among individuals, whereas variable regions have nucleotide sequences that differ among individuals. PCR is used to make copies of the variable regions to create a DNA profile.

By the way, one mistake that appears in mystery stories is a reference to the PCR analysis of DNA. Forensic scientists do not analyze DNA with PCR; they use PCR to duplicate selected regions of DNA. These duplicated regions are then analyzed by various techniques.

Collecting DNA Evidence

Courts have recognized the validity of the underlying theory and technique of DNA typing. However, the quality of particular DNA profile evidence must always withstand judicial inspection and assault by defense attorneys. In the agency's online *Handbook of Forensic Services* (2003), the FBI warned that DNA evidence must be properly documented, collected, packaged, and preserved, or it will not meet the legal and scientific requirements for admissibility in a court of law:

• "If DNA evidence is not properly documented, its origin can be questioned.

• If it is not properly collected, biological activity can be lost.

• If it is not properly packaged, contamination can occur.

• If it is not properly preserved, decomposition and deterioration can occur."

Contamination is a particular concern with DNA evidence. PCR technology revolutionized forensic DNA analysis by offering a method to produce millions of copies of DNA from a minute amount of biological material. But PCR can also duplicate a minuscule amount of contaminating DNA. Issue 249 of the *National Institute of Justice Journal* includes the feature "DNA Evidence: What Law Enforcement Officers Should Know," which provides tips on collecting DNA evidence at a crime scene, such as avoiding a sneeze or cough that can contaminate DNA evidence, or using police radios instead of crime scene telephones, which may have DNA evidence on a mouth or earpiece.

In fiction, police detectives often acquire a biological sample by collecting a suspect's discarded coffee cup, chewing gum, or cigarette butt. Although surreptitious DNA collection incites protests from members of the public, law enforcement agencies argue that the practice is justified, because an individual has no privacy interest in an abandoned DNA sample.

Current Techniques of DNA Analyses

"'All we need to do an STR, which is the name of the test, is a saliva sample.'"

— Police Chief Lew Ferris in Victoria Houston's *Dead Water* (2001).

Today, DNA typing usually relies on the PCR technique for duplicating locations on chromosomes that contain short tandem repeats, or STRs. Human chromosomes have thousands of different types of these short repeating sequences, and on each chromosome, the number of repeats varies greatly from person to person. STRs typically have repeating sequences of two to five bases, and the total size of a DNA region containing particular STRs is small, usually less than 500 bases. The small size means that only minute amounts of DNA are required for analysis and that analysis can be performed on partially degraded DNA.

The FBI selected 13 STRs to serve as a standard battery of repeated sequences for DNA typing. Why bother analyzing more than one STR? DNA typing results are expressed as probabilities. A DNA profile probability indicates the likelihood that a person chosen at random from a certain population can provide the DNA profile of the sample obtained from the crime scene. Suppose that a lab performs STR analysis for a single location in one chromosome. In this case, there is only a small probability that two random DNA samples will produce the same profile. But the probability of two random DNA samples producing the same profile becomes infinitesimal after combining results of STR analysis from multiple chromosomal locations. If a lab generates a DNA profile by analyzing all 13 STRs, then the probability that DNA from an unrelated person would provide the same profile as the suspect's DNA may be less than one in 10 billion.

STR analysis is also used to identify the gender of a person who left a DNA sample at a crime scene. More than 20 STRs have been mapped on the Y chromosome. As an alternative, a crime lab may analyze the amelogenin gene in a DNA sample to determine gender. Although both X and Y chromosomes contain the amelogenin gene (which encodes tooth pulp), the gene is six bases shorter in the X chromosome than in the Y chromosome. Consequently, DNA from a male will produce DNA fragments of two sizes, since he has one X chromosome and one Y chromosome. In contrast, a female's DNA will produce one size of a DNA fragment from the X chromosome-linked gene.

Analysis of single nucleotide polymorphisms, or SNPs, is another DNA analysis method. The SNP technique examines single nucleotide differences in DNA among individuals. These variations can occur during the lifetime of an individual due to errors in DNA synthesis and DNA damage.

An advantage of the SNP method is that it requires even less intact DNA than STR analysis. Orchid Cellmark used SNP analysis to identify World Trade Center victims.

Mitochondrial DNA Analysis

"'For him to be absolutely certain, he'd have to perform mitochondrial-DNA testing, which again would require the complete destruction of the teeth.'"

— Medical Examiner Roger Duff in Alice Blanchard's *The Breathtaker* (2003).

Common STR and SNP techniques rely upon the analysis of nucleotide sequence variations that occur in chromosomal DNA found in a cell's nucleus. Human cells also contain DNA in small structures called mitochondria. A typical cell contains one nucleus and hundreds or thousands of identical mitochondria. This means that investigators can perform mitochondrial DNA, or mtDNA, analysis with samples containing insufficient nuclear DNA, including small or degraded biological samples. For example, investigators can perform mtDNA analysis on shed hairs that lack root bulb cells; bones or teeth that have been subjected to long periods of high acidity, high temperature, or high humidity; charred remains; and other samples that have been unsuccessfully analyzed for nuclear DNA.

Mitochondrial DNA analysis does have several significant drawbacks. In contrast to nuclear DNA, the DNA of mitochondria has a limited number of locations that can be tested for variations. Also, mitochondrial DNA, unlike nuclear DNA, is typically inherited only from the mother. This means that mitochondrial DNA nucleotide sequences obtained from maternally related individuals, such as a brother and a sister, or a mother and a daughter, should exactly match each other. And while this makes mtDNA analysis useful for associating persons related through their maternal lineage, mitochondrial DNA cannot be considered a unique identifier. Nevertheless, mtDNA analysis is an excellent technique for obtaining valuable information in cases where nuclear DNA analysis is not feasible, such as old evidence in cold cases.

Computer Analysis of DNA Evidence

". . . I put them both in an envelope. I didn't lick the seal so they couldn't find me through the DNA in my saliva."
— Grayson Guillory in Elizabeth Dewberry's *Sacrament of Lies* (2002).

The U.S. forensic science community has standardized a 13 STR series for entry into the FBI's national database structure, the Combined DNA Index System Program. The CODIS Program uses two systems to generate leads in crimes where there is DNA evidence. The Convicted Offender Index contains more than 10 million DNA profiles of individuals, while the Forensic Index contains more than 409,000 DNA profiles from crime scene evidence. CODIS also contains an Arrestee Index of DNA profiles of people arrested in states where local law allows the collection of samples, a Missing Persons Index of DNA reference profiles generated from people reported missing, a Biological Relatives of Missing Persons Index of DNA profiles obtained from samples volunteered by relatives of missing persons, and an Unidentified Human Remains Index.

The FBI has structured CODIS as a distributed database in which local authorities generate DNA profiles that flow to state and national levels. At the local level, a DNA Index System (Local DNA Index System, or LDIS) is typically installed in crime labs operated by police departments, sheriff's offices, or state police agencies. Each state participating in the CODIS Program has a single State DNA Index System, or SDIS, which allows DNA profiles submitted by different laboratories within the state to be compared against each other. All states have established DNA databases for law enforcement purposes. The Commonwealth of Virginia's DNA Databank, for example, stores over 345,000 profiles. Virginia's Department of Criminal Justice Services claims more than 7,000 matches (or hits) between a DNA profile from a crime scene sample in a case with no suspect and a DNA profile of an individual or of evidence collected from another crime scene. At the highest level of the CODIS Program, the National DNA Index System, or NDIS, provides a mechanism for crime labs throughout the country to exchange and compare DNA profiles. The National DNA Index System participants include all 50 states, the FBI and the U.S. Army. In short, the CODIS Program links the three types of

DNA databases—LDIS, SDIS, and NDIS—and transfers data between the databases.

Briefly, here's how CODIS works. When a biological material is recovered from crime scene evidence, the DNA is analyzed to generate a DNA profile, which is then expressed as a series of numbers and entered into the CODIS system. The CODIS software stores DNA profile data, an identifier of the agency that submitted the profile, and a specimen identification number. The DNA profile is searched against records of convicted offender DNA profiles, and possibly, arrestee DNA profiles. If DNA profile comparisons uncover a 13 STR match, or "hit," then the result can be used as probable cause to seek a new DNA sample from the suspect. The new sample will be used in a confirmation test and, possibly, during a trial.

If no match is found between crime scene evidence and the known offender database, then the DNA profile is compared with profiles obtained from other unsolved crimes. The comparison may provide a link between two crime scenes previously considered to be unrelated. Linking crimes in this way can help law enforcement officials in multiple jurisdictions to coordinate their investigations and share leads that they developed independently. A perpetrator may be linked to a number of crime scenes before that person's identity is known.

Summary

"'A familial search, Judge. It's a new forensic technique, and we'd like to use it in this matter. The warrant requests the DNA profile of Jamal's brother, Wesley Griggs, which we believe is in the crime scene evidence database of California.'"

— Alexandra Cooper in Linda Fairstein's *Lethal Legacy* (2009).

In this chapter, you've looked at several methods for DNA analysis, and you should appreciate the sensitivity of modern PCR-based techniques. We've also looked at that essential component of forensic DNA profiling: computer analysis. Where might things go from here? In a 2000 report entitled "The Future of Forensic DNA Testing," the U.S. Department of Justice predicted a trend toward enhanced nucleotide sequence automation and miniaturization, leading to transportable devices for DNA analysis. Crime scene investigators do not yet benefit from miniaturized, handheld DNA analysis chips. Nevertheless, researchers at Oak Ridge National Laboratory have been developing a lab-on-a-chip technology for rapid analysis of DNA at a crime scene. These improvements, coupled with advances in communications technology, should allow investigators to test DNA samples at a crime scene with remote links to the U.S.-based CODIS system, as well as national DNA databases located throughout the world.

Originally, the FBI would not issue the results of a CODIS search unless it yielded a complete, 13 STR match. In 2006, the FBI announced a temporary plan to release partial matches detected with CODIS. Law enforcement agencies use partial matches for "familial searching," a method to identify possible relatives of a suspect in a criminal investigation. Familial searching is based on the fact that individuals who are related are more likely to have similar DNA profiles than people who are unrelated. United Kingdom law enforcement agencies have used familial searching for years, and some U.S. states have laws that authorize the technique.

Law enforcement officials and prosecuting attorneys argue that familial searching generates new leads, which can result in arrests and convictions. Privacy advocates protest that familial searching places innocent people under surveillance. One concern about familial searching is that a partial match may not identify a genetic relative. Two DNA profiles can partially match statistically even though the profiles were generated from DNA samples of unrelated individuals.

Despite objections to familial searching, the technique may become more common after success achieved in capturing the Grim Sleeper. For 20 years, an investigation of a serial killer called the Grim Sleeper failed to generate useful leads. Then, the Los Angeles Police Department requested a familial search with DNA profiles stored in state databases. The search yielded 200 DNA profiles of people who might be related to the unknown serial killer. One DNA profile shared genetic markers with DNA recovered at 15 of the Grim Sleeper's crime scenes. Further analyses suggested that they had identified the suspected serial killer's son, whose DNA profile had been added to the database following a felony weapons conviction. The investigation led to an arrest of the alleged Grim Sleeper serial killer in 2010.

Is it beginning to sound as if the villain in your story doesn't have a chance, while your investigator has it too easy? As mentioned before, investigators face the problem of DNA analysis backlogs. Insufficient funding of state and local crime labs combined with the skyrocketing increase of submissions for DNA analysis ensure that detectives will have to wait for results of DNA testing. That's fine for the fiction writer, who can create a twist by revealing test results that undermine assumptions by the story's hero.

The double helix itself can offer a few plot twists. For example, you know that one DNA profile can—more or less—fit at least two people: identical twins. Can one person have two DNA profiles? Surprisingly, the answer is yes. A November 2003 report from the *New Scientist* relates the story of a 52-year-old woman whose genetic tests indicated that she is not the mother of two of her three sons. Further investigation showed that the mother, "Jane," is a tetragametic chimera, a person whose body is composed of two genetically distinct lines of cells. The most likely explanation for this situation is that Jane's mother conceived nonidentical twin girls, who fused at an early stage of the pregnancy to form a single embryo. Around 30 people who are tetragametic chimeras are known, people who can leave biological evidence of two distinct DNA profiles.

Of course, DNA evidence can be deliberately misleading. Suppose that your villain decides to con investigators by planting DNA evidence. Harry Rowan took this tactic to extremes in the *Law and Order: Criminal Intent* episode "Dead" (2002). Harry's cousin Russell worked at Fox Hills Crematorium, and Harry convinced him that, rather than cremate bodies, he should bury the corpses in shallow graves behind the crematorium. Harry was a hit man who hated to see DNA go to waste. By seeding his crime scenes with samples from the corpses, Harry ensured that the police chased phantoms, not him. John Sanford's *Broken Prey* (2005) also has a killer who uses another person's DNA to mislead an investigation.

In real life, a Canadian doctor misled investigators about his DNA profile. The doctor was accused of sedating and sexually assaulting two of his female patients. Three times, investigators removed blood from the doctor's arm and each time, his DNA profile did not match the DNA profile of sperm found in the victims. Seven years later, one of the women hired a private investigator, who took a licked envelope from the doctor's car. This time, DNA testing indicated that the doctor had assaulted the women. What happened before? The doctor had prepared for the three scheduled DNA tests by surgically inserting a plastic tube into his left arm, a tube filled with a patient's blood and anticoagulants. When the lab technician removed blood from the doctor's arm, the blood came from the implanted tube, not the doctor's blood stream. This trick found its way into the *Law and Order: SVU* episode titled "Serendipity" (2003).

What about the DNA evidence that should be present but is not? Suppose that a person claims that he was injured when an air bag exploded during a car accident. DNA analysis of the biological residue on air bag fragments should indicate the truth of the claim.

A final twist to consider is the use of animal DNA to track a criminal. As an example, the Royal Canadian Mounted Police found the body of a murdered woman. Near the body, they discovered a leather jacket covered in the woman's blood. The jacket also contained strands of cat fur. The police suspected that the woman's ex-husband was the killer, and they obtained a blood sample from Snowball, a cat that lived in the same house as the ex-husband. STR analysis of DNA extracted from the cat's blood and DNA from a partial root of one of the strands of cat fur matched. The ex-husband was convicted of second-degree murder.

The cat fur in this case is one type of trace evidence. In the next chapter, we'll survey the types of information that investigators glean from hair, synthetic fibers, glass, soil, and other forms of trace evidence.

A Few FAQ from the Course

You mentioned that a person who is a tetragametic chimera can produce two DNA profiles. Can acceptance of donor tissue affect a person's DNA?

There is a phenomenon called microchimerism, which is the presence of a low number of circulating cells transferred from one person to another. This type of transfer takes place naturally during pregnancy, between mother and fetus. In 2004, researchers reported that fetal cells can transfer into maternal blood and can persist in bone marrow. These fetal cells, of course, have half of the DNA representing the father's genes. Microchimerism can also occur during blood transfusion, as well as during bone marrow and solid-organ transplants. Scientists reported in 2005 that white blood cell microchimerism persisted at least two years after trauma patients received transfusions.

Has DNA analysis been used to free people from prison?

Yes. DNA evidence has been used to exonerate people convicted of crimes, an effort spearheaded by the Innocence Project at Yeshiva University. According to the Innocence Project, post-conviction DNA testing in the United States has led to the exoneration of more than 250 people in 34 states.

CHAPTER 5

Without a Trace?

"Wherever he steps, whatever he touches, whatever he leaves, even unconsciously, will serve as silent witness against him. Not just his fingerprints or his footprints, but his hair, the fibers from his clothes, the glass he breaks, the tool marks he leaves, the paint he scratches, the blood or semen he deposits or collects – all of these bear mute witness against him. This is the evidence that does not forget."
— Paul L. Kirk, *Crime Investigation, Second Edition* (1974).

Edmond Locard taught that whenever two people, places, or things interact, trace materials transfer from one to the other. In this chapter, we'll survey trace evidence, those small fragments of material that shift between people, places, and objects. In particular, we'll look at how trace evidence specialists investigate hair, fiber, glass, paint, and soil.

Unlike nuclear DNA, trace evidence does not identify a suspect. Trace evidence is primarily class evidence, not individualizing evidence. Yet trace evidence can provide a link between a suspect and a crime, and prosecutors use it during trial to corroborate other evidence. Developing a link requires the identification of trace evidence and a comparison with a reference sample. For instance, a suspect's clothing may contain trace material from the victim or from the environment. Investigators can take trace material samples from the suspect and compare these with material found on the victim and at the crime scene. Similarly, trace materials on the victim might have come from the suspect. Again, trace evidence must be collected from the victim and compared with material found on the suspect.

While investigating the murders of Ronald Goldman and Nicole Brown, O.J. Simpson's ex-wife, police officers covered Nicole Brown's body with a blanket found inside her condominium. In their book, *Blood Evidence* (2003), Henry C. Lee and Frank Tirnady say that while "that decision was certainly a gesture of respect and concern for the victim and her family, it was an action that they would come to regret." Crime scene trace evidence had become compromised by cross-contamination.

The prosecution probably would not have faced a significant problem with a primary transfer of evidence; that is, blanket fibers transferred from the blanket. The real problem was caused by the possibility that the blanket transferred fibers or hair accumulated from other sources. This is secondary transfer. As we saw in Chapter 2, people who examine a crime scene must not contaminate evidence. This is why the first responder to a crime scene must isolate the area and why protective clothing is necessary.

Hair is the primary type of trace evidence. So we'll start there.

Analysis of Hair

"The rivers left no fingerprints, no trace evidence of hair or fiber."
—Thomas Harris' *The Silence of the Lambs* (1988).

A hair found at a crime scene may belong to the perpetrator, the victim, or an animal associated with either person. If a suspect's hair has sufficiently similar properties to be consistent with a hair found at a crime scene, then this provides strong corroborative evidence to place that person at the crime scene. With one exception, analysis of hair provides class characteristics, but cannot point to a particular individual. The exception, of course, is that hair may provide nuclear DNA for analysis. Nuclear DNA can individualize a human hair.

Hair grows from a hair follicle located in the skin, extending from the root embedded in the follicle to the hair shaft and to the hair tip. The hair shaft is composed of a cuticle, cortex, and medulla. The cuticle is formed by transparent overlapping scales that point to the tip of the hair. The cortex lies inside the cuticle and is a regular array of cells that run along the length of the hair and give hair its pliability. The cortex also contains pigment that gives hair its color. The color, shape, and distribution of pigment granules can help to associate a hair with a certain person. A canal called the medulla may be present in the middle of the cortex and contains cellular debris and some pigment granules. This structure can have a continuous form, a fragmented form, or can be absent. Generally, a strand of human head hair has no medulla or has a fragmented medulla.

Hair growth progresses through three phases. During the anagen phase, which may last up to six years, the hair root is attached to the follicle. When pulled from the root, anagen hairs may include a follicular tag, which contains a good source of nuclear DNA. During the catagen phase, hair continues to grow, but at a slower rate. This phase lasts about two to three weeks. The telogen phase begins when hair growth ends. The hair will be pushed out of the follicle during a two to six month period.

A comparison microscope allows an examiner to view a crime scene hair and a hair from a suspect side by side. The characteristics that an examiner will want to match are color, length, diameter, presence or absence of medulla, and the distribution, color, and shape of pigment granules. Scale patterns can be viewed directly with a microscope or by embedding the hair in a soft medium, such as softened vinyl, to make a cast. After the medium has hardened, the hair can be removed and its impression examined with a microscope.

Often, the structures of different hairs from the same individual show significant variation. This is particularly true if the hairs are from different parts of the body. For this reason, investigators typically obtain the widest range of comparison samples for analysis. According to one recommendation, a head hair sample should consist of at least 20 hairs from each of the center, front, back, and sides of the scalp. That's correct. One hundred hairs are collected by pulling, combing, or by cutting at the skin line. An examiner will select a portion of these as representative samples.

Human hair identifications are subjective interpretations, and the value of a microscopic examination of hair relies upon the skill and experience of the examiner. In the September 2002 issue of the *Journal of Forensic Sciences*,

Max M. Houck and Bruce Budowle reported significant error rates in microscopic examinations of hairs. The authors reviewed 170 hair examinations submitted to the FBI between 1996 and 2000. Eighty microscopic examinations indicated a match between questioned and reference hairs. Yet mitochondrial DNA analysis showed that nine of these matches were incorrect. The authors suggest combining microscopic examination with mitochondrial DNA analysis.

What story can a hair strand tell? First, an examiner will want to know if a strand of evidence is a natural hair or synthetic. This does not pose a serious challenge. Synthetic hairs and other fibers lack natural hair's cuticle and cortex layers.

If the evidence is a natural hair, then an examiner will want to know if it originated from a human or other mammal. For this question, an examiner has many characteristics to consider.

- The medulla layer is narrower in humans than in most other animals. The diameter of the medulla relative to the diameter of the hair shaft is the medullary index. This index typically has a value less than one-third for humans and is one-half or greater for most nonhuman mammals.
- Human hairs are generally consistent in color and pigmentation throughout the length of the hair shaft, whereas animal hairs may have drastic color changes in a short distance, a phenomenon called banding.
- In humans, the cortex layer contains most of the pigment granules. Other mammals have the granules primarily in the medulla.
- Human hair has cuticle scales that overlap smoothly, while other species have scales that form a rough, serrated edge.
- Human hair gradually tapers to a point, while animal hair comes to a point abruptly.
- The root of human hairs is commonly club-shaped, while the roots of animal hairs are highly variable in shape.

By the way, differentiating hairs among nonhuman mammals can be difficult. There can be a great deal of variation in hairs from one animal, while hairs from different species can appear similar.

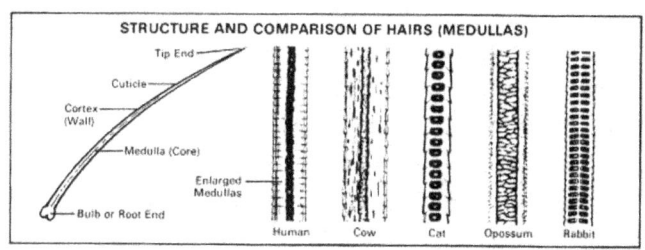

Figure 5.1. Hair details. Source: *Law Enforcement Investigations, U.S. Army Field Manual No. 19-20* (November 25, 1985).

A hair's shape indicates which part of the human body that the hair came from. Generally, hairs from the head have a circular cross section and a more uniform distribution of pigment particles. Hairs from eyebrows and eyelashes also have circular cross sections, but these hairs tend to have more tapering tips. Hairs from a beard are typically triangular in cross section with blunt tips from shaving, whereas armpit hairs tend to be oval. Pubic hairs are typically short and coiled with a continuous medulla.

Other clues gleaned from hair include the manner in which the hair was removed. A hair root with follicular tissue indicates that the hair was pulled out by brushing, combing, or perhaps by another person. Hairs pulled quickly from the head are more likely to have root sheath cells than hairs removed slowly from the scalp. Naturally shed hair has a bulbous-shaped root without adhering tissue.

So far, we've considered naturally colored hair, but microscopic examination can also reveal whether a hair has been artificially colored or bleached. Often, dyed hair will have the color present in the cuticle as well as the cortex. Bleaching tends to remove pigment from the hair and give it a yellow tint. An examiner can provide an estimate about the last time that the person bleached or colored the hair by measuring the distance between the hair root and the end of the bleached or colored zone. Hair grows at a rate of about one centimeter a month, although there is considerable variation.

In sum, a combination of physical characteristics can impart a degree of uniqueness to a hair sample. According to a study performed by the Royal Canadian Mounted Police, the probability that a crime scene hair came from someone other than the suspect is 4500-to-1 if the hairs match in color, width, distribution pattern of medulla, color and distribution of pigment granules in the cortex, and cuticle pattern. Artificial coloration, bleaching, or abnormalities in hair structure can further identify a hair sample. In Patricia Cornwell's *Black Notice* (1999), for example, Medical Examiner Kay Scarpetta tracks a killer who leaves strands of peculiar thin, pale hair.

Fiber Evidence

"'And here . . . another bit of reddish leather. From the glove. And . . . We've got another fiber. A different one.'

Criminalists love fibers."

—Forensic Scientist Mel Cooper in Jeffrey Deaver's *The Bone Collector* (1997).

"'The report states that the fibers were from a very costly cashmere-merino blended-wool fabric made for only a few years in the 1950s in a factory outside Pato, Italy.'"

—Detective Captain Laura Hayward following fiber evidence in *Dance of Death* (2005) by Douglas Preston and Lincoln Child.

Like hair, fibers can be found in many places: a victim, a suspect, a crime scene, a murder weapon, or a vehicle used in a crime. Fibers can be important in a variety of investigations, such as a hit-and-run where fibers from the victim's clothing adhere to the vehicle, fibers left behind after a burglary, or any close contact between a victim and suspect. One of the most famous cases involving fiber evidence is the 1982 trial of Wayne Williams in Atlanta, Georgia. The prosecution presented 62 fiber comparisons to link Williams to 12 murders.

Fibers used in clothing and furnishing fabrics are natural, regenerated, synthetic, or a combination.

- Natural fibers include silk, vegetable fibers (such as cotton, flax, hemp, sisal, and jute), and animal hair or fiber derived from animal hair (for example, wool, cashmere, camel hair, and mink fur). Microscopic examination of the morphological characteristics and color can distinguish between these types of natural fibers. Vegetable fibers, for example, can be distinguished from animal fibers because the textile industry uses animal hair that has a medulla and cuticular cells.

- Rayon, acetate, and triacetate are "regenerated fibers" because they are manufactured by extracting cellulose from raw cotton or wood pulp and reforming the cellulose into the fibers.
- Synthetic fibers are polymers, which are substances composed of repeating units of atoms. Examples of synthetic fibers include nylon and polyester.

Another type of fiber is the mineral fiber, such as glass wool, asbestos, and fiberglass. Mineral fibers are found in insulation.

The usefulness of fiber evidence depends upon its rarity. Cotton is so common that it's of little use unless the fiber has been dyed in an unusual way. No method has been devised to differentiate between fiber products made by different manufacturers. To have value for an investigation, the examiner must be able to narrow the fiber's origin to a limited number of sources and, ideally, to one source.

Fibers are first examined for color and diameter using a comparison microscope. Other standard tests include cross-section appearance, reaction to dyes, refractive index, density, and melting point. The colors of fibers can be compared using microspectrophotometry, a technique in which the absorption spectrum is recorded after a beam of visible or infrared light is shined on a fiber sample. Dyes can also be extracted from fibers and analyzed. These characteristics of a fiber produce class evidence, not individuating evidence. Even if the physical and chemical properties of a fiber from a suspect and a victim match, this is not sufficient to say that the fibers came from the same source. Can fiber evidence positively point to a source? This is possible if that evidence is a piece of fabric. For example, a convincing argument can be made if the tear lines of fabric found in the suspect's vehicle match tear lines of fabric found at the crime scene and both pieces of fabric have identical physical and chemical properties.

Trace Evidence in Jeffery Deaver's Lincoln Rhyme Novels

Deaver's novel, *The Twelfth Card* (2005), covers a large number of forensic techniques, and offers a brief review of the forensic scientist's task when analyzing evidence: identify, classify and individuate. *The Broken Window* (2008) shows how an accumulation of class evidence can lead to a conviction. *The Burning Wire* (2010) again illustrates how trace evidence analysis can drive an investigation. Deaver also makes an interesting point about many TV detectives. Often, a fictional police detective will pull latex gloves from her/his pocket before handling evidence. This is not a good practice, because the detective transfers traces from the pocket onto the evidence.

Glass Evidence

"'Very well,' said Thordyke; 'now observe' . . . He laid the little splinter in a gap in one of the lenses and then gave it a gentle push forward, when it occupied the gap perfectly, joining edge to edge with the adjacent fragments and rendering that portion of the lens complete."

—Dr. Thordyke using a glass splinter to identify the scene of a murder in R. Austin Freeman's short story "The Case of Oscar Brodski" (1912).

Like many types of trace evidence, glass cannot be individualized to one source—unless certain circumstances exist. An examiner can make a positive identification if a piece of glass recovered at crime scene fits with a known source. For example, large glass fragments can be fitted into a lamp or window pane from which they were broken. Dr. Thorndyke was able to use this jigsaw puzzle approach with a glass fragment from a pair of eyeglasses.

Although the majority of glass evidence doesn't allow individualization, the composition of glass evidence can corroborate other evidence. The glass fragments found on a suspect may match the composition of glass found at the crime scene, and this helps to place the suspect at the scene. How does a criminal acquire these unwanted bits of glass? Small particles of glass are sprayed back toward the direction of applied force. Due to this "blow-back" effect, glass particles may become lodged in the hair or clothing of the person who broke the glass.

Examiners classify glass particles using the class characteristics of density and refractive index, a measure of the degree to which glass bends light. The analysis can yield two possible outcomes. The analyst may find significant differences in the density or the refractive index of the glass particles. If so, then these glass fragments do not have a common origin. Suppose that the fragments have the same values for density and the refractive index. This does not necessarily mean that the fragments share a common origin. But this possibility becomes more likely if the glass is a rare type. The FBI created a databank of density and refractive index values from glass submitted to its lab for evaluation. The databank, which U.S. crime labs can access, provides a correlation between these values and their frequency of occurrence in glass samples found in the United States. The frequency of occurrence allows an analyst to assess the probability that two glass fragments had a common origin.

The appearance of glass can also tell a story: direction and sequence of impact. Determining the direction of impact can be useful, for example, in a case where a break-in was faked. Glass is elastic, but it has its limits. When force is exerted on one side of a window pane, the surface on the side opposite to the applied force stretches and then begins to crack as the elastic limit is exceeded. On the surface opposite that of the exerted force, radiating lines develop that look like the spokes of a wheel. These are called radial fractures. Continued force places tension on the front of the glass, and this causes the formation of circular lines, or concentric fractures.

According to the Three-R Rule, "Radial cracks will have right angles on the reverse side of the applied force." If you look at the edge of a radial crack, you'll notice arch-shaped stress marks that are perpendicular to one surface and curved almost parallel to the opposite surface. The perpendicular edge faces the surface opposite the applied force. On the other hand, stress marks associated with concentric fractures have right angles on the side of the applied force.

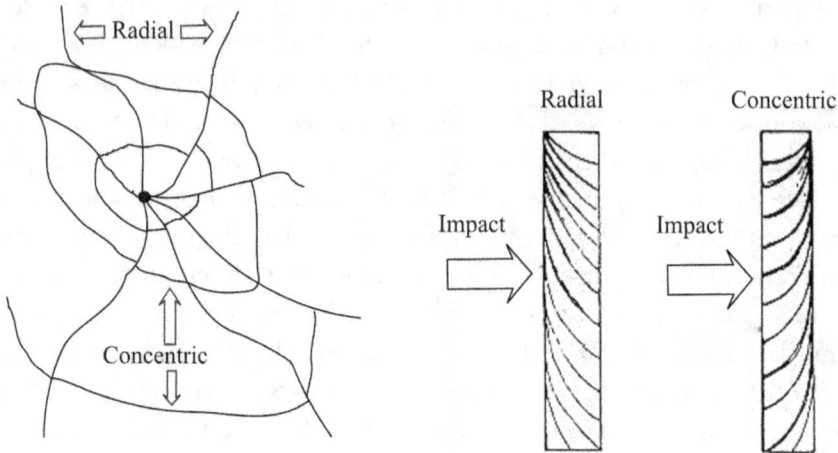

Figure 5.2. Glass fractures. Left panel: An impact produces radial and concentric fractures visible on the surface of a glass sheet. Right panel: Side
views of glass sheets, illustrating differences between radial and concentric
fractures. Adapted from the U.S. Navy's *Master at Arms Training Course*,
NAVEDTRA 14137 (April 1994).

Let's suppose that high-velocity projectiles, like bullets, flew through
that glass window. A bullet leaves a round, crater-shaped hole surrounded
by a pattern of radial and concentric cracks. The hole is wider on the exit
side. Again, the glass evidence indicates direction. But suppose that an
object moving slower than a bullet broke the window. The irregularity of
the hole in the glass will increase as the speed of the projectile decreases.
This means that the shape of the hole will not indicate direction for slow-
moving projectiles.

Glass also gives clues about the sequence of events. Let's consider bullets again. When glass is penetrated by bullets, the first bullet makes a hole
surrounded by radial fractures that are linked by concentric fractures. At
this time, any new fractures will stop at the point of any existing fracture
line. Therefore, radial fractures from a second bullet end where they meet
the radial fractures of the first bullet hole. Fractures produced by additional bullets also stop where they meet existing fractures. Consequently,
an investigator may be able to determine the sequence of impact by noting
fracture lines and their points of termination.

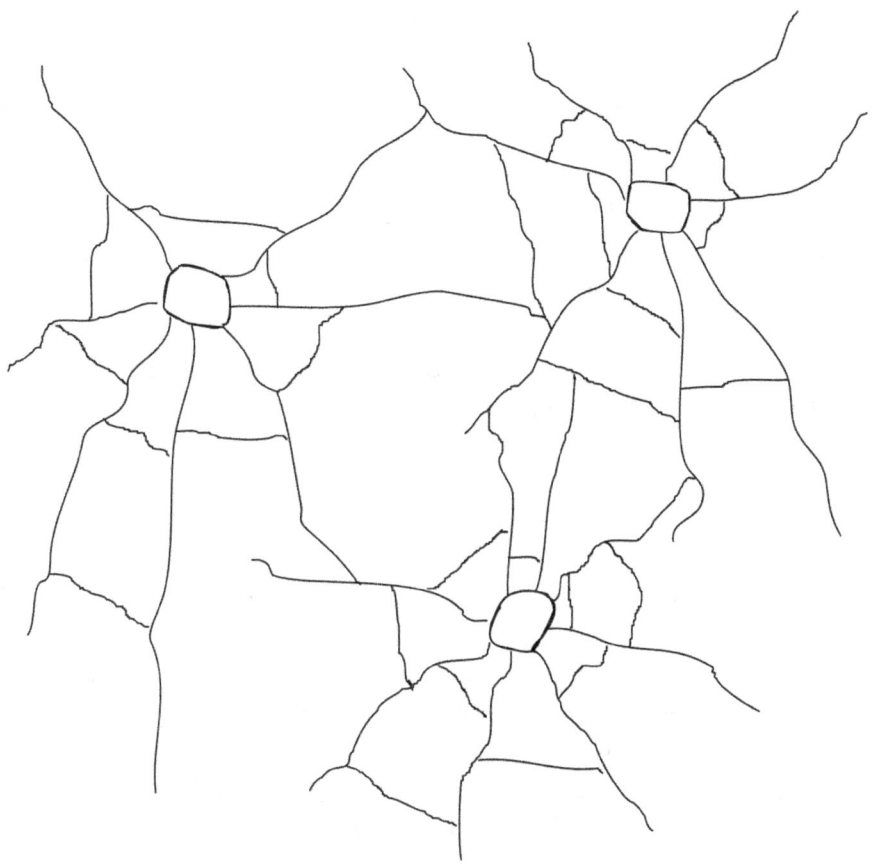

Figure 5.3. Bullet holes in glass. The first bullet created the hole in the upper right, the second bullet went through the lower right and the third created the hole on the left.

Not all glass is amenable to analysis of impact fractures. For about 50 years, U.S. auto manufacturers have used tempered glass in side and rear windows. Tempered glass does not produce radial or concentric fracture lines, because tempered glass fragments into small pieces with little splintering.

Paint and Soil Trace Evidence

Paint is one of the most common types of physical evidence analyzed by crime labs. After all, paint is everywhere. Paint evidence may be used to establish that a person was at a particular place, that a certain vehicle struck a person or an object, that a weapon inflicted injury, or that a tool was used in a forcible entry. Often, paint evidence plays a role in investigations of burglaries and in hit-and-run cases.

A particle of paint is seldom unique. A positive link between a paint chip and a source can only be made by matching a precise fracture along the line where the paint chip separated from the source. Nevertheless, a comparison between a paint chip associated with a suspect and paint found at a crime scene may provide a link between the two.

During a burglary, for example, paint on safes, window sills, and door frames can be transferred to and from burglary tools. Using a microscope, an analyst can compare paint obtained from the tools with paint at the crime scene, noting color, surface texture, and color layer sequence. There are no rules about how many layers and colors must match before an examiner can conclude that they came from the same source. The examiner's experience in this area is important.

Investigators also analyze the chemical composition of paint. Paint contains pigments and additives suspended in a binder, which provides the support medium. In pyrolysis gas chromatography, paint chips are heated to release their components as gases, which are then sent to a gas chromatograph. The recorded results, the chromatogram, can distinguish one binder—and therefore, one paint formulation—from another. This technique can differentiate most paint formulations. Infrared spectroscopy is another technique that provides information about the binder composition of paint.

A paint chip from a vehicle is especially informative. Car manufacturers apply a variety of coatings to a vehicle. The automobile finishing system for steel often consists of at least four coatings. The first layer is the electrocoat primer, which may be a gray or black color. A highly pigmented primer surfacer is applied next; this coat covers imperfections in the surface. Next, the basecoat, or colorcoat, is applied to provide color to the finished car.

Finally, an unpigmented clearcoat is applied to improve gloss and durability. The physical and chemical properties of the combination of these coatings can allow a lab to identify the make and model of the source vehicle.

Since 1975, the Royal Canadian Mounted Police Forensic Laboratories have collected color and chemical information on auto paints. This effort evolved into the Paint Data Query database, which contains chemical and physical information about thousands of paint systems used on most domestic and foreign vehicles manufactured in North America after 1973. The PDQ allows an investigator to obtain data on paints related to auto make, model, and year, such as paint layer colors, primer colors, and binder composition. The PDQ software has become an international standard used by police departments in Canada, the majority of U.S. states, the FBI, Australia, Japan, and European countries.

Soil, like paint, is everywhere. The perpetrator of a crime can inadvertently deposit soil at a scene or carry away a sample from the scene. A criminal may momentarily place an instrument or weapon on the ground, transferring traces of soil. The color, texture, and composition of soil samples may associate a suspect with a crime scene.

Soil analysis may also indicate that a suspect is innocent. Sir Arthur Conan Doyle became involved in several criminal investigations. In one, he fought for the release of George Ernest Thompson Edalji, who was convicted in 1903 of maiming cattle and horses. Conan Doyle had many reasons for believing the man innocent; among them was an observation about soil. In a January 1907 edition of the *London Daily Telegraph*, Conan Doyle wrote that "the mud at the place of outrage was yellow-red, a mixture of clay and sand, quite distinct from the road mud, which the police claim to have seen upon the trousers."

In general, the usefulness of physical evidence depends on the number of significant differences that exist in the material. That is, the material may have various characteristics, each pointing to a broad class. However, the combination of class characteristics can make the physical evidence a uniquely identifiable material. Soil can contain a plethora of components: eroding rocks and minerals, plant spores, plant particles, insects, microorganisms, decomposing animal matter, and artificial materials. The variations in the types and quantities of these components provide the means for an investigator to make a meaningful comparison of soil samples and to draw a conclusion.

Dust is another form of trace evidence. Particles of concrete, flour, or brick that the criminal leaves behind can establish a connection between that person and a place or an occupation.

During August 1960, the Scientific Investigation Bureau of Sydney, Australia, examined trace evidence found with the corpse of a young boy who had been kidnapped several months earlier. Investigators found a pink substance encrusted on certain items of clothing, as well as plant material. The curator of the Geological and Mining Museum identified the pink substance as a mortar used in house construction. The staff at the National Herbarium identified the leaves, twig particles, and seeds found on the body, including a rare cypress seed. This evidence led police to a pink house that had the rare cypress and other plants that could have produced the material found on the body. The killer was caught and sentenced to life imprisonment. This case also illustrates the value of botanical evidence. Pollens and spores can help to identify a site or region, link suspects and objects to a crime scene, and may indicate the travels of a suspect or objects.

Bits of metal can also provide important clues. In an Idaho mining town around 1916, a woman awoke in the early morning. Feeling hot breath on her face, she screamed and startled a would-be burglar. The intruder became confused, struck a match to find the doorknob, and threw it on the floor before leaving the room. The sheriff requested the help of Luke S. May, a bona fide scientific detective. May's microscopic examination of the match revealed a stain of grease or machine oil and a speck of coal dust. He also found a crystal composed of brass and iron. Investigation of seven nearby mines showed that an engine had been recently repaired with brass. The police questioned the repairman, who confessed.

Summary

"'Tell me more about our phony sand.'

'It's mixed with a little dirt. There's loam, flecks of quartz, feldspar and mica. But minimal leaf and decomposed plant fragments. Flecks here of what could be bentonite.'"

—Lincoln Rhyme and Mel Cooper discussing a bogus soil sample in
The Bone Collector (1997).

"Line cords, coaxial cable, T1 line, and all of used stock, with a smor-
gasbord of trace evidence. Fibers, animal hair, paint, plasterboard, human
hair. The one from the hair-styling salon should give the FBI lab weeks and
weeks of nerdy fun."

—Barbara D'Amato's *Help Me Please* (1999).

In this chapter, we've looked at various forms of trace evidence, especially hair, fiber, glass, paint, and soil. As you'll recall from the previous chapter, analysis of nuclear DNA can lead to the identity of a person involved in a crime. Trace evidence lacks this individuating quality except for rare "jigsaw puzzle" circumstances. A glass fragment
found on a suspect fits into a broken glass object at the crime scene,
for example. As we've seen, the value of trace evidence more commonly lies in an accumulative effect. Here's one more illustration of
this point.

On the night of September 5, 1958, a group of burglars broke into
the Rollaway Service Station in St. Louis, Missouri. They entered by
breaking a window, and then smashed an inside lock on an overhead
door so that they could steal a panel truck that they loaded with a safe.
Around 3 a.m., police responded to a complaint about a pounding noise
coming from a baseball field. Here, they found the stolen truck and the
badly damaged safe. They also found a man walking nearby, who was
promptly arrested.

During the defendant's trial, William Secunda, a police lab chemist,
testified about the following trace evidence.

- Secunda found particles of putty with red paint on the defendant's
  clothing. A comparison between these particles and samples taken
  from the rim of the broken window showed that they were identical.
- Small fragments of glass found on the defendant's clothes had the
  same density and index refraction as samples removed from the filling station window.

- On one of the defendant's shoes, Secunda found a particle of paint consisting of three layers: black over yellow over gray. Samples of paint taken from the shoe and from the stolen truck matched in thickness, sequence of color, gloss, and texture.
- Secunda compared a flake of green paint found on the defendant's pants with a specimen taken from the panel of the inside door of the filling station. Both specimens were olive green over pastel green, followed by white. They were also identical in texture and gloss.

In Secunda's opinion, when considered in combination, the odds against all of the items found on the defendant's clothing originating from a place other than the filling station would be one chance out of a billion. Note that this cumulative effect benefits writers who can trickle discoveries of trace evidence into a story, slowly drawing attention to the culprit.

During the 2011 Trace Evidence Symposium, Skip Palenik presented a seminar entitled "Microscopic Trace Evidence: The Overlooked Clue." Palenik, founder and senior research microscopist at the Illinois-based private independent laboratory Microtrace LLC, said that in the past, trace evidence analysis played a vital role in ongoing investigations, whereas today, trace evidence is used almost exclusively to try to establish associations for presentation at trial. Still, law enforcement may turn to trace evidence analysis if other leads turn cold. Maryland police, for instance, contacted Palenik's company to help an investigation of an unsolved series of rapes carried out over the course of two and one-half years by someone using a similar modus operandi in every case. Although investigators recovered the rapist's DNA from each victim, CODIS did not contain a matching DNA profile with a suspect's identity. The victims could not offer a description of the attacker.

The police asked Microtrace to analyze possible food stains on shirts that the rapist had left after two of the attacks. Company analysts found that the stains had been almost totally removed from the material. However, they discovered a sufficient amount of dust for analysis. Based on their study of the dust, they concluded that the same person had worn both shirts, that the person worked indoors, that the person worked as a drywall installer and finisher on large-scale commercial projects, and that when he had lost one of the shirts, he had been working during the spring season near an oak tree. The police released photos of the shirts and information gleaned from dust analysis to newspapers and television stations. Soon, a suspicious neighbor reported a man who left the apartment of a young girl. Police officers caught up to the man, who was driving a commercial drywall contractor's van. During questioning, the van driver confessed to the rapes, saying that he knew that his time was running out when he saw a TV report that police were searching for a drywall installer.

Keep in mind that trace evidence can mislead your fictional investigators. The villain who has some knowledge about forensics can plant trace evidence at a scene to deceive the police. And the story's criminal can find ways to avoid leaving trace evidence behind. In Val McDermid's *The Mermaid's Singing* (1996), a serial killer describes precautions taken with Adam, one of the victims:

> A criminal will always take something away from the scene of his crime and leave something behind. With this in mind, I had carefully chosen my wardrobe for today. I was swearing Levi 501s, the same brand that I'd seen Adam wear often. I'd topped it with a baggy V-neck cricket sweater, the exact double of one I'd watched him buy in Marks and Spencer a couple weeks before. Any stray fibres I left behind would inevitably be ascribed to the contents of Adams's own wardrobe.

Did a warning bell toll when you read that passage? The killer seems to have taken care of a primary transference of fiber evidence from the clothes, but what about a secondary transference of trace evidence? The killer might inadvertently transfer hairs, fibers, or dust from the carefully selected clothing to the crime scene. Even a seemingly perfect crime should have a few flaws for investigators to detect.

In the next chapter, we'll survey three instances in which forensic chemistry comes into play: arson investigation, examination of an explosion, and that favorite of classic mysteries, poisoning.

A Few FAQ from the Course

Is it possible to compare a hair dye substance used on a hair? Also, would freshly-dyed hair foil comparison to a hair sample obtained previously from the same person?

Examiners can analyze hair dye from hair samples. According to FBI guidelines published in 2005, this type of chemical analysis is not used very often today. Mitochondrial DNA analysis is more commonly used as an aid in identification. With regard to the second question, even freshly dyed hair can provide information, such as hair shape and mitochondrial DNA analysis.

I have a question about the illustration of bullets breaking a window. I understand the rule about radial and concentric lines, but how do I apply the rule to find the bullet hole sequence?

When studying the sequence of bullet holes in the window, the trick is to forget the rules about concentric and radial fractures. Here, the important rule is that a fracture progresses through glass unless it hits another fracture. This means that fractures caused by a second bullet will stop at the older fractures. The illustration shows that the fractures created by the bullet in the upper right did not stop at other fractures, fractures created by the bullet in the lower right stopped only at fractures created by the upper right bullet, and fractures created by the bullet on the left were stopped by fractures created by the other two bullets. So, the sequence is: upper right, lower right, and left.

How do crime scene investigators prevent contaminating the crime scene that they're working on?

CSIs wear protective clothing and are careful to minimize contamination. Some level of contamination will occur, and CSIs will leave some amount of trace evidence. However, we know that the CSIs visited the scene. Often, the question is whether trace evidence places a suspect at the scene. By the way, contamination of a crime scene by law enforcement officials has been used several times in fiction. In one case, a police officer was the killer who revisited the scene in his official capacity. It was not surprising when CSIs found that some trace evidence could be linked to the police officer.

CHAPTER 6

Fire, Bombs, and a Poison Chaser

"I could continue to live in the quiet fashion which is most congenial to me, and to concentrate my attention upon my chemical researches. But I could not rest, Watson, I could not sit quiet in my chair, if I thought that such a man as Professor Moriarty were walking the streets of London unchallenged."
—Sherlock Holmes in Sir Arthur Conan Doyle's *The Final Problem* (1893).

Sherlock Holmes eagerly pursued knowledge of chemistry, a discipline that aided many of his investigations. In this chapter, we'll survey several aspects of forensic chemistry, including arson investigation and analysis of explosives. Fires and explosions have much in common: Either can occur by accident or by design, a fire can cause an explosion, and an explosion can cause a fire. A prosecutor typically relies upon circumstantial physical evidence to make a case for arson or the use of explosives because direct evidence—such as eyewitness testimony—is often unavailable. Fire and explosions have another point in common. A criminal might choose fire or explosives to directly achieve an objective, such as to destroy a building or to kill a target. A fire or explosion can also disguise a crime, such as murder.

After surveying fire and explosions, we'll take it down a notch with a quieter topic: poisons and toxins. Although these classic murder weapons have lost popularity in real life, they're still very popular in fiction.

Arson Investigations

"Arson sites, aside from their naturally dirty nature, are notoriously abused by others: Firemen, rescuers, cops, medical examiners, homicide teams, and sometimes even insurance adjustors and gawkers trampling on the evidence before the arson investigator gets his first glimpse. More often than not, important details that could have told the story of the fire right off are ground into oblivion."
—Lieutenant Joe Gunther in Archer Mayor's *Borderlines* (1990).

"All Banks knew, as he forced himself to be detached and concentrate on the job at hand, was that a fire scene was unique and presented a number of problems he simply didn't encounter at other crime scenes. Not only was fire itself incredibly destructive, but the act of putting out a fire was destructive, too."
—DCI Banks in Peter Robinson's *Playing with Fire* (2004).

A combination of three elements produces a fire: heat, fuel, and oxygen to combine with the fuel. Heat is required to initiate combustion and sufficient heat must be generated later to sustain the reaction. After combustion starts, the fire becomes a chain reaction, absorbing some of its own heat to generate more heat. A fire continues to burn until it exhausts the supply of oxygen or fuel.

To produce a flame, fuel must be available in a gaseous state to react with oxygen. If the fuel is liquid, then the temperature must be high enough to vaporize the fuel. This vapor burns when it mixes with oxygen and combusts as a flame. The flash point is the lowest temperature at which a liquid fuel produces sufficient vapor to burn. The ignition temperature—the minimum temperature at which fuel spontaneously ignites—can be much higher than the flash point. For example, gasoline has a flash point of about -40 F and an ignition temperature that varies up to 495 F.

A solid fuel must be exposed to sufficient heat to decompose into gaseous products, a process known as pyrolysis. The gaseous products combine with oxygen to produce a fire. A glowing fire, such as a charcoal fire, results when a solid fuel produces an insufficient quantity of flammable gases to sustain a flame.

Most fires leave a clue about the heat source that started them. The cause of an accidental fire is often very clear. A fault in an electrical system, an overheated electric motor, a lightning strike, a discarded cigarette, a volatile material stored near a heat source, or a gas leak may be discovered as the cause of an accidental fire. It's up to arson investigators and forensic chemists to determine if a fire was accidental or deliberate.

An arson investigator wants to determine the cause of a fire and find its origin site, which is typically the area of greatest damage. Ideally, the investigator arrives at the scene before firefighters have completely extinguished the fire. This way, the investigator can observe characteristics of the fire, such as the color of the flames and smoke. Depending upon their fuel, fires burn at different temperatures, producing flames and smoke with certain colors. Wood and cloth fires can burn with reddish-yellow flames and gray-brown smoke. Gasoline and kerosene fires can burn with yellow-white or blinding white flames and black smoke, whereas a cooking oil fire can produce yellow flames and brown smoke.

A fire that is very difficult to extinguish can indicate the presence of an accelerant, a substance used to initiate or promote the spread of a fire. Arsonists typically start their fires with a petroleum accelerant, such as gasoline or kerosene. Other common accelerants include paint thinner, charcoal lighter, diesel fuel, and alcohol.

An investigator seeks the origin of the fire, because this is the location that will contain accelerant traces or the remains of an ignition device. Fires tend to spread upward and outward, leaving a cone or V pattern after the fire is extinguished. When the V pattern is distinct, the bottom of the cone can point to the fire's origin. Many factors, however, can cause a fire to deviate from this pattern, such as a draft, a secondary fire caused by a collapsing roof, or the efforts of firefighters. Distorted shapes of objects can indicate the origin. When heat partially melts the glass housing of a light bulb, the misshapen bulb will point to the direction of the fire. Extreme heat can also increase gas pressure in a light bulb, causing a blow-out toward the fire.

After the origin has been located, the investigator can search for ignition sources. If no possible source of heat can be found at the origin, such as an electric or gas outlet, then a deliberate source must be considered. A pile of ash at the base of the fire, for example, may indicate that an arsonist stacked material before lighting it.

The investigator must be skilled to interpret the often ambiguous signs of arson. For example, the presence of several origin sites suggests a deliberate fire, but this sign can be misleading. Multiple fires can arise from flashback, which occurs when a flaming fire has been extinguished and the debris continues to smolder. During this period of glowing combustion, flammable gases are produced, and a fire can reignite with adequate ventilation.

Another sign of a deliberate fire is the odor of an accelerant. An arsonist may try to mask these odors with chemicals, such as ammonia. After an arsonist pours accelerant on a floor, its vapors burn and leave an outline around the outer edges of the spill. The outline, or pour pattern, is considered to be a signature of an accelerant-induced fire. Yet these pour patterns can also be caused by plastic materials that drip and melt onto a surface, where they burn.

Heat produces a blistered pattern, called alligatoring, on the surface of partially burned wood. If these blisters are large and shiny, an investigator may conclude that the fire spread quickly, a sign of an accelerant-fueled fire. Dull blisters that appear baked can indicate a slow-developing fire.

For reconstruction of a fire scene, investigators may use measurements of the char depth of burned wood. The char depth is the depth to which wood has been converted to charcoal by pyrolysis. As charring occurs, the char forms a barrier that insulates subsurface wood from the action of fire. As a result, progressively longer periods are required to char the wood at deeper levels. Char depth can be affected by such factors as the species of wood, its age, and the temperature of the fire. Consequently, investigators compare the char depth measured at a fire scene with that obtained using the same species of wood burned under similar conditions. The depth of char has been used as evidence of the duration of a fire. This gives an investigator a method to estimate when the fire started.

Evidence of streamers or trailers—material used to spread fire from one area to another—is another sign of arson. An arsonist might have used a trail of gasoline, sawdust, rope soaked in oil, or paper to cause the fire to move through various locations in a building. Investigators may also find evidence of a plant, which is a device that ignites accelerant or assists the initial flame to build in intensity.

Other arson indicators include signs of a break-in, the presence of containers that could have held an accelerant, and an ignition device. A candle, a time delay apparatus, and an incendiary mechanism, such as a Molotov cocktail, are examples of ignition devices.

An arson investigator may use a vapor trace analyzer, or sniffer, to detect minute amounts of flammable liquid vapors and gases. This portable detector pulls in air around a questioned sample and passes the air over a heated filament. If a combustible vapor is present, then the oxidation of the vapor increases the filament's temperature, which is then indicated on the instrument's meter. Since a sniffer can respond to vapors other than flammable liquid vapors, a positive result from a sniffer is not proof of accelerant traces. It's like the screening—or presumptive—tests that we considered for detecting blood at a crime scene. An arson investigator may decide to use another type of sniffer at the site of a fire: a dog trained to recognize the odor of accelerants.

Time is of the essence for an arson investigation. Any petroleum residue remaining after a fire is extinguished can evaporate in a few hours or days. Since accelerants are volatile, fire debris must be packaged in vapor-tight containers for transport to a laboratory. This also applies to a suspect's clothing. If arrested within a few hours of setting a fire, an arsonist's clothes may contain accelerant traces.

The crime lab's first challenge in analyzing fire debris is to separate accelerant residues from ashes and other material obtained from the scene. One classic approach is the heated headspace method, in which debris is heated in an airtight container to release volatile accelerant residues. The vapor can be removed with a syringe and injected into a gas chromatograph, where it is separated into its components. Each component peak is recorded on a chromatogram, and the chromatogram pattern can be compared with patterns produced by known products to identify the volatile residue.

The pattern may be difficult to interpret if the arsonist used a combination of accelerants or if the accelerant residue was mixed with breakdown products of materials at the scene. In this case, a forensic chemist may decide to simplify analysis by passing components that emerge from a gas chromatography column through a mass spectrometer. This device fragments a component into ions and allows the analyst to filter out certain ions, eliminating extraneous peaks.

Forensics under the Microscope

Forensic science continues to generate controversies. In the August 2009 issue of *Popular Mechanics*, Brad Reagan's "Reasonable Doubt" explores debates about perceived pitfalls of various types of forensic analyses. The article highlights the following quote: "Forensic science was not developed by scientists. It was created by cops – often guided by little more than common sense." For another view on recent debates, take a look at the interview ("Implementing the Recommendations Laid Out in the National Academy of Sciences Report") with Detective Lieutenant Kenneth F. Martin, Commanding Officer of the Crime Scene Services Section of the Massachusetts State Police in the July-August 2009 issue of *Evidence Technology Magazine*, which is available online.

Investigation of an Explosion

"The bomb detonated at a rate of twenty-seven thousand feet per second, twenty-two times faster than a nine-millimeter bullet leaves the muzzle of a pistol. Heat flashed outward in a burst of white light hot enough to melt iron. The air pressure spiked from a normal fifteen pounds per square inch to twenty-two hundred pounds, shattering the iron pipes into jagged shrapnel that punched through the Kevlar suit like hyperfast bullets."

—Robert Crais' *Demolition Angel* (2000).

There are four types of explosions: mechanical, electrical, nuclear, and chemical. A mechanical explosion, like a boiler failure, occurs when a high pressure gas bursts from a container. An electrical explosion can be produced by a high-energy electrical arc—such as a lightning strike—that generates sufficient heat to cause a mechanical explosion. A fission or fusion process sets off a nuclear explosion. The chances are that your fictional investigators will be examining the fourth variety of explosion, the chemical type.

A chemical explosion is a rapid transformation of unstable compounds into stable compounds accompanied by the release of gas and heat. Expanding heated gas increases pressure inside a bomb's container until the casing bursts, blasting pieces outward at high speed. Damage is inflicted by these fragments and by the blast pressure effect, a violent pressure exerted by expanding gases that shatters objects in its path as it rushes from the point of origin.

Explosives can be classified according to the speed of the chemical reaction. A low explosive reaction produces light, heat, and a subsonic pressure wave that flies in all directions from the detonation. The speed at which a low explosive decomposes, called the speed of deflagration, or speed of burning, can reach 1,000 meters per second. Black powder and smokeless powder are examples of low explosives. Smokeless powder typically consists of nitrocellulose and is the most powerful low explosive.

A detonator of a low explosive may be homemade. For example, an electrical detonator may be linked to a battery through a device—such as an alarm clock—that allows the bomb to detonate at a particular time. If a bomb contains a mercury tilt switch, movement will complete a detonation circuit. A car bomb can be wired to the ignition switch so that the bomb goes off when the driver starts the engine.

Another type of low explosion is caused by the detonation of gaseous fuels in combination with oxygen, such as the ignition of a natural gas leak. This type of explosion will not leave a crater.

High explosives detonate almost instantaneously at rates from 1,000 to 8,500 meters per second. In this case, the speed of decomposition is the speed of detonation, which refers to the creation of a supersonic shock wave in the explosive charge. A high explosive can be classified as a primary or secondary explosive. Primary explosives are extremely sensitive to heat, shock, or friction and are used to detonate other explosives. Primary explosives provide the major component of a blasting cap, which in turn can be triggered by an electric current or by lighting a fuse.

Secondary explosives are relatively insensitive to heat, shock, or friction and will typically burn rather than detonate if unconfined and ignited in a small quantity. This is why secondary explosives must be detonated by an initiating explosion provided by a primer or booster charge of a primary explosive. Dynamite is one example of a secondary explosive. Cyclotrimethylenetrinitramine (RDX) is a powerful military high explosive, which can take the form of a pliable material known as composition C-4. Other high explosives include trinitrotoluene (TNT), pentaerythritol (PETN), and Semtex, which is a blend of RDX and PETN.

In a criminal case involving an explosion, the investigation will typically center on a homemade bomb. The most common explosives of homemade bombs encountered by U.S. law enforcement personnel are black powder and smokeless powder, the low explosives. However, ammonium nitrate—available as fertilizer—has also been used to create a type of high explosive for a homemade bomb. The 1995 Oklahoma City explosion, for example, resulted from an ammonium-nitrate-based bomb.

A bomb-scene investigator's search for the origin of destruction is usually easier than that faced by an arson investigator; a crater typically marks the center of an explosion. Explosives are not completely consumed in the detonation, and residues remain at the scene. Near the center of the blast, soft debris, such as wood, can absorb traces of explosives, while hard debris like metal may have traces deposited on the surface. Fragments of detonating devices and bomb containers can be found at a distance from the crater and in a circular pattern. Sometimes, the perpetrator may decide to disguise the bomb as an innocuous object rigged to detonate at a certain time or by a certain action. Fragments of this "infernal machine" may be found as well.

At the bomb scene, investigators can use an ion mobility spectrophotometer, a screening tool that detects a wide range of explosive residues. This portable detection device uses a vacuum to collect residues from surfaces. In the ion mobility spectrophotometer, the residues are vaporized and converted to electrically charged molecules, which are then analyzed. Like the arson investigator's sniffer, any positive results need to be verified by confirmatory tests. And, like the sniffer, the ion mobility spectrophotometer has a canine counterpart: dogs trained to detect explosives.

In the lab, microscopic examination can reveal particles of unconsumed explosive and, possibly, components of the detonating mechanism. While black powder and smokeless powder have characteristic shapes and colors, high explosives usually must be detected with other methods.

An analyst may decide to screen evidence with a color test, which is presumptive because it's not specific for explosives. For example, in the presence of nitroglycerin, the Griess reagent transforms from pink to red.

After microscopic examination, an analyst can rinse debris with a solvent to extract residues of explosives and analyze the extract using thin layer chromatography, high-performance liquid chromatography, or gas chromatography-mass spectrometry. Depending upon the amount of residue recovered, the lab may also confirm results with infrared spectrophotometry or X-ray diffraction.

Organic residues may also be detected on the hands and clothes of anyone handling explosives. Nitrate-based commercial explosives like nitroglycerin are absorbed into the skin and cannot be entirely removed by simple hand washing. The test may yield a false positive result if the suspect is a firearm enthusiast who loads his own ammunition or someone who takes nitroglycerin tablets for a heart condition. Therefore, the detection of nitroglycerin on the hands of a suspect is only presumptive evidence that the suspect handled an explosive.

To assist the investigations of explosions and arson, the Bureau of Alcohol, Tobacco, Firearms, and Explosives launched the Bomb and Arson Tracking System in 2003. Participating local, state and federal law enforcement agencies can gather, store, and exchange information, such as the type of incident, target, location, date, and time. This system also uses Geographical Information System technology to create maps and confirm incident locations.

In the future, investigators may be assisted by a requirement for manufacturers to tag explosives with a liquid, solid, or vapor-emitting substance for identification or detection. The U.S. government has considered adding color-coded, 10-layer plastic particles, called taggants, to commercial explosives. A taggant includes magnetic and fluorescent layers as well as a color sequence indicating the manufacturer and date of production. In a study reported in 1998 and funded by the Department of the Treasury, the National Research Council recommended delaying a taggant program until more research could be performed to study the effect of taggants on the stability of explosives. High explosives manufactured outside the United States, however, may contain microscopic tags or chemicals that produce a distinctive, identifying odor.

Forensic Toxicology

"Having sniffed the dead man's lips I detected a slightly sour smell, and I came to the conclusion that he had had poison forced upon him."

—Sherlock Holmes in Sir Arthur Conan Doyle's *A Study in Scarlet* (1887).

"'We know next to nothing of the composition of the protein bodies in the snake venoms which had such terrific and quick physiological effects on man,' Kennedy went on.

'They have been studied, it is true, and studied a great deal, but we cannot say that there are any adequate tests by which the presence of these proteins can be recognized.'"

—Craig Kennedy in Arthur B. Reeve's *The Film Mystery* (1921).

It's time for a brief tour of forensic toxicology, which encompasses the analysis of poisons and drugs in bodily tissues and fluids. Poison has been a favorite murder weapon since humans established civilization. Historically, arsenic has been the most popular poison; it's sometimes called the "inheritance powder" for its ability to initiate changes in fortune. Cyanide and strychnine have also been popular poisons.

Why have killers favored poisons? In *Criminal Poisoning* (2007), John Trestrail suggests that the reason lies in the following advantages of poisons over other weapons:

- Invisible weapon
- No protection (everybody needs to eat, drink, and breathe)
- No noise
- No gore
- Depersonalization (no personal contact required)
- If the poison doesn't work the first time, then the poisoner can try again
- Precise targeting
- Easy to overcome a stronger person

In addition, the physical symptoms of poisoning can resemble those of common diseases and mislead medical examiners. The plant extract atropine, for example, kills by inducing heart or respiratory failure. Antimony produces symptoms resembling a stomach illness and leads to heart failure. Ricin, obtained from castor oil plant seed, causes the victim's red blood cells to aggregate and also leads to heart failure.

Killers have a generous medley of poisons to choose from. Just to name a few, there are metals like thallium, mercury, antimony, and arsenic; bacterial toxins like botulinum toxin (now widely known as BOTOX®); alkaloid toxins from plants, such as strychnine; and venoms from snakes, frogs, and spiders. Poisoners may select a toxic substance based on a convenient mode of administration. Poisons can be administered in food and drink, in the air, or absorbed through skin. And, on top of this, for most of recorded history, poisoning went undetected.

But then in 1836, the English chemist James Marsh developed a test for arsenic, and this became the first toxicological test presented during a criminal trial. Scientists soon found methods to detect other minerals and metals used in poisoning. With the invention of these detection methods, toxic metals soon lost popularity. Criminals then turned to poisons derived from plants, such as morphine.

The poisoner's lot became still more difficult during the late 1940s and early 1950s with the availability of gas chromatography and high-pressure liquid chromatography. These analytical tools were followed by gas chromatography coupled with mass spectrometry and assays using antibodies that bound specifically to toxic compounds.

Although postmortem forensic toxicology remains an important part of death investigation, using poison to kill is relatively rare today. Yet it still happens. For example, Donald Harvey was convicted for 24 murders committed from 1983 to 1987, some with arsenic or cyanide. Another killer selected thallium to poison Robert Curley, who entered a Pennsylvania hospital in 1991, complaining about a variety of symptoms. His condition soon worsened, and he slipped into a coma, never to recover. Urinalysis showed that Curley had 900 times the expected amount of thallium in his system. Three years later, the state exhumed his body, and a forensic toxicologist created a timeline for Curley's thallium exposure by analyzing hair, skin, and other tissues. Curley seemed to have been exposed to thallium starting at about six to 11 months before his death and, surprisingly, this exposure continued during his hospitalization. Curley's wife was one of the few people who could have dosed Curley with thallium at this time. During her trial, she pleaded to murder, and when asked why she poisoned her husband, she reportedly said that she wanted the insurance money. Motives aren't always complicated.

A forensic toxicologist follows three general steps for detecting drugs and poisons: Extract the victim's tissue or biological fluid, analyze the extract with a screening test, and verify screening test results with a confirmation test. For small organic compounds like drugs, the analyst can screen extracts with thin-layer chromatography, an immunoassay technique in which antibodies bind to drugs or poisons, a color test, or a microcrystalline test in which chemical reagents are added to a sample to produce characteristic shapes of microscopic drug crystals. The identity of the poison or drug can be confirmed with a combination of gas chromatography and mass spectrometry. A lab may also use gas chromatography-mass spectrometry to identify drug metabolites, the breakdown products of drugs. High-performance liquid chromatography is another technique used to identify drugs or classes of drugs.

To screen for heavy metal poisons, such as arsenic or thallium, the forensic toxicologist may use the Reinsch test. In this test, the chemist dissolves a tissue or bodily fluid sample in acid and then places a copper strip in the solution. If heavy metals are present, then the copper acquires a silver or dark coating. A positive result must be confirmed by a test such as spectrophotometry, emission spectroscopy, atomic absorption, or X-ray diffraction.

Immunoassays have been a traditional technique for detecting toxic proteins, such as ricin and botulinum toxin. These tests can take a day or more to produce results. Concerns about bioterrorism have spurred research into quicker methods for detecting protein toxins. The U.S. Department of Homeland Security funds research on miniature sensors for a wide variety of poisons. One of these lab-on-a-chip sensors can provide test results in minutes.

Summary

"'Anyhow,' Jake went on, 'the C-four explosive used in the West Hollywood bomb was not the run-of-the-mill C-four. It contained an unusual mixture of RDX and PETN, which were its two major ingredients.

The mix was so unusual that the people at the ATF laboratory believe it was custom-made.'

'So?' Joanna asked, hearing nothing new thus far.

'So that same C-four was recently used in another crime.'"

—L.A. medical examiner Joanna Blalock and homicide detective Jake Sinclair in Leonard Goldberg's *Lethal Measures* (2000).

In this chapter, we've looked at the basic principles of fire and how arson investigators use technology and their own senses to distinguish between an accidental fire and one set deliberately. If arson plays a role in your story, you might consider creating an arson expert who has been trained with, or who consults with, the Bureau of Alcohol, Tobacco, Firearms, and Explosives' Fire Research Laboratory. The Maryland-based facility operates as a testing laboratory for reconstruction analysis and has a storehouse of fire investigation research data.

We've also surveyed aspects of bomb investigations: the cause of an explosion, the types of explosives, and the clues that allow investigators to trace a bomb. As the quote from *Lethal Measures* shows, an unusual explosive can yield a "fingerprint" that links crimes. By adding your own—perhaps imaginary—ingredient to the explosive, you can create a trail for investigators to follow. And if you plan to feature a bomb expert in your story, then you should decide if your expert is a chemist with the forensics lab. Or, is your expert a member of the local police department's bomb squad, someone who must know how to secure a bomb scene and collect evidence? You can find an example of this type of expert in Robert Crais' *Demolition Angel* (2000), which features bomb squad veteran Carol Starkey.

Finally, we took an overview of forensic toxicology, including the classic types of poisons and their modern counterparts: drugs. While the classic poisons have fallen out of favor in reality, they're still very popular in fiction. For example, a killer used cyanide in TV's *Law and Order* episode "Compassion" (2003), in *Law and Order: Criminal Intent*'s "Poison" (2001), and the *Silent Witness* episode "Intent" (2010). Arsenic was the poison of choice in the *Law and Order: Criminal Intent* episode "Sound Bodies" (2003). Maybe you're thinking about setting your murder mystery in the past, a time when classic poisons were in vogue. If so, you may want to look at Deborah Blum's *The Poisoner's Handbook* (2010), which details the battles between toxicologists and criminals during the early 1900s in New York City.

Perhaps, the enduring attraction of poison in detective fiction stems from the typically ordered investigation of a poison homicide case and the challenge of tracing the poison. If your story includes a homicide-by-poison, then your investigator should consider these points.

- Determine if the suspect had access to the poison. Was the poison readily available? Would the suspect's occupation offer an opportunity to obtain the poison? Could the suspect have purchased the poison? Is there a physical link between the suspect and the poison, such as fingerprints on the poison container?
- Determine if the suspect had access to the victim.
- Determine how the suspect could have obtained information about the effects of the poison. Sources include formal education, printed material (from both standard and "underground" presses), and the Internet.
- Have the crime scene specialists collect items that might have been used to administer the poison, such as beverage containers, partially eaten food, and medicine. Check areas where the killer could have disposed of poison, including trash containers and sink traps.
- Compile a detailed medical history of the deceased. Did this person suffer a lingering illness or a prolonged poisoning?

Of course, your story's not limited to any existing poisons; your villain can devise a new one. If you plan on inventing a new toxic substance for your antagonist, then you might want to look at *Book of Poisons* (2007) by Serita Stevens and Anne Bannon, which offers tips on formulating fictional poisons. Keep in mind that contemporary possibility: poisoning by combining two or more relatively innocuous compounds. Lincoln Child used this approach in his novel, *Death Match* (2004).

It's time to leave the subtle craft of the poisoner. In the next chapter, we look at the forensic analysis of firearms, from the time-honored examination of gunpowder residue to current computer analysis techniques.

A Few FAQ from the Course

Can you comment on the physical effects one might have if killed with a fast-acting poison? Also, I assume that if a person dies instantly then an investigator will be able to see that poison was involved. James Patterson does this in one of his Alex Cross books.

Cyanide can take effect within 30 seconds. Initial symptoms include headache, nausea, vomiting, difficulty in breathing, and confusion. These effects can be followed by seizures, gasping, cardiovascular collapse, and coma. Some people detect the presence of cyanide as the odor of almonds. Strychnine poisoning symptoms can occur within 15 to 30 minutes if taken orally or within 5 minutes if administered intravenously. Initially, the drug causes muscle stiffness and painful cramps, which then proceed to muscle contractions. The victim's body can take the form of an arch with the head and heels touching the floor. The face may have a forced smile called *risus sardonicus*. Serita Stevens' *Deadly Doses* (1990) includes an appendix that categorizes many poisons by the time they take to produce symptoms. By the way, I think that the Patterson book that you mentioned is *Roses are Red* (2000) in which victims die in less than 15 minutes from Anectine poisoning. This drug is succinylcholine, a classic neuromuscular blocking agent.

Please explain flash point.

Certain liquids, such as ether, can be ignited, but it is not the liquid itself that burns. The combustion of an ignitable liquid occurs in the liquid's vapor phase. The flash point is the temperature at which the concentration of vapors above the liquid in a still pool of the liquid will ignite when exposed to a flame. Flash point is sometimes confused with the ignition point, which is the temperature required to ignite those vapors. For example, gasoline has a flash point of -40 F, which means that at that temperature and above, gasoline produces sufficient vapors to burn. Those vapors will burn if exposed to a source of heat that is hotter than gasoline's ignition point, which runs around 500 F (depending on the particular mix of gasoline).

CHAPTER 7

Bullet Points

"He went to the ledge that overlooked the entrance to the Criminal Courts Building. The area was littered with .30-caliber shell casings, from a Springfield rifle, maybe. Using his handkerchief he picked the casings up and dropped them in his pocket. The Ghoul had recently bought a new invention called a comparison microscope for conducting ballistics tests. They hadn't used it much yet, but Rourke still had high hopes for it."

—Detective Daman Rourke in Penelope Williamson's 1927 mystery *Wages of Sin* (2003).

It was 1794. In northwestern England, someone shot Edward Culshaw through the head. While examining Culshaw's body, a surgeon found a wad of paper in the wound. This wasn't unusual; paper wads sealed gunpowder in a firearm's barrel until firing. But the paper found in Culshaw had an unusual characteristic: It included a segment of a street ballad. The police questioned John Toms about the shooting and found a piece of paper in his coat pocket that contained the rest of the ballad. They charged Toms with murder. The Culshaw case is considered to be the earliest application of forensic ballistics. Since that time, many more tools have become available to forensic firearm examiners, who no longer have to rely on fitting together pieces of paper.

In this chapter, we'll look at forensic examinations of firearms, including the determination of the type of weapon used in a crime, how investigators can link bullet fragments to a weapon, and an overview of methods for reconstructing a shooting. Strictly speaking, firearms identification focuses on the determination of whether ammunition was fired from a particular weapon, while ballistics is the study of projectiles in motion. However, these activities are often lumped together as firearms identification or forensic ballistics.

We'll begin by surveying firearms and ammunition.

Firearm Basics

During 2004, European law enforcement officials initiated a change in the rules of engagement for dealing with suspects: Now police must draw their weapons when a suspect reaches for a cell phone. This is not because they find cell phones obnoxious or because they want to stop the suspect from contacting a lawyer. Rather, cell phone guns have become a problem. In these weapons, the digital phone face conceals a .22-caliber handgun, which can fire four rounds.

Despite the increasing variety of firearms, there are still only four types that most commonly appear in criminal cases: revolvers, pistols, rifles, and shotguns. Revolvers and pistols are handguns. A revolver is a repeating handgun that stores extra cartridges in multiple chambers within a revolving cylinder. When the trigger is pulled, the hammer falls from its cocked position and strikes the firing pin, which in turn, impacts the cartridge and causes the bullet to discharge through the barrel.

A semiautomatic pistol is a handgun that loads itself from cartridges lodged in a magazine located in the hollow handle grip. When the trigger is pulled, the hammer strikes the firing pin. The pin hits the cartridge in the chamber, initiating a discharge that propels the bullet through the barrel. The force of the discharge causes the slide to recoil backward, opening the breech and ejecting the casing. As the slide closes, a new cartridge automatically enters the chamber from the magazine. Since a semiautomatic pistol automatically ejects spent cartridges, while a revolver retains the cartridges in its cylinder, a cartridge case from a semiautomatic weapon is more likely to be found at a crime scene than spent ammunition from a revolver.

The third common type of firearm is a rifle, or long gun, designed to be fired from the shoulder using both arms. Types of rifles include pump or slide action, lever action, bolt action, and single-shot action.

Revolvers, semiautomatic pistols, and rifles share a common feature: They have rifled barrels. Rifling is the process of cutting spiral grooves in the barrel of a firearm. After a bullet is fired, these screw threads cause the bullet to spin as it emerges from the barrel. The spinning prevents the bullet from tumbling in flight, increasing both range and accuracy. The original barrel surfaces that remain between the cut grooves are called lands. In general, the diameter of the barrel—or bore—measured between opposite lands determines the caliber of the weapon, which is usually expressed in hundredths of an inch or in millimeters. For example, a .45-caliber gun has a bore diameter of forty-five-hundredths of an inch.

A shotgun is a shoulder weapon with a smooth bore. Like rifles, shotguns are classified by the way that the weapon is loaded: semiautomatic, pump or slide, lever, bolt, or single-shot. The size of large-bore shotguns relate to the weight of lead balls that can fit into the bore. A 12-gauge shotgun can accommodate a lead ball that weighs one-twelfth of a pound. The higher the gauge number, the smaller the diameter. The .410-caliber shotgun is an exception to this scheme; it has a bore size of 0.41 inches.

Ammunition

"'Based on amounts of trace levels of bismuth and antimony, the lead was mined at a location in southwestern Saskatchewan.'"

—Chief of Police Scott Parris discusses a forensics report about bullet fragments with tribal investigator Charlie Moon in James D. Doss' *Dead Soul* (2003).

The two basic forms of ammunition are bullets and shot. Your investigator will probably find one of four common types of bullets at a crime scene:

- full jacketed, nonexpanding: a one-piece metal jacket encloses the lead slug, except for its base;
- lead alloy: an unjacketed lead slug alloyed with other metals to increase the hardness of the bullet;
- round-nose, soft-point, expanding or mushrooming bullets: lead is exposed at the tip of the bullet, and a metal jacket covers the base and side of the bullet; and
- expanding, open, hollow-point: a one-piece metal jacket—nicked to weaken its structure—encloses the base and side of the bullet.

In general, pistols and rifles used for sport fire lead bullets that are round-nosed, sharp-nosed, cylindrical, or hollow-pointed. Military rifles and automatic pistols typically fire bullets with a lead or steel core that is wholly or partially enclosed in a jacket made of aluminum or an alloy of copper with zinc or nickel.

Let's consider a generic bullet. A cylindrical cartridge case, which is often made of brass, contains the propellant charge. A bullet seals the front end of the cartridge, while the back of the cartridge includes a small cap with a primer charge. Some cartridges have a small metal cup with primer placed in the center (a center-fire cartridge), while others have primer along the outer rim of the cartridge case base (a rim-fire cartridge). Pulling the trigger causes the firing pin to strike the cap and detonate the primer. The primer's flame ignites the main powder charge and propels the bullet down the barrel.

Shotgun cartridges contain a primer, a brass case, gunpowder, and a plastic or cardboard case. The front end of the cartridge is sealed with a disk of compressed cardboard, and the plastic or cardboard body is filled with lead shot, which are small pellets or balls. A wad, which may be made of paper or greased felt, lies between the shot and the gunpowder. After the cartridge's powder charge ignites, the wad pushes the pellets through the barrel. A cartridge may contain a polyethylene sleeve called a shot collar instead of a wad.

A shotgun can also discharge an elongated hollow rifled slug loaded in a shotgun cartridge. For example, the Remington® Copper Solid sabot shotgun slug, first distributed in 1993, is a solid copper, hollow-point slug with longitudinal slots cut into the nose. The slug is fitted into a hard plastic sabot and loaded into a shotgun shell with two plastic wads that separate it from the gunpowder charge.

Firearm Identification

"'You played it smart down there at Realito, brother. Not trying to cover up. We keep a file on unidentified bullets nowadays. Someday you might use that gun again. Then you'd be over a barrel.'"

—Captain Gregory warns Philip Marlowe in Raymond Chandler's *The Big Sleep* (1939).

The objective of firearms identification is to determine if a certain weapon fired a bullet or cartridge found at a crime scene. To achieve this objective, examiners study marks created by a weapon on the surface of the bullet and the cartridge case. These marks can represent class characteristics or individual characteristics.

When bullets are fired through a rifled barrel, the barrel's lands and grooves create marks on the bullet. Since bullets are made of a softer material than gun barrels, any bullet fired from a weapon will have a similar pattern of marks.

Class characteristics include the bullet diameter and features of the weapon's barrel: the number of lands and grooves, the width of the lands and grooves, and the direction in which the grooves spiral from breech to muzzle. These are the characteristics common to weapons having the same make and model. The table below illustrates some of the variation of rifling characteristics among firearms. The FBI maintains a General Rifling Characteristics File, which the agency distributes to law enforcement offices.

Table 7.1. Examples of Rifling Characteristics.

Make – Caliber	Twist Direction – *Amount	Number of Lands	Approximate Lands/Grooves Width (inches)
Colt – .22	L – 1/14	6	0.5
Luger – 9 mm	R – 1/9.84	6	1
Luger – 7.65 mm	R – 1/9.84	4	1
Smith & Wesson – .44	R – 1/20	5	1.1

*One turn in the indicated inches of barrel length.
Source: Paul L. Kirk, *Crime Investigation, Second Edition* (Krieger Publishing Company 1974).

An examiner cannot use class characteristics to identify a particular weapon. In addition to class characteristics, however, every weapon bears unique traits initially introduced during manufacture and later caused by wear. The individual characteristics of a bullet or cartridge case enable an examiner to identify a round of fired ammunition as coming from a particular gun. Individual characteristics can be provided by striated marks and impressed marks.

The interior of a gun barrel has fine lines, or striations, unintentionally created by the particular cutting tool used to make the rifled barrel. These striations impart individual characteristics because they have a random distribution and irregular shape that will not appear in two barrels. As a bullet travels through a gun barrel, it acquires a characteristic set of marks from the barrel's striations.

An impressed mark is created when a hard surface, such as a firing pin, imprints its shape into a softer material. The impressions produced by two weapons will differ but are virtually identical on case cartridges used in a particular weapon. Let's go back to the firing of a gun. A charge that explodes in a gun barrel expands in both directions. While the bullet is propelled toward the muzzle, the explosion drives the soft metal of the cartridge case backward against the rear of the barrel, the breechblock. Here, the case acquires an imprint of imperfections in the face of the breechblock. The force of the explosion also expands the cartridge case within the chamber, and this may impress any irregularities of the chamber onto the casing. In semiautomatic firearms, extractor and ejector markings are engraved into the cartridge cases.

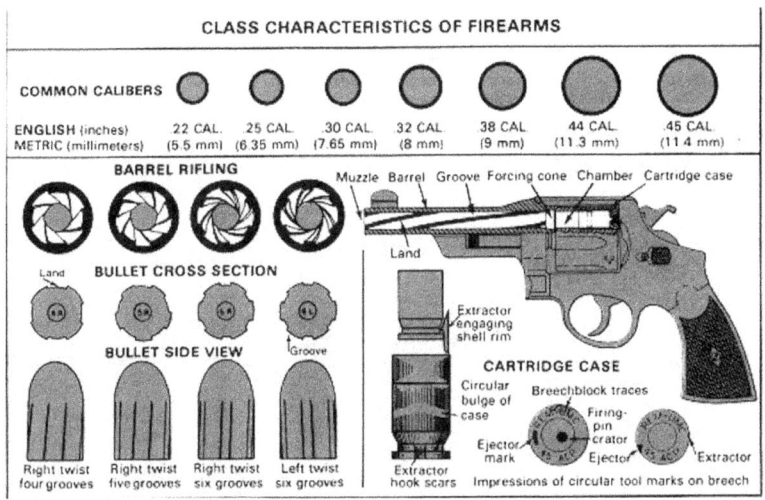

Figure 7.1. Firearm characteristics. Source: *Law Enforcement Investigations,* *U.S. Army Field Manual No. 19-20* (November 25, 1985).

Shotgun pellets lack characteristic markings that can be linked to a weapon. However, the brass portion of shotgun shells may contain marks from the firing pin, breechblock, extractor, or ejector. An examiner may be able to use these marks to individualize a shell to a weapon. The size and shape of the wad may also tell a story: the gauge of the shotgun and the manufacturer of the fired shell.

A suspect can be linked to a crime if a bullet found at a crime scene and a bullet test-fired from the suspect's gun have the same markings. To obtain a test bullet, a firearms examiner shoots the suspect weapon into an object that protects the bullet, such as a water tank (a bullet recovery tank) or a box filled with cotton (a bullet trap).

For about 80 years, the comparison microscope has been the primary tool of forensic firearms examiners. This instrument is composed of two microscopes connected by an optical bridge, which allows the examiner to view two bullets simultaneously. An examiner will place a bullet into each of two cylindrical bullet holders located beneath the lens system and then rotate one bullet until a prominent land or groove comes into view. The other bullet can be rotated to find a matching region. After the examiner has determined that two bullets share the same class characteristics (such as six lands and grooves with a right twist), the examiner will study the striated markings on the bullets.

An absolute match is not always possible. Powder residues, grit, or rust particles in the barrel can alter markings on bullets fired at different times. A bullet found at a crime scene may also be distorted after passing through obstructions, such as the victim's body. Whether two bullets match is a determination made by the expert; firearms experts usually don't require a predetermined number of points of similarity.

Computer Analysis

"He knew that IBIS stood for Integrated Ballistic Identification System, a new computer program that the Bureau of Alcohol, Tobacco and Firearms used to store bullet and shell casings. Part of ATF's new Ceasefire program."
—Special Agent Nick Carlson in Harlan Coben's *Tell No One* (2001).

The U.S. Bureau of Alcohol, Tobacco, and Firearms developed a computerized system for firearms analysis called CEASEFIRE in 1992. Eventually, the agency incorporated the Integrated Ballistics Identification System, or IBIS, a system developed by the ATF and Forensic Technology (Montreal, Canada). IBIS includes two software programs: a bullet-analyzing module called Bulletproof, and Brasscatcher, a cartridge-analyzing module. Law enforcement agencies in over 30 countries have adapted IBIS technology.

During 1992, the FBI launched its own imaging system with networked search capabilities. This system, DRUGFIRE, emphasized cartridge case markings. In 1997, the FBI and ATF decided that the two competing systems need to be interoperable so that an image captured by one system could be analyzed and correlated on the other. ATF agreed to stop referring to its program as CEASEFIRE and the FBI agreed to stop using the term DRUGFIRE. The agencies initiated the National Integrated Ballistics Information Network, or NIBIN.

In the NIBIN program, images of fired bullets and cartridge casings are electronically scanned, and this information is converted into a set of numbers. When an examiner loads a new image into the system, regional and national databases are searched for a match. If a possible match is found, a firearms examiner will scrutinize the actual evidence with a comparison microscope. Computer analysis allows law enforcement agencies to connect shooting incidents by matching projectiles and shell casings recovered from seemingly unrelated occurrences. Like CODIS in DNA analysis, NIBIN creates links between investigations across jurisdictional boundaries.

The Rise and Fall of Bullet Composition Analysis

Suppose that investigators cannot associate a gun with a suspect, or that the crime scene yields only bullet fragments too small or distorted for analysis of markings. In these cases, investigators may find a suspect with unfired ammunition and can compare these chemically with bullet fragments found at the crime scene. Using the compositional analysis of bullet lead, or CABL, technique, bullets or bullet fragments collected from a crime scene or from a body can be compared with unused cartridges in the possession of a suspect. Developed in the 1960s, the technique is based on the assumption that two bullets probably came from the same source if they share identical concentrations of contaminants in the lead: arsenic, antimony, tin, copper, bismuth, silver, and cadmium.

A 2004 report from the National Research Council cast doubts about CABL's reliability. According to the council, batches of melted lead may not contain uniform profiles of contaminants, and bullets from identical batches could be sold in different boxes. Furthermore, different batches could match by chance. The National Research Council concluded that the FBI's technology for measuring contaminants (inductively coupled plasma-optical emission spectroscopy) is the best available for bullet composition analysis. But the council recommended improvements in quality assurance and statistical analysis practices. The NRC also suggested that experts should testify in terms of the probability that two bullets came from the same source rather than state that they had positively identified a match.

The FBI performed a 14-month review to study the NRC's recommendations. On September 1, 2005, the FBI announced that it has discontinued bullet lead examinations. The agency stated in a press release that a significant factor in this decision was that "neither scientists nor bullet manufacturers are able to definitively attest to the significance of an association made between bullets in the course of a bullet lead examination."

Perhaps, testimony about compositional analysis of bullet lead played a key role in the conviction of one of your characters. Would his release from prison serve justice or unleash a killer?

Reconstructing a Shooting

"The forensic analysis report contained a subreport labeled GSR, which I knew meant gunshot residue. It stated that a neuron activation analysis of leather gloves worn by the victim found particles of burned gunpowder on the right glove, indicating he had used that hand to fire the weapon. GSR and gas burns were also found in the victim's throat. The conclusion was that the barrel had been in Sean's mouth when the gun discharged."
—Journalist Jack McEvoy in Michael Connelly's *The Poet* (1996).

Your investigators find a shooting victim. Was this an accident, suicide, self-defense or a murder? Differentiating among these scenarios may require a determination of the distance between a weapon's muzzle and the victim.

When a firearm is discharged, smoke and gunpowder particles accompany the propelled bullet. The distribution of these residues provides clues about the distance from which a shooter fired the weapon. Like many of the forensic examinations that we've seen, certainty comes from a comparison of evidence. The best way for a forensic examiner to determine the muzzle to target distance is to compare powder residue patterns on the victim and patterns obtained after firing test shots with the suspect weapon from various distances into cloth similar to the victim's clothing.

If no suspect weapon is recovered, then the examiner can only state whether or not the victim was shot from a certain broad distance. Was the shooting a contact shot, a close-range shot, or a distance shooting?

Let's consider a contact shot, in which a gun is fired with the muzzle pressed against the victim's body. Hot gases burn the edges of the bullet wound, and a corona of gray or black powder (soot) is present in about the size of the weapon's barrel. The muzzle sight of the weapon may be stamped in soot on the skin. Gunshot residues will be found along the bullet track in the victim's tissues.

Suppose that a gun is fired near the body, but no more than two feet away. Soot and stippling can be observed around the entry wound. Stippling, or tattooing, occurs when gunpowder particles are driven into the skin, creating hemorrhages in a spotted pattern. An abrasion collar will also be present; this is a discolored circle around the entrance wound caused by bruising of the skin by the bullet.

With distances up to three feet, scattered particles of unburned and partially burned powder grains are sometimes found on the victim. Beyond that range, the only marks typically found around a bullet entry wound are an abrasion collar and a dark ring created when the bullet's surface brushes against the body. This bullet wipe can contain lead, carbon, lubricant, primer residue, and dirt.

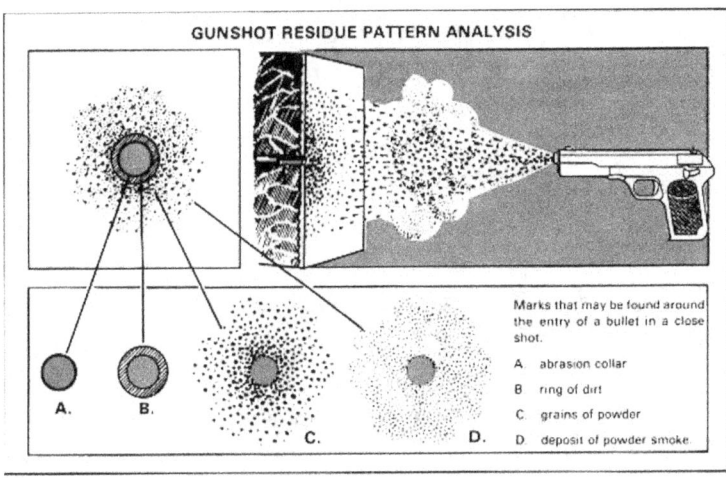

Figure 7.2. Gunshot residue patterns. Source: *Law Enforcement Investigations, U.S. Army Field Manual No. 19-20* (November 25, 1985).

A bullet wound also yields information about the position of the victim. As a bullet passes through a victim's body, it may tumble or become distorted after impacting bone. This can produce an exit wound larger and more irregularly shaped than the entry wound. The size difference is often used as the definitive marker for direction in fiction. However, this sign is not foolproof. More reliable ways to distinguish entry and exit wounds are:

- exit wounds will not have soot or tattooing,
- exit wounds typically do not have an abrasion collar, and
- exit wounds may have triangular skin tears.

A bullet creates additional signs about direction if it impacts bone structures. At the entry site, bone chips are knocked inward, producing a sharp-edged hole on the entry side and a larger beveled-out hole on the inside. The opposite occurs when the bullet leaves the bony structure: The impact produces a sharp-edged hole on the interior entry side and a larger beveled-out hole on the exit side.

Shotgun wounds provide information as well. At a distance of about four to five feet, the shot tears a concentrated wound and leaves scorching and tattooing. If the weapon is fired more than three feet away, shotgun pellets create a spreading pattern. At distances less than ten feet, the wad used in ammunition may be found inside the body or partially embedded in the entry wound. At 10 to 20 feet, the wadding still travels with the shot and may cause an abrasion.

In a shotgun blast, the spread of shot particles can indicate the range at which the weapon was fired. However, distance is not the only variable; the spread pattern also depends on the weapon design and the constriction of the barrel. This constriction, or choke, extends the weapon's range by reducing the spread of the shot after leaving the muzzle.

To locate gunpowder residue not observed with visual examination, an investigator may use the Greiss test. This test detects nitrites produced by an incomplete combustion of smokeless powder. The examiner transfers nitrite particles from cloth to a chemically treated photographic paper and then treats the paper to develop the nitrite pattern. This pattern can be compared with the pattern obtained with a test firing from a suspect gun to determine shooting distance.

The location of gunshot residues is not limited to the victim; gunpowder and primer particles can be found on surfaces within a few feet of the sides of the firearm and on the hands of the shooter. The classic dermal nitrate test (paraffin test) was developed to detect unburned gunpowder or nitrates. However, the test also detected the presence of common substances, such as fertilizer, cosmetics, and tobacco.

A more modern approach focuses on the detection of primer residues, not gunpowder residues. An examiner may use adhesive tape to remove a sample from a suspect's hands. The tape can be analyzed with a scanning electron microscope coupled with energy dispersive X-ray analysis. Using a scanning electron microscope, the examiner can determine primer particle size and shape. The examiner uses an X-ray detector to obtain elemental data about a sample. Typical elements found in most currently manufactured primers are lead, barium, and antimony. These elements are also found in the environment, so the examiner must take into account any background particles found on the hands.

Primer residues remain on the hands for a brief time and can be difficult to detect several hours after a shooting. A higher rate of positive findings has been achieved in the examination of hands from suicide victims, as long as samples are taken before the victim is moved or if the hands are protected with paper bags.

Summary

"'Assuming the evidence was collected correctly, there are plenty of things that can match up the gun as the homicide weapon. Evidence techs can study the striations taken off the barrel. Groove impressions can also be linked, and bullet landmarks can be identified by their patterns. Sometimes the lab techs will even compare and link cartridge cases by looking at microscopic details in the marks of the firing pin on the primer. Weapons have their own fingerprints, and ballistics can match them.'"

—Captain Lou Bohannon of the Buffalo Police Department in Alan Russell's *Political Suicide* (2003).

In this chapter, we've surveyed the basic principles of firearm identification. We've looked at general rifling characteristics determination, which provides the probable identity of a firearm's model based on the measurement of class characteristics found on fired bullets. And we've seen how spent ammunition can carry individuating characteristics that link the ammunition with a suspect firearm. We've also considered clues provided by projectile wounds that allow a reconstruction of the shooting.

Let's go back to the scene of a shooting. Your investigator will want to know whether the victim was murdered or committed suicide. Here are a few points that the investigator may consider.

- Multiple gunshot wounds suggest homicide.
- The area of injury may preclude the possibility of suicide.

- Establishing the distance from the muzzle to target may indicate homicide. (Your investigator can probably rule out suicide or accidental shooting during a struggle if the firing distance exceeded the victim's reach.)
- An autopsy may reveal that the trajectory of the bullet is inconsistent with suicide.
- The position of the victim at the time of injury—established by blood spatter analysis, gunshot powder residue, and bullet trajectory—may indicate either homicide or suicide.

Of course, the victim might have been shot accidentally, perhaps while cleaning or unloading a firearm. A firearms expert can examine a weapon to determine the likelihood of an accidental firing. Was the weapon predisposed to fire accidentally? The firearm should not have a trigger pull that is less than the weight of the weapon. The examiner will also determine if the weapon fires when dropped or when it strikes an object.

You've probably seen many films and TV shows in which an investigator directly handles a weapon found at a crime scene. This may eliminate fine particles of blood spatter, destroy fingerprints, and disturb fibers, hair, and other trace evidence. Sometimes the fictional investigator carefully lifts the weapon by placing an item, such as a pencil, in the barrel. This is no improvement. Sticking an object in a weapon's barrel can eliminate dust, which would have indicated that it had not been fired recently, as well as destroy and create rifling characteristics that may affect the identification of the weapon. Maybe the investigator avoids the barrel and places a pencil in the trigger guard to examine the gun. This really isn't a good idea; the pencil may discharge the weapon and wound a colleague. If handling the weapon is necessary, the investigator should do so using a checkered portion of the handgrip, edge of a trigger guard or other area less likely to contain evidence.

Remember those scenes in which a diver finds a suspect weapon in a river or lake and triumphantly waves the weapon in the air to show those on shore? If the firearm is recovered in water, then the weapon should be placed in a container and kept submerged in the same water. If exposed to air, the firearm will begin to rust, a process that destroys rifling characteristics.

Your crime scene specialists will probably want to protect firearm residue on the victim's hands by covering the hands with brown paper bags.

They should not use plastic bags to protect the hands, because condensation forms as the body is refrigerated in the morgue. Also, the shooting victim's clothing must be preserved to prevent a disruption of firearm residues.

We'll leave this survey of firearms identification and look at another type of identification in the next chapter: fingerprint determination, a long-established technique that has come under fire in recent court cases.

A Few FAQ from the Course

From time to time, a story line revolves around a bullet made of a material that disappears after wounding the victim. The classic is the ice bullet, but a criminal on a popular forensic TV show used a frozen piece of ground beef as a bullet. Would this really be effective?

The heat of discharge would render an ice bullet ineffective. The rare, or at least medium rare, ground beef bullet would also be ineffective. In the first episode of Discovery Channel's *Mythbusters*, you'll see that an ice slug or a frozen ground beef slug cannot penetrate like a bullet.

Is it possible to restore serial numbers on firearms?

The identification of a weapon's serial number can lead investigators from a firearm found at a crime scene to the manufacturer, seller, and the person who purchased the weapon. But sometimes, serial numbers have been filed off and even phony replacement numbers stamped in their place. Serial numbers may be restored with chemical etching agents, such as strong acids. The process of stamping the original serial number places metal under a permanent strain that extends beneath the original serial numbers. Etching agents dissolve a strained area at a faster rate than unaltered metal. Metal stamped with a serial number also has magnetic properties differing from surrounding metal. Missing serial numbers can be revealed by applying magnetic particles to the surface of a magnetized gun.

What is a ballistic fingerprinting law?

Maryland adopted the nation's first ballistic fingerprinting law in 2000. The law requires manufacturers to test-fire all handguns shipped into the state and to send a spent shell casing to the purchasing firearms dealer. After selling the gun, the dealer must forward the casing to state police, who record the casing's markings in a database for possible use in criminal investigations. New York has a similar scheme called COBIS, or the Combined Ballistic Identification System. However, some experts consider ballistic fingerprinting impractical, because firearms change with use and can be deliberately altered.

CHAPTER 8

Whorl-wind Tour of Fingerprinting

"Wilson examined the finger marks on the knife handle and said to himself, 'Neither of the twins made those marks. Then manifestly there was another person concerned, either in his own interest or a hired assassin.'"
—*The Tragedy of Pudd'nhead Wilson* by Mark Twain (1894).

"'I never pass anything, however trifling,' said he with some pomposity. 'That is my advice to you, Mr. Holmes. In twenty five years' experience I have learned my lesson. There is always the chance of finger-marks or something.'"
—Police inspector lectures Sherlock Holmes in Sir Arthur Conan Doyle's "The Adventure of the Three Gables," included in *The Case Book of Sherlock Holmes* (1927).

In this chapter, we'll survey one of the oldest types of evidence used in criminal investigations: fingerprints. Fingerprint evidence entered the criminal investigation arena in the 1870s. Henry Faulds, a Scottish doctor working in a Tokyo hospital, began studying fingerprints as identifying marks, a pursuit known as dactyloscopy. Then he became involved in a case in which a thief left a fingerprint on a whitewashed wall. When a suspect was caught, Faulds noticed that the patterns on the suspect's fingers were very different from those found at the crime scene. The police interrogated another suspect; this time, the fingerprint patterns matched. When confronted with this evidence, the suspect confessed. Enthusiastic about this new method of identification, Faulds offered to fund a fingerprint bureau at Scotland Yard. But police officials declined his offer, favoring a popular identification method devised by French policeman Alphonse Bertillon.

The Bertillon System, or bertillonage, is considered to be the first widely accepted scientific method of biometric identification. Bertillonage relied on a combination of physical measurements (e.g., height, skull width, and foot length), full-length and profile photographs, and information such as hair color and eye color. Law enforcement agencies throughout Europe and in the United States adopted this system.

In 1880, Faulds published his observations about fingerprints in a scientific journal. He forwarded a copy of his paper to Charles Darwin, who passed it on to Francis Galton, his nephew. Galton researched fingerprints and determined two of the basic principles that underpin fingerprinting practice: Fingerprints remain the same during an individual's lifetime, and no two fingerprints are identical. He published *Finger Prints* in 1892, which presented his findings and suggested a system of fingerprint identification.

In 1900, the British government created a committee to investigate fingerprinting as a means of identification. Around this time, Edward R. Henry, Commissioner of the Metropolitan Police, published his book, *The Classification and Use of Finger Prints*, which proposed a method of fingerprint classification and comparison to replace the Bertillon system. Following the recommendations of the committee, a three-person Fingerprint Branch opened in July 1901 at New Scotland Yard. The small department used the Henry system of classification, which has become the core of fingerprint systems in most English-speaking countries.

Meanwhile, only a few U.S. agencies explored fingerprinting. The New York City Civil Servant Commission used fingerprints to certify civil service applications. James Parke, an identifications clerk with the New York Bureau of Prisons, had learned about fingerprinting from Henry's book and had tested the classification system. Parke presented an exhibit on fingerprinting at the 1904 World's Fair in St. Louis. His demonstration, though a success, was upstaged by a presentation on fingerprinting by Detective John Kenneth Ferrier of New Scotland Yard. Ferrier stayed in the United States for a while, teaching the Henry system to identification clerks from police departments and prisons.

One trainee, Constable Thomas Alfred Edward Foster of the Dominion Police, returned to Canada and pressed for the creation of a fingerprint system. His efforts engendered the national fingerprint bureau at the Royal Canadian Mounted Police headquarters in Ottawa. Established in 1911, this is the oldest central fingerprint bureau in North America.

In 1904 the penitentiary at Leavenworth, Kansas, and the St. Louis, Missouri, Police Department established fingerprint bureaus. During the following years, other U.S. police departments adopted fingerprinting systems. The demand for a national repository of fingerprint records led to a 1921 Act of Congress, establishing the Identification Division of the FBI. Today, the FBI has the largest collection of fingerprints in the world.

Detecting Prints at the Crime Scene

"Using porcelain-tipped forceps, Cooper picked up the stone and examined it. He slipped on goggles and hit the rock with a beam from a PoliLight – a power pack the size of a car battery with a light wand attached.

'Nothing,' Cooper said.

'VMD?'

Vacuum metal deposition is the Cadillac of techniques for raising latent prints on nonporous surfaces. It evaporates gold or zinc in a vacuum chamber containing the object to be tested; the metal coats the latent print, making the whorls and peaks very visible.

But Cooper didn't have a VMD with him.

'What *do* you have?' asked Rhyme, not pleased.

'Sudan black, stabilized physical developer, iodine, amido black, DFO and gentian violet, Magna-Brush.'"

—Lincoln Rhyme and identification expert Mel Cooper in Jeffrey Deaver's *The Bone Collector* (1997).

Skin, the largest organ of the body, performs many functions. It contains internal organs and the skeleton, it provides sensory information about the environment, and it eliminates waste products—salts, amino acids, ammonia, and urea—as sweat. The palms of the hands and soles of the feet are covered with a particular type of skin: friction ridge skin, raised layers of skin with openings for sweat glands. Friction ridge patterns, which develop during fetal life, expand as a person matures and may shrink in old age. Yet the pattern remains unchanged until decomposition destroys the skin.

Two general categories of fingerprints are inked (or direct) prints that are intentional impressions made with ink, powder, or a similar material, and unintentional impressions found at crime scenes. A crime scene fingerprint may be one of two types of patent (or visible) prints:

- a transfer print, which is made by fingers that contacted a visible material such as blood, wet paint, soot, grease, or wet ink; or
- a plastic, or impression, print, which is created when fingers press against a pliable material, such as putty, dust, or wax.

Latent (or invisible) prints may be present at a crime scene. A latent print is created when the natural oils and perspiration present between friction ridges are transferred to a touched surface. The quality of a latent print can be affected by the surface of the object touched and by the rate of sweat secretion, which, in turn, is affected by health, emotional state, occupation, and weather. Porous surfaces generally absorb sweat and often do not hold a fingerprint impression, whereas a hard, smooth surface of a nonporous material is ideally suited for retaining latent impressions.

Where should your evidence specialists—who are wearing gloves, of course—search for fingerprints at a crime scene? They will be guided by the suspected nature of the crime. If the crime appears to be a burglary, then they will scrutinize points of entry and exit, as well as any area rifled by the burglar in the search for valuables.

Your crime scene specialist may search for latent prints with laser light, which causes chemicals in human perspiration to fluoresce in the dark. Instead of a laser, your specialist may locate prints with an alternate light source. These forensic lights emit high-intensity light covering a range of wavelengths from the near-infrared to the ultraviolet.

Tactics for visualizing latent fingerprints depend upon whether the print lies on a nonabsorbent or absorbent surface. Hard and nonabsorbent surfaces like glass, painted wood, tiles, or metal are usually dusted with fingerprint powder that sticks to oil and perspiration traces. Although fingerprint powders are available in a variety of colors, the basic materials are a fine carbon powder for light-colored surfaces and a gray aluminum dust for dark surfaces. A print left on a patterned or brightly colored surface can be dusted with a fluorescent powder and photographed under ultraviolet light. A latent print can also be revealed by spraying with a magnetic powder and removing excess powder with a magnet.

Yet another option for fingerprint visualization is superglue fuming, which develops prints with the active ingredient in superglue, cyanoacrylate. A crime scene specialist might use a handheld wand that heats a small cartridge containing a mixture of cyanoacrylate ester and a fluorescent dye. Alternatively, prints can be visualized by placing an object in a fuming tank. Cyanoacrylate evaporators can be used to fume entire rooms, as well as the interior and exterior of a vehicle.

Fingerprints on soft or porous surfaces, such as cloth and paper, can be visualized. A classic approach is to place the item inside a closed cabinet with iodine crystals. When heated, the crystals give off an iodine vapor that combines with traces in the print to leave a visible mark. Another method is to spray the item with ninhydrin, which produces a purple-blue color when combined with traces of amino acids in human sweat. The ninhydrin method is very sensitive and easy to use, almost eliminating the use of iodine. Superglue fuming is yet another option for visualizing prints on porous materials.

Physical Developer, a reagent that contains silver nitrate, reacts with the salt in perspiration to form silver chloride, which can be viewed under ultraviolet light. This technique can develop latent fingerprints on porous articles even if they have been wet. Since Physical Developer eliminates traces of proteins from the tested object, this reagent is usually used as a follow-up to ninhydrin treatment.

If other techniques have failed to recover a latent print, then vacuum metal deposition, or VMD, may provide an expensive solution. In this process, an item of evidence is placed under vacuum, and an invisible layer of evaporated gold uniformly deposits on the surface and penetrates the fingerprint. A second layer of metal, typically zinc, is evaporated and deposits preferentially on the exposed gold but does not penetrate the fingerprint deposit. Consequently, friction ridges are left transparent while the background becomes coated with a layer of zinc. This method can detect latent prints that are decades old.

Patent prints and visualized latent prints must be photographed. If a print is on a small object, then the crime scene specialist may simply cover the object with cellophane and transport it to the lab for photography. If the print is on a large object, then the specialist may choose to preserve the print by lifting it with tape or a plastic sheet.

Corpses are also fingerprinted. During an autopsy, fingerprints may be taken after any trace evidence has been removed from the fingers and fingernails. To obtain fingerprints from a corpse, the examiner dries the fingers and palms, inks the fingers, and then presses them into a fingerprint spoon, a curved metal plate that holds a fingerprint card. If the body is decomposed, the outer layer of skin will peel off, or deglove. As Dr. Michael Baden and Marian Roach explain in their book *Dead Reckoning* (2001), "You just need to put your own gloved finger into it and roll off a print or two."

What about latent prints left on a corpse by the killer? This is a challenge. Human skin is a porous surface covered with sweat and oil, the same components of latent fingerprints. In the early 1970s, examiners searched for latent prints on human skin by covering the skin with a fine lead powder, which would be brushed away to reveal fingerprints. Improvements include the use of magnetic powder, the superglue method, and a laser technique combined with a fluorescent powder.

Bacterial Betrayal

A person who touches an object with a bare hand not only leaves fingerprints and DNA, but also bacteria. Researchers at the University of Colorado, Boulder, discovered that about 150 bacteria species thrive on a typical human hand. The types of skin-dwelling bacteria vary greatly from person to person; two people share only about 13% of bacteria species. An investigation of bacteria species living on the hands of 51 people revealed more than 4,700 different bacteria species, and only five species lived on the skin of every participant of the study.

To test one application of these discoveries, the scientists analyzed DNA traces of bacteria that computer users had deposited on computer mice and keyboards. The DNA traces more closely matched the DNA of bacterial colonies that inhabited the hands of the individual who used the computer, compared with bacterial DNA traces of randomly selected people. The scientists obtained useful samples of bacterial DNA two weeks after an individual touched a computer mouse.

Characterizing Fingerprints

"'I have noticed that the minute whorls on the fingertip offer amazing variety. I believe some attempts have been made in India and Japan to systematize the phenomenon, and I intend to experiment once I am back in Baker Street with my equipment at my own fingertips.'"
—Sherlock Holmes in *Femme Fatale* by Carole Nelson Douglas (2003).

A fingerprint is an individuating characteristic because every finger has a unique and complex pattern of friction ridges that divide, cross, and end. These ridge patterns, combined with the number and locations of certain ridge characteristics, provide the basis for fingerprint identification. The probability that two fingers will produce the same fingerprint pattern is extremely small. This has been borne out over a century of experience. At the same time, fingerprints share general characteristics that allow a systematic classification.

The 10-fingerprint classification systems currently in use rely on three ridge patterns: loops, whorls, and arches.

- About 60% to 65% of the population has ridge patterns that form loops, in which ridges enter from one side of the pattern and curve to exit from the same side. About 60% of loops are ulnar loops, which open toward the little finger; a radial loop opens in the opposite direction. A loop has two focal points: the core and the delta. The core is the center of the pattern, and the delta is the area in which ridges divide to form a triangular shape.

- About 30% to 35% of the population has whorl ridge patterns, which have at least two deltas. A plain whorl can look like a collection of concentric circles or a spiral. A whorl pattern may also appear as a double loop, a central pocket loop, or an accidental loop.

- About 5% of the population has arch-shaped ridge patterns, which lack any deltas or cores. Here, ridges enter on one side of the impression and usually flow out the other side, with a rise in the center. These are plain arches if they have a wavelike pattern or tented arches if they end in a sharp point in the center.

Most U.S. agencies use the FBI's modification of the Henry classification system, in which possible impression variations are split into 1,024 groups. We'll look at the FBI's fingerprint analysis process in the next section. For now, let's focus on the FBI's primary fingerprint classification method.

Table 8.1. Scheme Used by the FBI to Classify Fingerprints.

Right index finger	Right ring finger	Left thumb	Left middle finger	Left little finger
Right thumb	Right middle finger	Right little finger	Left index finger	Left ring finger

Fingerprints are arranged in a double row with the sequence shown in the table. Each of the 10 fingerprints is assigned a numerical value, depending on the pattern of the print and the particular finger. If either of the fingers in the first column has a whorl pattern, it gets a value of 16. If either fingerprint in the second column has a whorl, it gets an eight. If any of the third, fourth, and fifth pairs has a whorl, it scores a four, two, and one, respectively. Any finger without a whorl pattern is given a zero. After adding the scores, an additional point is given to each row, unless all fingers in the row have whorl patterns.

Here's an example. Suppose that whorls are present on the right middle finger and left thumb. Using the formula, we get (0 + 0 + 4 + 0 + 0 +1)/(0 + 8 + 0 + 0 + 0 +1), or a primary classification of 5/9. This is a class figure and a starting point in the search for a matching print.

Fingerprint Individualization and Analysis

"'How many points does the FBI use to compare prints?'

'We don't rely on any individual number at all. We rely on the expertise and overall impression of the examiner.'

'So, examiners are allowed to make matches based on, say, six points?'
'Theoretically . . . .'"

—Defense attorney cross-examines a fingerprint expert in the *Law and Order* episode, "Myth of Fingerprints" (2001).

The fingerprint classification system provides a means to search for candidates with a positive match. Overall ridge patterns impart class characteristics, while the type and position of ridge characteristics (minutiae) impart an individuating character. Identification relies upon the comparison of individual ridge characteristics, such as bifurcations and ridge endings, features sometimes called Galton points.

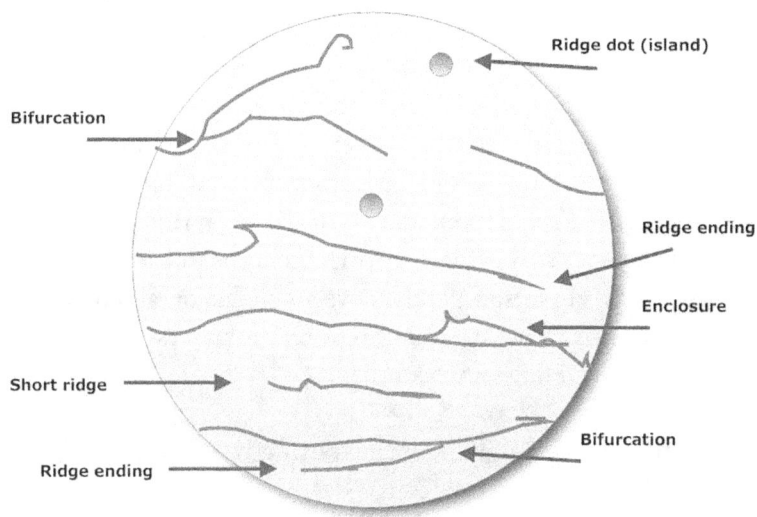

Figure 8.1. Examples of ridge characteristics.

The average fingerprint can contain as many as 175 individual ridge characteristics. Yet the odds are that a print found at a crime scene will be partial. In fact, a typical latent print may represent about 20% of a full fingerprint. How many ridge characteristics must two fingerprints share before an expert declares them identical? Opinions vary.

Examiners in certain countries rely on a point system, in which a fingerprint examiner declares a positive match only after identifying a minimum number of corresponding Galton points in the correct geometry between an evidence print and a reference print. In Italy, examiners want to see 16 or 17 points of similarity; in Argentina and Brazil the number is 30. Swedish examiners prefer 7, while Australians prefer 12.

David Ashbaugh, a constable with the Royal Canadian Mounted Police, published a book entitled *Ridgeology* (1983) on the process of individualization through friction ridges. Ashbaugh claimed that matches are not established by the accumulation of points of similarity. Instead, the examiner must consider ridge detail in its totality, including location of points, the size and orientation of points, the locations of pores along ridges, and the characteristics of ridges between points. Canada does not have a minimum point threshold for identification, and the United Kingdom eliminated its point system. The International Association for Identification does not find a valid basis for requiring a particular minimum number of friction ridge characteristics before concluding that two fingerprints are identical. Rather, fingerprint identification should rely upon the experience of the fingerprint examiner. Some U.S. examiners, however, still prefer a point system.

Currently, the FBI uses an identification process known as ACE-V, or analysis, comparison, evaluation, and verification. In this process, an examiner assesses reference and evidence prints (analysis), observes recognizable features in both (comparison), and draws a conclusion about the evidence print (evaluation). Another examiner repeats the process to perform a peer review (verification). Here's an example:

- Candidate matches are identified using the patterns of loops, arches, and whorls (Level 1 detail).
- The examiner then analyzes the evidence print to identify Level 2 detail: the points where ridges terminate or bifurcate, as well as patterns of islands, dots, and forks. The examiner also notes variations in the ridges, such as the slight turns of the ridges (the ridge path) and the locations of sweat pores (Level 3 detail).
- The examiner then compares these features to the Level 2 and Level 3 details of an ink print.
- If the examiner decides that the evidence and ink prints are sufficiently similar to declare a match, then another examiner must verify the match.

This method combines quantity and quality. The quality of Level 3 detail—the information most likely lost in a latent print—is unimportant if there are abundant ridge characteristics. On the other hand, a low number of ridge characteristics can be compensated by high-quality Level 3 detail.

Automated Fingerprint Identification Systems

"Though Gladden was fingerprinted upon his arrest, Santa Monica does not have its own fingerprint computer and relies on use of a Department of Justice computer and other departments, including the LAPD, to run prints on the AFIS network. The process usually takes days because departments run their own prints as priorities."

—Michael Connelly's *The Poet* (1996).

Throughout most of its history, fingerprint examination required a scrutiny of paper records. Fingerprints recovered from a crime scene could be used in a number of ways. If investigators identified a suspect, then they could make inked prints from the suspect, and an examiner could compare the suspect's fingerprints with an evidence print. If no suspect had been identified, then an evidence print would be filed until a suspect came to light. Alternatively, an evidence print could be used to perform a search of fingerprints on file. This manual search would have a low likelihood of success. During the 1950s, experts worked on systems to store fingerprint information on punch cards, which could be mechanically searched. Twenty years later, optical scanners and computers revolutionized fingerprint record keeping and analysis.

Law enforcement agencies now rely on Automated Fingerprint Identification Systems, or AFIS. These systems can scan fingerprints and convert the image into digital ridge characteristics that contain data about ridge termination points and the branching of ridges into two (bifurcation). The relative position and orientation of ridge characteristics are also determined. The system stores both an optical image and data describing geometric patterns. At a rate of thousands of comparisons per second, the analysis part of the system compares the digital record of the description against the new print to produce candidate matches. Optical images of these potential matches are retrieved and displayed for a fingerprint examiner. An examiner, not a computer, performs the final comparison to determine if fingerprints match.

Investigators can perform three types of automated searches.

- A 10-print to 10-print search compares the complete set of prints from a suspect against the database of 10-prints. The purpose of this search is to determine whether the suspect is using an alias or has a previous conviction under another name. This type of search can also identify a nameless corpse.
- An evidence print to 10-print search is run when crime scene technicians record an evidence print from a crime scene, and the suspect is not apparent or does not match the print. If there is no hit, then the evidence print is retained by the system as an unsolved file.
- When new 10-prints are entered into the system, they are automatically searched against the unsolved files (sometimes called a 10-print to latent print search). A hit with this search reveals that the suspect may be involved in a previously unsolved crime.

Various companies manufacture AFIS computers, which differ in the way that fingerprint information is recorded. This has created a compatibility problem. To promote the sharing of fingerprint data, the FBI developed and initiated in 1999 the Integrated Automated Fingerprint Identification System, or IAFIS. This system provides a national storehouse of criminals' fingerprints, which can be accessed by other federal, state, and local law enforcement agencies. These agencies also submit fingerprints and corresponding criminal history information. As a result, the IAFIS maintains the largest biometric database in the world, with fingerprints and criminal history information for more than 70 million people.

The use of computers in fingerprint identification has had another effect. The age-old practice of inking a suspect's hands to obtain a fingerprint has been replaced with an optical scanning process. The electronic fingerprint image can be transmitted to an AFIS computer center for an assessment, which may reveal information about outstanding warrants and arrest history.

Summary

"'When those packets were sealed up, Jonas Oldacre got McFarlane to secure one of the seals by putting his thumb upon the soft wax. . . . It was the simplest thing in the world for him to take a wax impression from the seal, to moisten it in as much blood as he could get from a pinprick, and to put the mark upon the wall during the night, either with his own hand or with that of his housekeeper. If you examine among those documents which he took with him into his retreat, I will lay you a wager that you find the seal with the thumb-mark upon it.'"

—Sherlock Holmes explains a fingerprint fraud in Sir Arthur Conan Doyle's "The Adventure of the Norwood Builder," included in *The Return of Sherlock Holmes* (1905).

"'Thus there is produced a *facsimile* in relief of the finger-print having actual ridges and furrows identical in character with the ridges and furrows of the finger-tip. If an inked roller is passed over this relief, or if the relief is pressed lightly on an inked slab, and then pressed on a sheet of paper, a finger-print will be produced which will be absolutely identical with the original, even to the little white spots which mark the orifices of the sweat glands. It will be impossible to discover any differences between the real finger-print and the counterfeit because, in fact, no difference exists.'"

—Dr. John Evelyn Thorndyke on fingerprint fraud in R. Austin Freeman's *The Red Thumb Mark* (1907).

In this chapter, we've surveyed the basic principles of fingerprint analysis, including detection and characterization of fingerprints. Fingerprint evidence can identify a victim or criminal, and it can prove that a suspect was at the scene of a crime. The power of fingerprints derives from three basic principles.

- A fingerprint is an individuating characteristic due to the unique pattern of ridges and depressions.
- This fingerprint pattern develops during fetal life and remains unchanged until decomposition destroys the skin.
- Even though fingerprint patterns are distinct in ridge characteristics, their overall appearances are similar enough to allow a systematic classification.

Unless the criminal wears gloves, the odds are that the criminal will leave fingerprints at a crime scene. These bits of evidence are becoming easier to detect. In 2003, a new fingerprinting method was announced that would make it virtually impossible to erase fingerprints. Scientists at the University of Sunderland (United Kingdom) developed a dust made of millions of nanoparticles, each having a sticky surface that attaches to oily residues left in a fingerprint. These nanoparticles are glass spheres—about 200 to 600 nanometers in diameter—that are speckled with fluorescent dye. University of California scientists announced in 2005 that they had developed a novel method to visualize fingerprints. At Los Alamos National Laboratory, they found that they could focus a tight beam of X-rays on a surface and detect sodium, potassium and chlorine in sweat, which a fingertip deposits along its friction ridges. One advantage of micro-X-ray fluorescence is that it can be used to discover children's fingerprints, which can be difficult to detect due to the absence of oily sebum secreted by the sebaceous glands. The March-April 2012 issue of *Evidence Technology Magazine* includes an article ("Beyond Identification") about a new method for producing high-resolution fingerprints with antibody-coated nanoparticles. The technique also reveals drugs and drug metabolites in a latent fingerprint.

Despite advances in fingerprint detection technology, your mystery story doesn't end as soon as investigators identify fingerprints. After all, a fingerprint indicates that a suspect visited a particular place but does not indicate *when* the suspect left that fingerprint. A fingerprint match may not even indicate this much, because the identification may be due to fraud or an error.

As the above quotations show, Conan Doyle's and Freeman's detectives faced criminals who created false fingerprints to throw police off the track. In the days of paper records, this type of fraud was more successful in fiction than in real life. According to fingerprint examiners, no forgery will get past expert scrutiny. With the current dependency on electronic records, however, it does seem plausible that a hacker could modify a file or insert a new file.

Criminals aren't the only ones who want to fabricate fingerprint evidence. During the 1990s, officers and civilian employees of the New York State police were reported to have been faking fingerprints. Some staged photos by cutting pieces of inked prints and photographing them on top of the real evidence, or by lifting prints from nonevidentiary items and placing the tape on evidence prior to photography. The most common method of fabricating latent prints was to make a lift from a known print and label it as having been found at the crime scene. An investigation revealed that these people faked latent print evidence to lead others to the same conclusion that they had reached. They felt justified in faking evidence to lock up criminals. Undoubtedly, this case inspired the story about the similarly motivated fingerprint examiner Lisa Russo in *Law and Order*'s "Myth of Fingerprints" (2001).

Errors in fingerprint matching also occur. In May 2004, the FBI detained an Oregon lawyer as a material witness in the Madrid train bombings. This was based upon the FBI's identification of his fingerprints on a plastic bag of detonators. After several weeks, the agency released the lawyer because Spanish authorities announced that the fingerprint belonged to another man. Earlier in the year, a Massachusetts man—convicted on fingerprint evidence—was exonerated for shooting a police officer. DNA evidence had freed the man after he had spent six years in prison. Kasey Wertheim and Melissa Taylor offer their insights into causes for fingerprint analysis errors in their *Evidence Technology Magazine* (January-February 2012) article, "Human Factors in Latent-print Examination."

Here's a warning for those of you considering a mystery story set in the future: A clone of a human will probably have different fingerprints than the original. For about 100 years, muzzle prints have been used to identify sheep, cattle, and other animals. Like fingerprints, no two muzzle prints from different animals have been found to be identical, and a print remains the same throughout the animal's life. When researchers examined the muzzle prints of cloned, genetically identical sheep, they found differences, probably due to variations in the prenatal environment.

We'll continue a survey of impression evidence in the next chapter. This time, it'll be feet, shoes, tires, bites, and toolmarks. And we'll look at several odd impressions: lip prints and ear prints.

A Few FAQ from the Course

What was the first murder solved by fingerprints?

The credit for this goes to an 1892 investigation of two murdered children in the Argentinean town of Necochea. The local police sought assistance from the La Plata Bureau of Identification and Statistics, which was headed by Juan Vucetich. After reading Galton's book, Vucetich performed his own fingerprinting studies and devised a classification scheme. Police Inspector Alveraz, who was interested in Vucetich's experiments, was sent to Necochea, where he found the imprint of a bloodstained thumb on a bedroom door. He cut the section out, brought it to the police station, and ordered the mother of the children to be brought in as well. He used an ink pad to make an impression of her thumb, and Vucetich found it identical to the bloody thumbprint. Faced with this evidence, she admitted to killing her children.

Isn't fingerprint analysis being challenged in court?

The nature of fingerprint evidence analysis has left it open to recent court attacks. In *United States v. Byron C. Mitchell*, the defendants' attorneys argued that fingerprints could not be proven to be unique under the *Daubert* guidelines. The U.S. Supreme Court case, *Daubert v. Merrell Dow* (1993), concerned the standard for admitting scientific evidence in court. According to the *Daubert* guidelines, trial judges are responsible for determining the admissibility and reliability of scientific evidence and must consider a number of factors, such as whether the scientific technique can be tested, whether standards exist to control the technique's operation, and whether scientists have published reports on the technique. In the *Mitchell* case, the judge upheld the admissibility of fingerprints. One of the *Mitchell* appellate decisions, *United States v. Mitchell*, 365 F.3d 215 (3rd Cir. 2004), offers a detailed analysis about the admissibility of fingerprint evidence, and is available from the Third Judicial Circuit website (www.ca3.uscourts.gov).

In your quote from the Bone Collector, Mel Cooper has Sudan black, stabilized physical developer, iodine, amido black, DFO and gentian violet, and Magna-brush. How are these substances, other than physical developer and iodine, used in lifting latent prints?

Sudan black is a dye stain used on wet evidence. It is considered useful for wet items with surfaces contaminated with grease. Amido black is a dye used to enhance fingerprint detail in bloody impressions. The dye is sensitive to protein in blood. DFO reacts with amino acids in residue of a latent fingerprint and is used to enhance details of latent prints left on porous surfaces, such as paper. DFO is considered more sensitive than ninhydrin and is used before resorting to ninhydrin. Gentian violet is a dye stain used with surfaces contaminated with oils and grease. It is especially useful for visualizing fingerprints on nonporous surfaces. "Magna-brush" refers to a technique using magnetic powder. It can be used to visualize fingerprints left on human skin.

CHAPTER 9

Impressive Evidence

"Finally, there were the tool marks on the cotter pin, fresh and bright."
—*The Dead Cat Bounce* (1998) by Sarah Graves.

"The FBI laboratory's Firearms and Toolmarks section reported on the severed branch. The blades that clipped it were thick, with a shallow pitch: it had been done with a bolt cutter."
—Thomas Harris' *Red Dragon* (1981).

Impression evidence is created when an object contacts a surface capable of recording a recognizable pattern. Investigators can examine these three-dimensional patterns for identification of class characteristics and individuating characteristics. In the last chapter, we reviewed fingerprints, which is one type of impression evidence. Here, we'll survey other types of impression evidence, such as toolmarks, footprints, footwear impressions, bite marks, and tire tracks. We'll also look at two-dimensional imprint (or residue) evidence, which an investigator may find on hard surfaces.

Toolmarks

A toolmark—most often found at sites of forcible entry—is any impression, cut, scratch, gouge, indentation, or other mark caused by the contact of a tool with another object. Toolmark analysis has linked drills with holes bored in a safe; screwdrivers and crowbars with pry marks on doors, window frames, and safes; tire irons with doorknobs; and bolt cutters with locks.

There are three basic types of toolmarks. Force applied between two objects in an approximately perpendicular direction creates a compression, or indentation, mark. The harder material marks the softer material and leaves a three-dimensional replica at the point of contact. A sliding toolmark (an abrasion or friction-type mark) takes the form of scratches caused by a lateral movement of one object across another. A tool that slices through a material leaves a cutting toolmark. A wire cutter, for example, can create striations along the cut edge of a wire.

An impression left in a soft surface, such as wood, can indicate the size and shape of a tool. These are class characteristics. A comparison of a toolmark's class characteristics with marks made by a known tool may lead to an inclusion or exclusion of the tool as the source of the toolmark evidence. Tools also bear microscopic variations created during casting, grinding and polishing of metal components. Irregularities introduced at the time of manufacture or during subsequent wear can provide individuating characteristics.

Suppose that your crime scene specialists need to examine the site of a burglary. They may find toolmarks left on window sills, locked cabinets, and other objects. If possible, they will remove a piece of a damaged object that has toolmarks and transport it to the lab for examination with a comparison microscope. An examiner must rely on photos of the toolmark if the marked object cannot be removed to the lab or if the portion containing the toolmark cannot be cut from the object. Although liquid silicone or dental plaster may be used to make a cast of the mark, the process cannot capture many small details.

If a possible tool is found in a suspect's possession, then an examiner can make a test mark on material similar to that recovered from the crime scene (a standard mark) and compare it with the crime scene toolmark (the original mark). Usually, the examiner must prepare a series of test marks, attempting to duplicate the striking angle and amount of force that created the original mark.

Knowledgeable investigators will not attempt to fit a suspect tool into the original toolmark. This contact may alter the toolmark and raise questions about the reliability of the evidence. For that matter, a suspect tool found at a crime scene and a marked object must be packaged in separate containers for transport to the lab. Otherwise, a defense attorney can question whether the tool marked the object in transit.

Toolmarks in the Lindbergh Baby Kidnapping Case

On the night of March 1, 1932, a kidnapper crept toward the New Jersey home of Charles and Anne Lindbergh. He scurried up a homemade ladder to the second floor nursery and snatched the Lindbergh's twenty-month old son. The New Jersey State Police found shoeprints under the nursery room and two sections of the kidnapper's broken ladder. The kidnapper left a ransom note, the first of many demands. A baby's sleeping suit accompanied the seventh ransom note to confirm authenticity. On May 12, a trucker stumbled across a decomposed body of a small child partially buried about five miles from the Lindbergh home. A coroner determined that the child had died in early March. Now, this was a murder investigation.

The state police relied upon medical and science experts outside their organization. Dr. Erastus Mead Hudson, a New York City physician, who had learned about fingerprinting at Scotland Yard, used silver nitrate to uncover fingerprints on the kidnapper's ladder. Two New Jersey private labs scrutinized the baby's sleeping suit: the E.R. Squibb Laboratories of New Brunswick and the Albert E. Edel Chemical and Toxicological Laboratory in Newark. Edel lab scientists also examined the recovered bones and concluded that the remains could have come from a twenty-month old child. Colonel H. Norman Schwarzkopf, Superintendent of the New Jersey State Police, requested the assistance of Arthur Koehler, a wood identification expert with the U.S. Forest Service in Madison, Wisconsin. By identifying the type of wood and machine planing marks, Koehler traced part of the ladder's wood from the Dorn Mill in South Carolina to the National Lumber and Millwork Company in the Bronx, New York. Meanwhile, other investigators traced the ransom money to Bruno Richard Hauptmann, a German-born carpenter who lived ten blocks from the Bronx lumber company.

During Hauptmann's trial, the defense attempted to prevent Arthur Koehler from testifying. At this time, the evidence of a wood expert carried little weight in a criminal court. Yet the judge deemed Koehler qualified as an expert. Among other evidence, Koehler showed that marks in the ladder indicated that the defendant's hand plane had been used to dress the edges of several ladder parts. The jury found Hauptmann guilty of murder and, later, jurors said that the evidence linking Hauptmann to the ladder established one of the most convincing parts of the State's case.

Marks Made By Shoes

"'There is no branch of detective science which is so important and so much neglected as the art of tracing footsteps. Happily, I have always laid great stress upon it, and much practice has made it second nature to me.'"
—Sherlock Holmes in Sir Arthur Conan Doyle's *A Study in Scarlet* (1887).

"'That change in footprints, for example. What do you make of that?'
'Mortimer said that the man had walked on tiptoe down that portion of the alley.'
'He only repeated what some fool had said at the inquest. Why should a man walk on tiptoe down the alley?'
'What then?'
'He was running Watson – running desperately, running for his life, running until he burst his heart – and fell dead upon his face'"
—Sir Arthur Conan Doyle's *The Hound of the Baskervilles* (1902).

In the previous chapter, we explored fingerprint marks, a type of evidence that a criminal can avoid by wearing gloves. A shoeprint is another matter; a criminal must contact the ground. By the way, shoeprints are often incorrectly referred to as footprints, which are marks left by bare feet. Footwear evidence can take the form of a visible (or residue) print, a plastic print (or impression), or a latent print. A person can leave a two-dimensional visible print by depositing or transferring material, such as dust, blood, water, or mud. Impressions are made in a pliable material and are three-dimensional.

Your fictional investigators should assume that any crime scene contains visible or latent footwear evidence. Regions of a crime scene that merit close inspection include the place where the perpetrator committed the crime, the point of entry, routes to and through the crime scene, the exit point, and the area in and around other visible impressions. Your crime scene team will take general photos to relate any footwear evidence to the surrounding area and follow these with examination photos taken directly over the evidence and a scale marker.

Two-dimensional footwear evidence can be preserved by transferring the print with electrostatic, gelatin, or adhesive lifting. An electrostatic lifting device, sometimes called a dust electrostatic lifter, transfers dry dust or residue prints from porous and nonporous surfaces, including carpets, tile, floors, bodies, fabric, and newspapers. The device will not transfer a print that was wet or that had become wet. This technique is also useful in the search for a latent print. An electrostatic kit can consist of a high-voltage control unit, a nickel-plated steel ground plate, and a lifting mat with one side coated with metal. The mat is placed over the print—metallic side up—and is pressed into the print with a roller. When high voltage is applied to the lifting mat, it becomes negatively charged, while the ground plate becomes positively charged. Dust or residue present under the mat also becomes positively charged and is attracted to the negatively charged lifting mat, producing an image that mirrors the original. Other methods of preserving a print include gelatin lifters for transferring prints from both porous and nonporous surfaces, whether wet or dry. Black gelatin lifters can be used to transfer light-colored prints, while white gelatin lifters preserve prints developed with fingerprint powders or prints containing a dark residue. Adhesive lifters can transfer prints from smooth, nonporous surfaces. Again, the surfaces may be wet or dry.

If your forensic team finds a footwear impression, then they'll want to preserve it by making a cast with dental stone. Since gypsum-based casting materials, like dental stone, emit heat during the curing process, impressions in snow or ice must be sprayed with an insulating material to preserve detail, such as Snow Impression Wax or Snow Print Wax.

Shoeprints tell more than the likely size of a perpetrator's feet. Footwear manufacturers make soles in a variety of patterns, which can help investigators identify the make and model of the shoe. Class characteristics gleaned from a shoeprint include shoe type, shape, brand, and size. Examiners may be able to tell whether the person was walking, running, limping, or even carrying a heavy object. Unless the perpetrator wore new footwear, the shoeprint can reveal patterns of wear created by the owner's way of walking. A shoeprint's individual characteristics may be due to wear marks as well as random marks and scratches on the sole.

During the criminal trial of O.J. Simpson, William J. Bodziak, a special agent of the FBI and expert in questioned documents, footwear, and tire tread evidence, testified for the prosecution. The following excerpt of

Bodziak's testimony will give you an idea about how footwear evidence is put to use.

> [O]ne of the primary purposes of footwear comparison is ultimately to examine the footwear impressions from the crime scene, which is depicted here on the right side, with shoes of suspects that might be obtained during the investigation. In this particular chart I've shown, as an example on the right, an impression from a crime scene, a test impression made from the shoe of the suspect, and on the left side a reverse photograph of the shoe of the suspect. This comparison involves the class characteristics first of the shoe, that is, the physical shape and size, the design or pattern on the bottom of the shoe, which leaves its print in the impression, and then subsequently we will draw its attention to wear characteristics. Maybe the heel may begin to wear on the edge and other wear that might be evident and would change the pattern of the shoe. The fourth area of comparison, after the size design and wear, would be things such as accidental characteristics, such as a cut mark that would also show up in the impression and would be found on both the test impression and the known shoe. These cut marks or changes to the pattern of the shoe are what makes a shoe unique and would possibly enable, if there was an adequate number of these, the positive identification of this shoe having made the impression at the crime scene.

Law enforcement agencies can identify shoes from shoeprints with a commercial product, the Shoeprint Image Capture and Retrieval, or SICAR, network program. The system includes three databases:

- a crime database that stores shoeprints recovered from crime scenes, which is searched to link a suspect to a crime or to link crimes with a common print;
- a suspect database that may be searched with a crime scene shoeprint to link crimes to a suspect; and

- a reference database of shoe records that provides a method for identifying unknown shoes from a print.

Tire Tread Marks

"He had made castings of the tread marks, and had taken soil samples containing what appeared to be oil drips. All of this he had also sent along to the FBI for brand identification. He determined the tire type as F205 radials, matching any number of American and foreign SUVs. These particular F205s showed uneven wear on the front tires, indicating that the front-end camber was out of alignment."

—*L.A. Requiem* (1999) by Robert Crais.

Criminals can also leave tire tread marks at the scene of a crime. Tire manufacturing practices guarantee that tread leaves a distinctive pattern. Tire tread contains alternating ridges (ribs) and grooves, which channel water on wet roads. Transverse slots break the ridges into isolated segments called lugs, or blocks. A tire may have three to nine sizes of lugs. By including various sizes, manufacturers prevent the buildup of vibration and decrease tire noise. Manufacturers also include bars of rubber in the grooves at various points on the tire. These wear bars, or wear indicators, rise above the floors of the grooves and show the degree of tread wear.

Investigators preserve two-dimensional tire tread prints and three-dimensional tire tread impressions using the techniques that we surveyed for footwear evidence. Manufacturers and law enforcement agencies maintain records of tire patterns that can be traced to different sizes of tire, and possibly the make and model of the vehicle. In other words, a tire mark can provide class characteristics. Tire wear and tire damage also create potential marks for individualization.

Bite Marks

"There had been a few cases over the years where bite marks themselves had been as incriminating as a fingerprint – Ted Bundy, for one. But more often, unless the perpetrator had some unusual dental work, saliva was the better way to go."

—Anne Frasier's *Hush* (2002).

A criminal may leave bite marks in food and even in a victim. Two assumptions provide the foundation for bite mark analysis, or forensic odontology: teeth, like tools, leave recognizable marks unique to an individual; and this uniqueness is transferred and recorded in the bitten substance.

Bite marks must be preserved quickly, because they may change in shape and size from the time that they were inflicted. Marks in a body may also become distorted when the victim changes position. Bite marks may shrink in one dimension and expand in another. Investigators preserve a bite mark impression with photography and by using a high-resolution casting material, such as dental stone. An examiner may compare a photograph or model of the bite mark to a template of the suspect's arrangement of teeth through an overlay technique. Bite mark analysis can also be performed by comparing photographs or by comparing a photo with a model cast.

Class characteristics of human bite marks include a linear or rectangular discoloration at the midline of a bite mark arch, which is a class characteristic of human incisor teeth. The linear or rectangular shape of the marks distinguishes incisors from the circular or triangular shape of canines. Class characteristics distinguish between a human bite and animal bite, as well as the bite of an adult and that of a child.

Examples of an individual characteristic include rotated teeth, attritional wear, and congenital malformations. As we've seen before, the number and unusual appearance of individual characteristics determine the confidence with which an examiner can link a suspect with the evidence.

During the murder trial of Theodore Bundy, a dentist showed the jury enlarged photos of Bundy's teeth and bite marks left on a victim. He then showed how an acetate overlay of Bundy's front teeth fit on top of the photo of the bite marks. The jury convicted Bundy in light of peculiarities in the arrangement of his teeth, which exactly matched the injuries.

Marks Left by Lips and Ears

"'You won't believe this. I lifted an ear print from the door out there.'"
—Detective Kenneth Souter in *The Silent Bride* by Leslie Glass (2002).

In 1970, Japanese researchers reported that they could classify lip prints from over 1,300 people according to distinguishing features. Twenty years later, a U.S. researcher published findings of a 150-lip-print study in the *FBI Law Enforcement Bulletin*, concluding that:

- Every individual has unique lip prints;
- Unique features are distinguishable; and
- Heredity plays some role in lip pattern development, although even identical twins do not share identical patterns.

The author advised that the criminal justice community must seriously consider lip print evidence to win convictions. Law enforcement soon heeded this advice.

In December 1993, someone shot and killed Patrick Ferguson in Elgin, Illinois. Investigators found a roll of duct tape at the scene, tape that included a set of lip prints. During the criminal trial, an Illinois State Police lab forensic scientist testified that she had discovered an upper and lower lip print on the sticky side of the duct tape. When she compared the print with standards from the defendant's lips, she found them identical. Since the case presented lip print identification for the first time in the state, the judge held a hearing to determine whether the prosecution could introduce the evidence. The prosecution's experts testified that lip prints are unique and that an expert can make a positive identification by comparing a known standard to an evidence lip print. The experts also testified that the FBI considers lip prints as a means of positive identification and that the technique has been around since 1950. The judge allowed the lip print testimony, and the state's appellate court affirmed the decision in 1999.

Despite this exceptional case, there's no guarantee that lip print evidence would be accepted by a judge in other state courts or in a federal court. Consider lip print evidence a possibility for your story, but not as slam-dunk proof.

U.S. prosecutors have had little success convincing judges about the value of earology, the science of ear identification. A Florida court rejected ear print evidence in 1985. In 1999, a Washington State appellate court rejected the state's argument that ear prints offer conclusive identifiers like fingerprints. The court wrote that "an opinion of non-exclusion (e.g., that a particular person cannot be excluded as the maker of a latent print) can rationally be based on readily discernible class characteristics, but an opinion of inclusion (e.g., that a particular person made or probably made a latent print) cannot be." In other words, the court accepted the idea that an ear print could provide class characteristics but not individuating characteristics. According to the court's view, an investigator could reasonably use ear print evidence to exclude a suspect, but not to identify a suspect.

Courts outside the United States accept ear print identification. In 1998 a United Kingdom court sent Mark Dallagher to prison for murder. The prosecution argued that ear prints on a newly washed window of the victim's house could only have been left by Dallagher. By the way, DNA evidence exonerated Mark Dallagher in January 2004.

Palm Prints and Footprints

"'Dr. Stannard, sir. You couldn't hope for anything clearer. The palm print's on the stone wall to the right . . .'"

—Head of crime scene team Nobby Clark in P.D. James' *Death in Holy Orders* (2001).

Unlike lip prints or ear prints, courts have deemed palm print evidence acceptable for almost a century. In the United States, palm print evidence dates to a 1918 Nevada Supreme Court case. Here, the court decided that the characteristic friction ridge markings found on fingertips are continuous with the palmar surface of the hand.

Palm marks left at a crime scene represent certain areas of the palm more frequently than others. About 65% of latent palm marks represent the hypothenar region, often combined with part of the triradiate area. The triradiate area alone accounts for about 12% of palm marks recovered from a crime scene. Of the remaining palm regions, the thenar area occurs more rarely and contains numerous creases that make it difficult to define true ridges and minutiae.

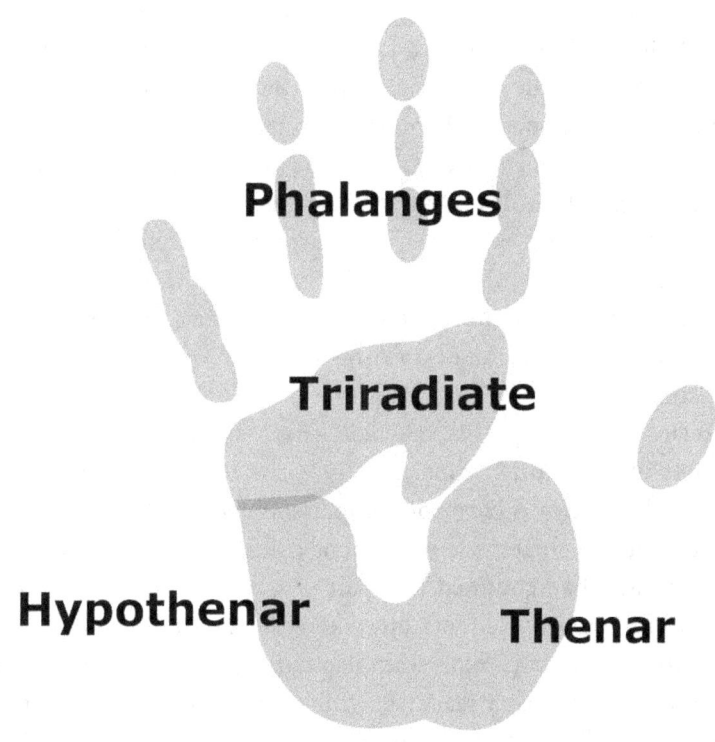

Figure 9.1. Regions of the palm. Adapted from Martin J. Leadbetter, "Use of automated fingerprint identification systems to process, search and identify palm prints and latent palm marks," *Journal of Forensic Identification* 49(1):18-36 (Jan/Feb 1999).

Although palm print patterns are considered unique to an individual and valuable for an investigation, few law enforcement agencies in the United States maintain accessible records of palm prints. In the United Kingdom, constabularies have taken palm prints from arrestees for about 50 years. Yet these records were of very little use because, unlike fingerprints, palm prints were not filed in a classified order.

Experts at the Fingerprint Bureau of the Cambridgeshire Constabulary (United Kingdom) devised a method to adapt an Automated Fingerprint Identification System to process, store, search, and identify palm print data. The Cambridgeshire Automatic Palms System became operational in 1997. A few years later, NEC Solutions America introduced the Automated PalmPrint™ Identification System, which is used by law enforcement agencies throughout the United States. Like AFIS, APIS scans a palm's characteristics and converts the information into data for storage. Crime scene palm prints can be scanned and entered into the database for matching.

Friction ridge patterns are not limited to the palms and fingertips; they also occur on the soles of the feet. So far, no two people have been found to have the same friction ridge patterns on their soles. Since records of bare footprints are not routinely stored, the value of an evidence footprint will rely on locating a suspect for comparison. A bare footprint found at the scene of a crime may also be used to eliminate a potential suspect.

Theoretically, investigators may identify a suspect by examining the footprint left in a discarded shoe. In 1995, the Royal Canadian Mounted Police released a study on barefoot comparison and identification research. They noted that the entire sole of the foot contains sweat pores that cause the foot to sweat when confined to a pair of shoes, and that this sweating, combined with thousands of footsteps taken each day, molds the shoe to the size and shape of the foot. Shoes can also damage the foot, causing callus buildup, bunions, and other features, which may provide a match to a foot when considered with details in the stained impressions left in the shoe. Nevertheless, the authors concluded that much research must be performed to establish this type of footprint comparison as a reliable piece of evidence.

Summary

"'Gentlemen, this is what the subject's teeth look like. The Smithsonian in Washington reconstructed them from the impressions we took of bite marks on Mrs. Leeds and a clear bite mark in a piece of cheese from the Leedses' refrigerator.'"

—A denture-wearing killer misleads Chief Medical Examiner Dominic Princi in Thomas Harris' *Red Dragon* (1981).

In this chapter, we've investigated various forms of print and impression evidence left by tools, footwear, tires, palms, bare feet, lips, ears, and teeth. While an investigator may benefit from any of these types of evidence, not all will be allowed in court. In the United States, the odds are that a judge will not let the state introduce evidence of lip prints or ear prints as proof of identity. At least, not yet.

Judges have been critically scrutinizing even more traditional forensic identification techniques. In 2001, for example, the Supreme Court of Florida decided *Ramirez v. State*, a case in which the court deemed a type of toolmark evidence inadmissible. Here, the state offered evidence that striations found in the cartilage of a knife wound identified a particular knife linked to the defendant.

In recent years, critics have cast doubt upon bite mark evidence analysis, arguing that the practice is subjective and has never undergone thorough experimental validation. A prosecution expert may expect a defense attorney to question the validity of a dental uniqueness determination and to be asked about the frequency of dental features identified in bite marks, data that may not be available.

If you plan to include print or impression evidence in your story, then don't forget about the types of evidence that we've covered in earlier chapters. Your investigators should be aware that a toolmark or a tool may contain trace evidence, such as paint, glass particles, blood, or foreign metal. These types of trace evidence may help establish identity. In the same way, your crime scene specialists should take samples from the area of a bite mark, which may provide a saliva sample susceptible to DNA and blood type analysis.

In the next chapter, we'll survey a very different type of impression evidence: magnetic impressions that computer forensic specialists hunt. We'll also look at the techniques of the forensic accountant, a specialty that continues to grab newspaper headlines about corporate scandals.

A Few FAQ from the Course

Was the knife mark analysis used in the Ramirez case the same technique featured in a CSI episode that has received a lot of attention?

In the *Ramirez* case, a toolmark expert witness identified a particular knife as the murder weapon based on a microscopic comparison of markings in a piece of cut cartilage. In one of the most criticized techniques of the TV show, the *CSI* forensic scientists cracked a case by injecting caulk into the fatal stab wound of a corpse to make a cast of a knife blade. Flesh doesn't hold a shape like this.

Will a footprint or footwear impression provide an exact size of the footwear or an estimate of the size?

An impression will often give an estimate, but not an exact size. For example, an impression in mud will shrink when the ground dries. On the other hand, a bare footprint made by a person in motion may be an inch longer than the mark that the foot would make if the person were standing still.

CHAPTER 10

Computer Tracks and Audit Trails

"'I've heard,' said Dougall, 'that even deleted files can be read off the hard drive using special software.'"
—Inspector Dougall in Peter Jamesson's *Unplayable Lie* (2002).

"'I have a friend who works fraud investigation for the U.S. Attorney's office. White-collar-crime stuff. A forensic CPA.'"
—CPA Melvin Bertram in Cathy Pickens' *Southern Fried* (2004).

In the last chapter, we surveyed tracks left by feet and tires. Here, we'll look at two very different types of tracks: computer traces and audit trails. First, we'll survey aspects of computer forensics, a specialty that encompasses the collection, preservation, and documentation of evidence obtained from a digital storage device in a manner that assures admissibility in a legal proceeding. This digital evidence is physical evidence; it's made of magnetic fields and electronic pulses that can be analyzed using special techniques.

Investigators use computer forensics to examine a broad range of criminal activities, including child exploitation, computer invasion, auction fraud, economic fraud, extortion, identity theft, narcotics, prostitution, and telecommunications fraud (such as telephone hacking). Electronic evidence can establish that a crime has been committed, or it can link a crime with a victim or its perpetrator. Electronic information may be the fruits of a crime, such as stolen software or trade secrets; it may serve as an instrumentality of a crime, such as a program that records other people's passwords when they log onto a computer; or it may provide evidence of a crime, such as an incriminating email message. Computer forensics also plays a significant role in many civil litigation matters, such as workplace disputes and bankruptcy.

We'll also take an overview of forensic accounting. Forensic accountants crack cases by detecting anomalies in financial records and by reconstructing a crime from the behavior of fraudsters. They track criminals by following the advice that Deep Throat gave *Washington Post* reporter Bob Woodward in the film *All the President's Men* (1976): "Follow the money."

Accessing Electronic Evidence

Constitutional law (federal and state), statutes, and court rules place limits on methods that law enforcement can use to acquire electronic evidence. Unlike the typical scenarios that we've considered, electronic evidence is not necessarily located at the scene of a crime. A computer may contain evidence of a crime committed elsewhere, including cyberspace. Police must access that evidence according to certain procedures if they plan to use it in court.

The Fourth Amendment of the Constitution guarantees protection against unreasonable searches and seizures. Unless a search falls within an exception to the rule, officers must have a search warrant signed by a neutral magistrate. A legal warrant is based upon the probable cause to believe that evidence of a crime will be found in the place to be searched. The identification of a place to be searched requires specific facts that point to the location. Any items to be seized must also be described with reasonable precision. If a search violates Constitutional protection, then a judge will probably not allow the State to introduce evidence obtained from the search.

There are a number of exceptions to the rule that evidence obtained without a warrant is inadmissible in court. Exceptions arise, for example, when the suspect or a person with authority over the property voluntarily and intelligently consents to the search. Since an employee may have a legitimate expectation of privacy with computer files in the workplace, a police officer must find out if the employer has authority to give valid consent to search or seize an employee's computer or computer files.

Officers normally cannot search or seize files stored in home computers unless they have a search warrant authorizing both entry into the house and a search of the computer. Again, an exception occurs when they have received consent to enter and search a computer from a person who has the authority to grant consent.

Another exception to the search warrant requirement occurs when an officer has probable cause and exigent circumstances exist. For example, in *United States v. David* (D. Nev. 1991), agents seized a computer memo book when they saw the defendant deleting files. The existence of exigent circumstances does not permit agents to search or seize beyond what is necessary to prevent the destruction of the evidence. Once the exigency ends, the right to conduct warrantless searches does as well.

Federal agents have yet another exception. The Patriot Act of 2001 created a new type of search warrant: surreptitious entry warrants, or sneak-and-peek warrants. Using information that meets a lower standard than that required for a standard search warrant, federal law enforcement agencies can obtain a sneak-and-peek warrant and enter a home or office while the occupant is absent. During the search, agents can take photographs, seize property, examine a computer's hard drive, and insert sniffer keystroke logger software. Once installed, the program creates a record of every keystroke. On another unannounced search, agents can download that information.

Securing the Evidence

"'Did you delete the files from the hard disk?'
'Yes.' I remembered Grady was a computer whiz. Did he know how to find hidden files, even in backup? 'Could the police retrieve deleted files, if they got to the computers in time?'"
—Lawyer Benedetta "Bennie" Rosato in Lisa Scottoline's *Legal Tender* (1996).

Electronic evidence is fragile; improper handling or examination can alter, damage, or destroy it. Law enforcement personnel take special precautions to document, collect, preserve, and examine electronic evidence. Often, examiners investigate computer evidence in a controlled environment, and this means that the recovery of electronic data takes place in two steps: acquiring the target media and performing a forensic analysis of the stored data.

The first step of acquisition is to secure the computer. People who are not processing an area that contains a computer should be removed to prevent tampering. Computers should be isolated from phone lines to thwart remote access. If the computer is off, then it should not be turned on. This prevents a modification of the computer's condition, including innocent alterations such as new date and time stamps. Switching on a computer can also trigger electronic booby traps, including viruses or logic bombs that alter the data stored on the hard disk. Another reason for approaching computers with caution is that physical bombs and booby traps are sometimes wired to an otherwise inoperable power switch. If the computer is running and it's not linked to a network, then crime scene specialists will photograph the monitor screen, disconnect the power cord from the computer, place evidence tape over drive slots, photograph the back of the computer to show components and connections, and label all connectors for later reassembly. Networked computers pose a greater challenge. Expert assistance may be needed because pulling the plug on a networked computer could destroy data stored on the computer and damage the network.

Computer accessories, such as keyboards, a computer mouse, flash drives, CDs, DVDs, or other removable media may have fingerprints or other physical evidence that must be preserved for analysis. Since chemicals required to develop latent fingerprints may damage the equipment and media, latent prints are typically visualized after completion of electronic evidence recovery.

All collected electronic evidence must be properly documented, labeled, and inventoried before packaging. Magnetic media are placed in antistatic packaging, such as paper or antistatic plastic bags. Standard plastic bags can produce static electricity and, therefore, should be avoided.

During transport, electronic evidence must be protected from magnetic sources. Common items such as radio transmitters and speaker magnets can damage electronic evidence. Exposure to excessive heat, cold, or humidity can also endanger magnetically stored data. Computers and electronic components must be secured during transport to avoid shock and excessive vibrations. And, as we've seen, the chain of custody must be maintained on all evidence.

Preliminary Analysis: From Mirror Imaging to Hashing

"I did a system search on files that had been modified in the past week. The results showed that files had been opened as recently as yesterday. I opened her email program. But the folders had been cleaned out. Incoming, outgoing, even the folder of deleted messages. Whoever had done the cleaning had been thorough. They'd probably swept the hard drive, too. I'd need sophisticated software to dig up the deleted files."
—James Calder's *About Face* (2003).

Before analysis can begin, a computer forensic specialist must ensure the integrity of the original copy of electronic media. The first recommended step in an examination of a hard drive is to make a byte-for-byte copy of the seized hard drive and to use the copy for analysis. One reason why a mirror image of the entire drive is preferred to a file-by-file copy is that an operating system like Windows® automatically overwrites each file's time and date stamp as the file copies are made. In addition, a file-by-file copy of a hard drive may leave behind the most important evidence: deleted files.

In computer storage devices, deleted files may be found in a temporary holding area, often designated as the Recycle Bin, or Trash Can. Certain utility programs install a second-level recycle bin to temporarily hold deleted files, which ensures that the user does not accidentally delete information. These safeguards help a computer forensic expert to recover files that the computer's owner might consider deleted. But what about those files that the computer user deletes from a recycle bin?

Delete does not always mean delete. To see why this is so, let's consider how information is stored on magnetic media. A hard drive contains flat disks (platters) coated on both sides with a magnetic material that can store information as binary numbers. Each disk's surface can retain tens of billions of individual bits of data, organized into groups of 8, 16, or 32 bits. Each of these groups forms a byte that represents an alphabetical character or a number. The disks are mounted on a spindle that rotates at high speed, and electromagnetic read/write devices (heads) are mounted on arms positioned over a disk's surface. The recording surface of a formatted disk is divided into concentric circles called tracks. These tracks are further divided into sectors and groups of sectors called clusters. The contents of a single file may be scattered among hundreds of sectors and clusters on various tracks.

When you click on a file that you want to open, the relevant program passes the file name to the computer's operating system and locates the track and sector that contain the first portion of the file. In a DOS environment and certain Windows® environments, the operating system keeps tabs on the locations of files with a file allocation table, or FAT. The operating system transmits the location of the first part of a file to a disk controller, which positions the read/write head over the correct location on a disk. This first cluster provides the address of subsequent sectors, and the controller retrieves the packets of data from various locations, reassembles them, and passes the file on to the central processing unit for display on your monitor.

When you delete a file, the operating system does not erase all segments of the file from the disk. Instead, the FAT entry for the file is modified by replacing the first letter of the file name with a special character. The altered file name instructs the FAT that the area of the disk occupied by the deleted file is now available to store new data. Consequently, portions of deleted files remain on a disk until they are overwritten by new files. This can take a while. Since files are randomly stored into many potentially available sectors, it's unusual for all sectors containing a certain file to be overwritten with new data. The data waits for discovery by a forensic specialist.

Even if a sector receives a new file, the sector may yield information about a deleted file that used to reside there. This is because an entire cluster is reserved for a file segment. If a new file segment requires less than one cluster, then the cluster will include extra or "slack" space. That slack space may store recoverable data from deleted files.

A simple copy of a magnetic disk will not include deleted information. For this reason, computer forensic specialists create a bitstream copy, which is also called a mirror or image copy. A bitstream copy is a byte-for-byte copy that contains all files on the original disk, whether the files are active, deleted, password-protected, hidden, or corrupted. It is this bitstream copy that a forensic examiner analyzes as the evidence copy.

Of course, a computer's owner can claim that investigators altered the bitstream copy by planting evidence. To provide proof of integrity, law enforcement computer forensic specialists compute a hash value for each file and for the entire image of the hard drive. A hash is a numerical computation based on every byte in the original. The most common algorithm for calculating a hash value is MD5, which accepts digital information in a file or hard drive and calculates a combination of 32 numbers and letters, which is often called a digital fingerprint. If a copy contains one altered bit of data, then MD5 will generate a different hash value, indicating that the evidence is no longer forensically intact.

Hunting the Data

"'He sometimes used my computer. That's how I got his letter. He thought he had deleted the file but I found it in the cache memory.'"
—Victor Verity in *Shattered* (2000) by Dick Francis.

The wealth of information stored on a hard drive can be categorized in various ways. Here's the scheme that we'll use:

- Active data
- Archived data
- Latent data (also called residual or ambient data, and includes swap files, deleted files, temp files, replicant data, and metadata)

A computer user can readily access active data, which include such common information as word processing documents, databases, graphics files, contact managers, and spreadsheets. Active data typically undergo multiple revisions until they reach a final form.

Archival data are data that have been intentionally backed up by creating a copy for safekeeping. A computer user may copy this backed-up information to removable media (such as a CD or flash drive) as insurance against a computer failure.

Latent data files appear to be absent but are still recoverable from the computer system. This category of data includes temp files, Windows® swap files, deleted files and the registry database of Windows® 95, 98, 2000, and XP. A swap file is a hidden file stored on the hard drive that Windows® uses to hold parts of programs and data files that do not fit in random access memory. The operating system moves data from the swap file to memory as needed, and the system moves data from memory to the swap file to make room for new data. Swap files may contain fragments of email messages, word processing documents, and other information.

A computer also contains replicant data files, which are created by the automatic backup feature of standard applications. Replicant data help users to recover information lost due to a user mistake or computer malfunction.

A file may include nonprinting or embedded information. This type of latent data (sometimes called data about data, or metadata) includes information in email headers, such as routing details and a list of associated file attachments. Software, such as Microsoft Office programs, can record the author's name, organization's name, designation of the network server or hard disk where the document is saved, names of previous document authors, document versions, when the file was last saved and by whom, and hidden text or cells. Much of this data is created by default, and users are often unaware of it.

Forensic search utilities locate relevant files by hunting for keywords, uncovering document drafts, back-up files, deleted files, temporary files, swap files, cache files, autosaves, and registry data. An examiner can also perform searches for general formats, such as telephone numbers, network Id numbers, logon records, or Internet protocol addresses, even when the specific number is unknown. Good resources for details about forensic software capabilities include the websites of Guidance Software™, which makes EnCase® Forensic; and AccessData®, which offers the Forensic Toolkit®. You may also wish to browse the Evidence Eliminator™ website. Robin Hood Software Ltd. offers this product to defeat computer forensic analysis.

Disguising the Evidence

"The key word *stego,* short for steganography, referred to computer programs that invisibly mingle data of one file within that of another carrier, usually a picture or sound file. Even on close examination, the data looks unchanged. An innocent digital snapshot of Aunt Martha could contain a stolen formula, a secret love letter, or the plans for blowing up New York."

—Ross LaManna's *Acid Test* (2001).

"'The menu is really a set of files encrypted with steganography. It means 'covered writing.' It's a way of hiding messages in pictures.'"

—Computer whiz Hiram Yaeger in *Fire Ice* (2002) by Clive Cussler and Paul Kemprecos.

We've seen how the normal operation of a computer can store information that is not readily apparent. A computer can also harbor data that a person deliberately concealed. Here are some common techniques for hiding data.

- Obscure placement of files: In this strategy, files are relocated to places where they normally shouldn't be.
- Misleading file names: For example, an image file may be renamed as a document file. Forensic software can match a file's extension (e.g., .doc) against the file's actual signature to determine if a computer user tried this tactic.
- Compressed files: Compressing a file defeats a simple keyword search.
- Password-protected files: If password guessing fails, an examiner can resort to software called a password cracker to access locked files.
- Using a code to hide information: For example, a person may include a certain phrase to indicate the time and place for a meeting.
- Encryption: In this approach, an encryption algorithm converts plain (or clear) text to cipher text. To reconstruct the original, an investigator must use a key—a sequence of bits—with the encryption algorithm used to create the cipher text. If a key is 40-bits long, then there is one

correct key among over a trillion possibilities. A 128-bit key is 309,485, 009,821,345,068,724,781,056 times more difficult to crack.

- Steganography: This strategy is used to hide data within files that appear innocent.

One drawback to encryption is that an encrypted file will seize an examiner's attention and inspire detailed inspection. Reportedly, a popular technique with terrorists and those engaged in industrial espionage, cryptographic steganography (stego) takes encryption one step further. Stego software encrypts secret information—a word processing document, a spreadsheet, an image or the like—and then embeds the file within an innocent-appearing carrier file, which is often a multimedia file, such as an image file (e.g., .jpg or .gif), a sound file (e.g., .mp3 or .wav) or even a video clip. After the file is hidden (or stego'd), the carrier file appears unchanged. The process is complex, but stego software is readily available as freeware.

If your investigator suspects that a person has used stego software, then the solution is more software. Special forensic software can detect the presence of information hidden in digital image or audio files and extract the hidden information by cracking the password. If you're interested in using steganography in your story, then take a look at StegoHunt™ featured on WetStone Technologies' website.

Forensic Accounting in the Past

The field of forensic accounting can trace its origins to the scribes of ancient Egypt who recorded the pharaoh's gold and other assets. Records from around 321–184 B.C. indicate that bookkeepers in India expanded the traditional scope of their duties to the detection of criminal acts, such as embezzlement. The first time that an accountant provided expert testimony during a court proceeding may be the 1817 Canadian case of *Meyer v. Sefton*, in which an expert testified about the value of a bankrupt's estate. Seven years later, accountant James McClelland started his business in Glasgow, Scotland, and offered to take cases before arbiters, courts, or councils. In the early 1930s, ties between accounting and criminal investigation strengthened when Elmer Irey, an accountant who headed the U.S. Internal Revenue Service's Investigation Unit, used his financial skills to bring down Al Capone for income tax evasion.

Forensic Accounting

"What he did find exciting and beautiful was the paper record of Grimaldi's account. Following the money was almost always revealing, and it was in the minutiae of spreadsheets and corporate shell games that he spent much of his time as an investigator, prising the secrets from the numbers."

—*The Genesis Code* by John Case (1997).

"'Boilerplate for money transfers to a bank in Canada with instructions to move percentages on consecutive days to an account in the Cayman islands.'

She sat back to look up at Lew and Osborne. 'In my line of work we call this money laundering. Couldn't be more obvious.'"

—Newspaper editor Gina Palmer in Victoria Houston's *Dead Water* (2001).

The American College of Forensic Examiners International defines a forensic accountant as "an accountant who performs an orderly analysis, investigation, inquiry, test, inspection or examination in an attempt to obtain the truth and develop an expert opinion in matters of dispute." In the United States, a forensic accountant is typically a Certified Public Accountant, who may also be a Certified Forensic Accountant and Certified Fraud Examiner.

The past decade has seen an increased demand for forensic accountants, a change attributed to two factors: terrorists and corporate scandals. Aiming to stop international money laundering that supports terrorist groups, the U.S. Patriot Act of 2001 imposes obligations on financial institutions to scrutinize potential money laundering schemes. In response to corporate scandals, Congress passed the Sarbanes-Oxley Act of 2002. The Sarbanes-Oxley law requires public companies to increase their monitoring of corporate transactions and accounting procedures.

Forensic accountants work with information that is incomplete and often inaccurate or misleading, hunting for anomalies in business deals and investigating circumstances surrounding transactions. The investigation of an economic crime also demands an ability to acquire information from those unwilling to provide it. A forensic accountant detects irregularities in financial records with traditional accounting techniques as well as data-mining software.

One data-mining technique relies on Benford's law (also called the first-digit law), an observation that numbers occur as the first or second digit at a predictable rate in a list of numerical data. For example, 1 appears as the first digit most frequently—about 30% of the time. The number 2 appears first about 18% of the time, whereas 9 appears first only about 5% of the time. Since fraudsters typically do not fabricate data according to Benford's law, the rule provides a simple screening method to uncover accounting fraud. Darrell Dorrell of Financial Forensics (Lake Oswego, Oregon) used a program that applied Benford's law to scan more than 21,000 payroll records of a healthcare company accused of defrauding investors. In this 2002 investigation, Dorrell found that certain numbers appeared as the second digits in payroll records more often than they should. In combination with other evidence, he could conclude that the records appeared contrived.

Forensic accountants play two main roles in legal investigations. Certain forensic accountants specialize in litigation support, providing expert testimony in cases dealing with financial disputes such as bankruptcy and divorces. Others conduct criminal investigations in private practice or with law enforcement agencies, examining crimes such as securities fraud, insurance fraud, and identity theft.

In the past, businesses would seek forensic accountants after the owners suspected that they were the victims of fraud. But now, a weakened economy and laws imposing financial responsibility encourage owners to request accountants to scrutinize their businesses for proactive fraud check-ups, such as investigating financial statement fraud or theft of assets.

A business can be a victim of internal or external fraud. Employees perpetrate internal fraud by stealing cash or by moving stolen goods. Fraudsters who take cash account for about 78% of asset misappropriations. Mechanisms include cash larceny and skimming, but the majority is accomplished via complex manipulation of billing and payroll systems or by falsifying expense reimbursements and check tampering. Payroll fraud is frequently committed using ghost employees, inflating hours of work or overtime, and by overstating expense accounts or medical claims. Fraudulent billing schemes often involve collaboration between employees and outside vendors, suppliers, and contractors. In these cases, the outsider submits false or inflated invoices for goods or services.

Senior management may commit fraud to benefit the company and themselves. Mechanisms include financial statement fraud, antitrust violations, securities fraud, and tax evasion. Enron Corp. managers, for example, were reported to have hidden over a billion dollars of debt in shell partnerships, allowing them to maintain inflated stock prices.

External fraud is committed by an outsider against a company. Targets of external fraud include government agencies and banks. However, the most common target is the insurance company through false claims.

A business can also provide the instrument for financial crime, particularly as a conduit for money laundering. According to a 2002 report by the Organization for Economic Co-operation and Development, more than $2 million in laundered funds flow through the U.S. economy every day. Illegal arms sales, smuggling, embezzlement, insider trading, computer fraud, and other illegal activities generate huge sums of money, which must be legitimized through money laundering. Dirty money is washed in three stages. In the first, or placement, step, the launderer breaks up large amounts of cash into less conspicuous smaller sums that are deposited in financial systems. One of the most common methods of placement is smurfing, the division of large sums of cash into amounts less than the currency transaction reporting requirement ($10,000). The bundles are distributed to a network of mules who deposit the cash into special accounts. In the second—or layering—step, the launderer converts or moves the funds to distance them from their source. Although electronic fund transfers are a common method of shifting money, the launderer might decide to disguise a transfer as payment for bogus goods or services. Finally, the funds re-enter the legitimate economy. This integration step can be achieved through large purchases, business ventures, or real estate investments.

And then there's reverse money laundering. After Sept. 11, forensic accountants traced financing for the attacks and found charitable organizations and businesses used as shelters to funnel money from outside the United States to terrorists inside the country. That is, money in legitimate entities was turned to illegal use.

Summary

"He knew they could get a forensic accountant to look into Masefield's finances and a computer expert to track down the Internet banking records, but that would all take time. There would no doubt be all kinds of false trails and blind alleys."

—*Playing with Fire* (2004) by Peter Robinson.

In this chapter, we've surveyed aspects of computer forensics—how law enforcement can gain access to evidence stored on a computer, procedures for acquiring a computer and preserving evidence stored within, methods for harvesting electronic evidence, and countermeasures used to conceal that evidence. Any investigation that takes place in modern times will probably require a look at some form of electronic evidence, whether stored on a computer or other device.

We've also briefly considered forensic accounting and the types of crimes that these specialists investigate. Tracking the public's awareness of financial crimes, forensic accounting is appearing more frequently in fiction. In Robert B. Parker's *Bad Business* (2004), for example, Spenser finds murder coupled with corporate fraud. Christopher Reich's *The Devil's Banker* (2003) details the efforts of a counterterrorist task force to follow a money trail and prevent a terrorist attack in the United States. The hero of the novel is Adam Chapel, a forensic accountant.

It's not surprising that forensic accountants can play roles in mystery stories. After all, greed typically motivates the commission of financial crimes. And greed inspires murder. Just consider James M. Cain's classic novel, *Double Indemnity* (1936). Here, femme fatale Phyllis Nirdlinger and insurance salesman Walter Huff commit murder to collect on a double benefit in an accident insurance policy.

In the next chapter, we switch from numbers to language. We'll investigate the world of forensic document examination, including handwriting analysis and tactics for detecting forged documents.

A Few FAQ from the Course

You mentioned file allocation table, or FAT, use in Windows®, but don't the new versions of the software use a different system?

Correct. Windows® 2000 and Windows® XP offer the option of the New Technology Filing System. NTFS also includes security features, such as the Encryption File System. Windows Vista™ has Transactional NTFS (TxF). Commercially available forensic analysis software can deal with NTFS and Transactional NTFS.

What are some examples of electronic evidence found on devices other than a computer?

Electronic evidence may be found on electronic organizers, electronic pagers, digital cameras, cell phones, off-site servers, mirror sites, backup tapes, and in the buffer memories of printers and copiers. A printer may have a sufficient amount of memory to store several hundred pages of text. Similarly, certain fax machines retain duplicates of the last several hundred pages of documents transmitted and received. Digital telephone systems may contain computer logs of all calls made and received. These systems also often store voice mail messages in digital form as .wav files. If your story concerns a computer linked to a network, then that network's audit programs may contain a history of all files accessed, downloaded or printed. The network's firewall monitors all websites visited and information transmitted or received from the Internet.

Is it possible to retrieve information from overwritten files?

Even data that have been overwritten several times may be recovered using advanced— and very expensive—techniques. "Shadow data" results from a minor imprecision that occurs when data are recorded: the read/write head does not record data in a perfect circle. For a crude analogy, think about how a bicycle tire track appears superimposed on a track made by a car. A magnetic disk can be examined for shadow data in a lab with advanced equipment (for example, a spin stand tester or a scanning probe microscope), and the recovered fragments can be pieced together to reconstruct parts of the original digital data. Thus, it may be possible to recover data from magnetic storage media even if the information has been deleted and the space reused, or if the user has overwritten the space with a "wipe" utility program. As hard drive memory size increases, however, the recovery of shadow data is becoming more difficult. This is because the track width is becoming so narrow that it's hard to recover off-track data. Nevertheless, data may be recovered even if it has been completely overwritten. When a "1" is overwritten by a "1," the strength of the magnetic field is slightly increased, whereas the magnetic field is weakened when a "0" is overwritten by a "1." A magnetic force microscope can measure how much the magnetic field for each bit is out from average.

CHAPTER 11

Paper Chase

"Alex had done his homework, and he knew that document examinations could be one of the most effective ways to link a suspect to a crime."
—Savvy reporter Alex Martin in Anne Frasier's *Hush* (2002).

In this chapter, we'll explore how a document examiner contributes to an investigation—from detecting hidden writing to unmasking forgeries. Frequently, document examiners analyze a questioned document, which is any type of paper object of doubtful authenticity that contains handwriting, hand printing, typewriting, printing or other graphic markings. The doubt about authenticity may concern the authorship of the entire document or whether someone altered a portion of the document. Document examiners are also requested to study writings or other marks left on walls, doors, and corpses.

In the United States, a document examiner may be employed by federal, state, or city crime labs, or may work in private practice. Typically, document examiners participate in investigations of forgery, kidnappings with ransom notes, and embezzlement. Yet a document examiner's skill may be required during the investigation of any crime, including homicide, arson, and burglary. Document examiners may also be hired to aid in civil cases, such as contested wills, disputed contracts, stock fraud, and divorces.

The objectives of forensic document analysis include:

- Distinguish a forged document from a genuine document.
- Attribute handwriting, signatures, printing, and other writing to a particular person.
- Detect alterations in a document.
- Authenticate and date documents.
- Restore obliterated writing.
- Reconstruct charred, water-damaged, or erased writing.
- Analyze ink, paper, and chemicals involved in document creation.

We'll start with an overview of methods to detect unintentional writings and techniques to reconstruct an attempted destruction of writing.

Hunting for Indented Writing

You've read about a certain technique for visualizing latent writing or you've seen it performed on many movies and TV shows. Detectives burst into a room, expecting to find a suspect, but their quarry has fled the scene. One detective finds a notepad near a telephone and rubs the top blank sheet with a lead pencil. The trick exposes indented writing created when someone wrote on a missing sheet. The trick also destroys evidence. And this is why real investigators would not rub the paper with a pencil.

Indented writing, or second-page writing, is the impression created by a pen or pencil captured on sheets of paper under the one that contained the original writing. Indented writing can aid identification in a case that involves an anonymous note and can indicate if a document—such as a business record—contains alterations. Additions to a medical record, for example, can produce impressions on pages beneath the altered page. Those impressions may be inconsistent with writing that appears on the surface of the official document.

Forensic document examiners use two basic techniques for recovering indented writing; neither requires a pencil. In the traditional method, an examiner shines oblique, or glancing, light at the grooves of indented writing to reveal shadowed depressions. Multiple photographs with a moving light source fill the indentations with shadows and reproduce the indented writing. The oblique lighting technique has a limitation: The method cannot recover minuscule indentations that can reside three or four pages below the original. Developed in England, the Electrostatic Detection Apparatus, or ESDA, can reveal indented writing four or more pages below the original writing. Not all documents are suitable for electrostatic detection. Thick cardboard documents, documents processed for latent fingerprints with ninhydrin, or documents that have been saturated with fluids are usually eliminated from analysis.

The basic process of electrostatic detection goes like this. An examiner places the paper evidence on an ESDA's porous brass plate, covers the paper with a thin transparent film, and then uses a vacuum drawn through the brass plate to pull the film into firm contact with the paper. The sandwiched page and film receive a strong electrostatic charge, which quickly dissipates except in the indented areas that come into closest contact with the charged mesh. The examiner applies black toner to the surface of the film, and this adheres to the charged areas, rendering the indented writing visible. The examiner photographs the impressions and may enhance the writing with digital imaging processing. Examiners have used ESDA to develop indented writing on documents 50 to 60 years old.

Reconstructing Text

An examiner may suspect that someone has altered a document by erasure or obliteration. Common mechanical methods for erasing parts of a document include eradicating ink or pencil marks with an India rubber eraser or scratching the paper's surface with sandpaper or a razor blade. These actions, however, remove the upper fibers of the paper, damage revealed by microscopic examination with direct or oblique lighting. An examiner can photograph the document under ultraviolet light, which may expose the original writing.

The chemical erasure of writing can be achieved with dilute acids and other substances. Yet microscopic examination will reveal a discoloration on the treated area of the paper. Ultraviolet or infrared lighting may reveal evidence of chemical treatment. Infrared luminescence may also expose residues of original ink that remain embedded in paper after erasure.

A less subtle means for modifying a document is obliteration, the over-writing or crossing out of writing or printing to render the original unreadable. An examiner may use a Video Spectral Comparator to uncover obliterated information. This instrument enables an examiner to view documents with various wavelengths of light. Since inks can differ in their ability to absorb infrared light, infrared illumination may reveal the presence of inks that have different compositions. An examiner may also be able to detect the original ink with blue-green light because some inks absorb blue-green light and re-radiate infrared light. These techniques for differentiating ink will not help if someone obliterated information with the same ink used to write the original.

Another way to eradicate writing is to burn the document. Even charred documents can yield some information. Infrared photography may reveal writing on a charred document. A burned document also may be read under oblique light that increases contrast between the writing and scorched surface.

Document Dating

"'Assuming the forgers weren't that good – that they might have made a mistake – what could you pick up?'

'I'm not a documents specialist, so this is an educated guess, but let's say they used a computer printer that generated a typeface that's common now but wasn't common then. That sort of thing would help date the document. Or, I don't know, maybe a reflection of the watermark on the paper came through on the copy. With a watermark the documents people can sometimes date the paper of the original.'"

—Crime scene specialist Flynn Coe explains tactics for analyzing a photocopy to date an original document in Stephen White's *Cold Case* (2000).

In a 1999 issue of the *Journal of Forensic Identification*, Detective Robert M. Hill, a forensic document examiner with the Scottsdale, Arizona Police Department, described the first recorded use of an Internet-based technique for dating a document. An attorney contacted Hill about a sexual harassment suit; the attorney represented the corporation defendant. To back up her claim, the plaintiff had supplied a hard-covered, lined journal with entries that she supposedly wrote between July 7, 1993, and March 6, 1994.

Hill found a manufacturer's label printed on the inside of the journal's back cover. Although scribbles in multiple inks obscured the label's printed information, a magnified examination exposed the Internet address of an online stationery store. Further investigation revealed that the company had not established a website until the spring of 1995, and that the company had not marketed the particular journal until September 1995. An Internet inquiry with the Whois file of InterNIC, an association responsible for the issuance and maintenance of URLs, confirmed that the stationery store's URL had been assigned on April 21, 1995. In short, the journal had been created long after the alleged sexual harassment had taken place. These findings inspired the plaintiff's attorney to drop the lawsuit.

The case shows how a document's content can indicate the earliest possible date that a document could have been executed. More traditional clues about document dates include printing or revision dates, and font or type styles. The issue dates of identifiers—ZIP codes and telephone area codes, for example—may also point to the creation date of a document. Content does not provide the only clues about a document's age; examiners also analyze the composition of paper and ink.

Paper analysis can provide information about its manufacture, which in turn can reveal the earliest date that the paper became available. Examination of a piece of paper reveals class characteristics such as weight, apparent color, and content of fiber and fillers. Fiber identification and classification can be performed with iodine stains, which may yield the following results: yellow (ground wood pulp), blue (wood chemically treated to remove undesirable materials), or red/purple (rag fiber). Additional characteristics include the presence of synthetic resins, starch, or optical brightening agents like fluorocarbons. Certain papers display a watermark, a design that some manufacturers change every year. The FBI maintains a watermark file with information from manufacturers on designs used in watermarks and unusual imprints.

The age of an ink sample may be determined by two approaches. One tactic is to analyze the compositional (or static) characteristics of an ink sample—using chromatography, for example—and to compare the results with compositions in a collection of inks, each having a known production date. The Forensic Services Division of the U.S. Secret Service maintains the Digital Ink Library. Considered to be the most complete forensic compilation of writing inks in the world, the library contains 10,000 ink samples and collections of toners and computer printer inks. Law enforcement agencies use the Ink Library to identify the type and brand of writing instrument used as well as to discover the earliest possible date that a document could have been produced with the ink.

Ink analysis may also reveal the presence of a chemical tag that fluoresces under long wave ultraviolet light. During the 1970s, certain ink manufacturers volunteered to add unique chemicals to inks and to change the tag every year. Ink manufacturers eventually stopped their tagging programs. Formulabs, for example, added tags to some ballpoint inks from about 1970 to 1994. Although ink manufacturers are reintroducing an ink tagging system, not all ink carries a tag. Nevertheless, analysis may reveal a tag in an ink sample, and this should allow an examiner to determine the ink's manufacture date.

An alternative tactic for dating a document's ink is to determine the aging (dynamic) characteristics that change with time. The properties of ink from a questioned document can be compared with known dated inks of the same formulation. Two key dynamic methods are the measurement of the time-dependent disappearance of ink solvents from paper and the measurement of time-dependent changes in ink extractability. Inks include coloring agents, such as dyes and pigments, and a volatile carrier solvent, which evaporates as ink ages on paper. One technique measures this loss of solvent. The other technique relies on the fact that ink manufacturers add resins to control viscosity. As ink ages on paper, resin hardens, and this hinders extraction of ink components. Although storage conditions affect the rate that ink ages, solvent evaporation and resin hardening generally contribute to the aging of inks placed on a document up to about one year. For older inks, examiners focus on resin hardening, a process that can level off after two years.

The investigation of the Hitler diaries illustrates how paper and ink analyses enable examiners to date documents. In 1981 a German publishing company paid about two million dollars for a collection of books that appeared to be Adolf Hitler's diaries. But then, forensic tests revealed that the paper contained a whitening agent first used in 1954, nine years after

Hitler's death. The books also included threads of synthetic materials introduced after the Second World War, and the ink had a formulation that was unavailable when the diaries were supposed to have been written. Finally, a test that measured the evaporation of chloride from ink showed that the documents had been created the year before.

Traces from Instruments That Produce Documents

"'It is a curious thing,' remarked Holmes, 'that a typewriter has really quite as much individuality as a man's handwriting. Unless they are quite new, no two of them write exactly alike. Some letters get more worn than others, and some wear only on one side. Now, you remark in this note of yours, Mr. Windibank, that in every case there is some little slurring over the 'e,' and a slight defect in the tail of the 'r.' There are fourteen other characteristics, but those are the more obvious.'"
—"A Case of Identity" by Sir Arthur Conan Doyle, included in *Adventures of Sherlock Holmes* (1892).

Changes in printing devices present challenges for document examiners. From a forensic viewpoint, the manual typewriter may be the most informative writing instrument. The analysis of text produced by a manual typewriter is based on the fact that different pressures on keys and different wear on particular characters create characteristics in text typed on a particular machine. In shift-key typewriters, certain letters may become displaced from the line of text, while others slant from the vertical due to twisted type bars.

In electric typewriters, a motor-driven mechanism lifts the type bar and strikes it against the ribbon, applying even pressure to all keystrokes. This convenience decreases variations in the typed text. Nevertheless, an electric typewriter's typeface characters, like those of a manual typewriter, suffer damage and wear that create individual features. In the early 1960s, IBM introduced the Selectric typewriter, which used a golf-ball-type head instead of type bars. Yet even these developed individual characteristics due to typeface imperfections, vertical misalignment, horizontal misalignment, and improper line spacing.

157

Typewriter ribbons also provide information. A crime lab may use a Ribbon Analysis Workstation to read letters left in typewriter ribbons and to prepare a printed version of the text present on the ribbon. Digital imaging processing can be used to match fractures found in a typewriter ribbon and a questioned typewritten document.

Early computer printers used a daisy wheel that contained type set on bars. Susceptible to wear and misalignment, daisy wheels offered individualistic characteristics. The occurrence of such helpful characteristics decreased with the use of inkjet, bubble jet, and laser printers. An inkjet printer can be identified as a class based on the lay of the ink on the paper and by the dotted nature of font formation. Ink examinations may also indicate that a printer using the same ink produced two documents. During 2010, Pennsylvania-based ChemImage Corporation announced the company's use of hyperspectral imaging to link documents printed from different inkjet printers to a common manufacturer or ink formulation. The identification of toner on a document created with a laser printer is usually of little value. Toners from various manufacturers are interchangeable among laser printers.

Photocopiers offer more clues. These machines can produce distinctive marks due to damage and imperfections in the drum, cover, glass plate, camera lens, and fusing rollers. A photocopier's class characteristics include photocopy process, method of fixing toner to page, enlargement and reduction capability, direction of feed, roller marks, fusion marks, brand markings, gripper and sorter indentations, and chemical properties of toner. After class characteristics are found to be consistent with a particular photocopier, an examiner can investigate the machine's individual characteristics, such as "trash marks" produced by wear, scratches, dirt and debris, streaks, smudging, speckles, and toner lines.

Facsimile machines create clues about the origin of a fax by the notched or stepped effect of printing, type of paper used (such as thermal), and substance left by a thermal ribbon. Laser fax printing is characterized by fine, grimy particles of toner forming the images. Fax machines print a header known as the transmitting terminal identifier (TTI) that can be seen at the top of a faxed page. The type of sending machine determines the fonts used in the TTI. The American Society of Questioned Document Examiners provides its members with access to the Fax Font III-TTI Data database, which contains an organized collection of TTIs.

In a 2004 article from the *Journal of Forensic Science*, U.S. Secret Service document examiner Gerald M. LaPorte noted that most inkjet and toner-based printing systems have three regions where hardware components of the paper transporting mechanisms are likely to make physical contact with the paper:

- when the paper is loaded and the intake begins,
- during the printing process when the paper moves through the system, and
- during transport of the printed paper to the output area.

LaPorte found that an electrostatic detection device reveals latent physical markings left on documents by inkjet printers, laser printers, and photocopy machines.

A Wealth of Data in Digital Copiers

During 2010, CBS News reported that almost every digital copier manufactured since 2002 contains a hard drive that stores an image of every document that the machine copies, scans or transmits via email. Accompanied by John Juntunen of the California-based company Digital Copier Security, a reporter bought four used copiers at a New Jersey warehouse. Juntunen used a free forensic software program to analyze the copiers' hard drives. In less than 12 hours, he had tens of thousands of documents.

CBS News announced that a copier used by the Buffalo, New York Police Sex Crimes Division yielded detailed domestic violence complaints and a list of wanted sex offenders. A machine discarded by the Buffalo Police Narcotics Unit produced a list of targets in a major drug raid. A copier from a New York construction company produced design plans for a building near Ground Zero in Manhattan, 95 pages of pay stubs with social security numbers and other personal data, and $40,000-worth of copied checks. The fourth copier, used by a New York insurance company, yielded 300 pages of individual medical records, including information about medical test results and drug prescriptions.

All major manufacturers of digital copiers informed CBS News that they offer security or encryption packages for their machines. The problem is that the majority of Americans simply are unaware that copiers store images on a hard drive.

Introduction to Forensic Handwriting Examination: What It Isn't

"'Graphoanalysis. You can't analyze personality from handwriting.'
She was put off by his peremptory tone. 'I thought a lot of people do it.'
'People read tarot cards too and talk to their dear departed. It's bogus.'"
—Forensic document examiner Parker Kincaid expresses an opinion in
Jeffery Deaver's *The Devil's Teardrop* (1999).

Although the two are often confused in fiction and news reports, the
aims of handwriting examination and graphology are distinct. Questioned
document examiners compare two sets of documents to determine whether
they were written by the same person. Graphologists study penmanship
characteristics and derive conclusions about the author's personality.

The methods are dissimilar as well. Graphologists typically work with
one document or with several written by the same person, seeking class
characteristics that reflect personality traits. Questioned document examiners compare details of individual characteristics found in a document of
disputed authorship with the individualistic marks of documents of known
authorship. This difference in training and perspective explains why graphologists may erroneously determine authorship of a document; they look
for characteristics common among a group of people, not detail that indi-
vidualizes a particular author.

In a 2002 issue of the *Journal of Forensic Identification*, George
Throckmorton, manager of the Salt Lake City Police Department crime
lab, published a scientific evaluation of graphology. He concluded that the
results "vividly demonstrate the lack of reliability in identifying personality traits from a person's handwriting." Throckmorton also revealed a conversation with forensic document examiner Art Walters:

> In May 1996, I had the opportunity to discuss the ongoing
> results of my research with Art Walters. He surprised me
> by telling me that he had changed his mind over the past
> several years and now believes that it is possible to identify
> certain personality traits from a person's handwriting.
> He told me that, if asked to analyze a person's handwriting,
> he would politely accept the request. He would look at the

writing for a couple of minutes and then, in a very serious tone of voice, he would say, "I can tell from your handwriting that you are very gullible!"

Keep these distinctions and attitudes in mind if you decide to include a questioned document examiner in your story.

What Forensic Handwriting Examination Is

"'I can read the first few lines, and these in the middle of the second page, and one or two at the end. Those are as clear as print,' said he; 'but the writing in between is very bad, and there are three places where I cannot read it at all.'

'What do you make of that?' said Holmes.

'Well, what do *you* make of it?'

'That it was written in a train; the good writing represents stations, the bad writing movement, and the very bad writing passing over points. A scientific expert would pronounce at once that this was drawn up on a suburban line, since nowhere save in the immediate vicinity of a great city could there be so quick a succession of points. Granting that his whole journey was occupied in drawing up the will, then the train was an express, only stopping once between Norwood and London Bridge.'"

—The amazing Sherlock Holmes instructs Inspector Lestrade in "The Adventure of the Norwood Builder" by Sir Arthur Conan Doyle, included in *The Return of Sherlock Holmes* (1905).

Questioned document examiners compare two sets of documents to determine whether they share common authorship. When the identity of the writer is questioned, the examiner needs to compare the questioned document with documents of known origin, called exemplars, standards, or known specimens. Known writings must show the examiner a range of natural variations in the suspected author's writing characteristics. Standards should date closely in time to the questioned document. For adults, writings within two or three years of the questioned writing are usually adequate.

In a criminal investigation, exemplar writings are known specimens from a suspect or victim. These give a document examiner writing samples that reveal individual writing habits and style characteristics, which then can be compared with the questioned document. A handwriting exemplar may be informal or formal. Informal exemplars (nonrequest writing) include routine business writings, education documents, credit applications, and government records. These are the best examples of natural handwriting but may be difficult to admit as evidence during a trial due to questions of authenticity. Investigators can ask a subject to provide a formal (request) writing. Both the paper and the writing instrument should be similar to those used to produce the questioned document. An investigator may periodically interrupt a writing session to make it more difficult for the subject to maintain a consistent modification of writing habits.

Handwriting examination is based on the theory that people automatically and subconsciously imprint their individuality in their writing. An examiner analyzes the class characteristics and individual characteristics of the writing. Class characteristics (sometimes called style characteristics) are features found in the writing of groups of people. In North America, for example, many have learned handwriting by imitating a certain traditional style (e.g., Palmer and Zaner-Bloser) or one of the newer italic handwriting styles, such as D'Nealian and Getty-Dubay. However, the decline in penmanship instruction in recent years has led to a decrease in the amount of class characteristics found in writing.

Although most people who still practice handwriting learned by copying standard characters, a person's handwriting style soon accumulates individual characteristics, either unconsciously or intentionally. It is this variation from a standard style that attracts the attention of handwriting experts. Many factors produce individuality in a person's handwriting: muscular habits, movement, skill, instrument used, and position. Experts study how letters have been formed, the proportion or relative height of different letters, embellishments, the overall slant from the vertical, pressure applied with the writing instrument, and the spacing of letters, words, and lines. A handwriting sample may also include idiosyncrasies that are neither class nor individual characteristics. An example of an idiosyncrasy would be a break in writing caused by a distraction, or, as Sherlock Holmes noted, writing during a jarring ride.

Forgeries

Signatures tend to reveal consistent characteristics, such as the placing of a signature relative to typed or printed text in a document, the shape of the signature, and the way that the signature as a whole ascends or descends from left to right. A microscopic examination may reveal differences between a carefully written forgery and a genuine signature, typically written quickly and with confidence. For example, a forged signature may have breaks in lines, tremors, correction of badly shaped characters (patching), and eraser marks.

Even when a person attempts to disguise handwriting, certain consistencies show through. Criminals may try to disguise handwriting by changing the direction that the letters slant, altering letter size, writing quickly or slowly, printing, or writing with the opposite hand. Yet examiners can detect the writer's own individual characteristics in the formation of individual letters, and in the way that the writer started or ended a particular letter. Altering the direction of slant does not help. The slant shifts back to the natural appearance as the writer unconsciously finds a way to ease the discomfort caused by forcing muscles into unnatural positions. Discomfort also creates an unusual number of points where the writer has lifted a pen or pencil from the paper.

Here's a quick overview of the eight basic forms of forgeries.

- Memory: A forger imitates handwriting observed at another time. Typically, the forgery contains distortions and features of the forger's natural handwriting style.
- Simulation: The forger attempts to imitate a handwriting sample using freehand simulation. This is characterized by slow writing with hesitations.
- Tracing: The forger places genuine writing underneath a piece of paper and traces over the writing, a tactic that also produces signs of hesitation. Infrared light can reveal an underlying pencil tracing of writing over which an inked copy was made. Another way to produce a tracing forgery is to place a copy of a genuine signature over a piece of paper, write over the genuine signature to produce an indented copy, and then fill in the indentations. Al-

though an examiner can detect a tracing forgery, this technique can disguise the forger's own individual characteristics.

- Freestyle: A person simply attempts to disguise their own handwriting with no idea about the appearance of the genuine writing. For example, a forger may fill out checks removed from someone else's checkbook. The free-style forger is likely to disclose individual characteristics.

- Auto-forgery: Here, a person forges his or her own signature by writing in an unnatural manner. The objective is to provide a basis for denying the authenticity of the signature, such as a signature on a contract or check endorsement. However, an examiner can usually associate the writer with the forgery.

- Writing lift: In this case, the forger photocopies a signature and then lifts the writing with a piece of tape before the toner sets. The forger then places the signature on another document.

- Photographic lift: A forger reproduces a signature—often of someone famous—on a forged document using photo-offset or a computer scanner.

- Signature machine: These machines are used to sign the name of a person for routine business correspondence. An unauthorized signing of a document with such a machine is usually a criminal act of fraud. These signatures are recognized by their bluntness of strokes and uniformity.

Summary

"He wondered if the unsub had tried to doctor his handwriting. Many criminals – say, kidnappers writing ransom notes – will try to disguise their writing to make comparisons more difficult. They'll use odd slants and formations of letters. But usually they can't do this smoothly; it's very difficult to suppress our natural hand and document examiners can usually detect 'tremble' – a shakiness in the strokes – when someone's trying to disguise his writing. But there was no tremble here. This was the unsub's genuine writing."

—Jeffery Deaver's *The Devil's Teardrop* (1999).

"Bowman put the note between two panes of glass to flatten the jagged edges of the hole. The tatters were smeared with vermilion ink. He was chanting under his breath. On the third repetition Crawford made out what he was saying. 'You're so sly, but so am I.'

Bowman switched filters on his small television camera and focused it on the note. He darkened the room until there was only the dull red glow of a lamp and the blue-green of his monitor screen.

The words 'I hope we can correspond' and the jagged hole appeared enlarged on the screen. The ink smear was gone, and on the tattered edges appeared fragments of writing.

'Aniline dyes in colored inks are transparent to infrared,' Bowman said.'"

—Document examiner Lloyd Bowman reveals obliterated writing in Thomas Harris' *Red Dragon* (1981).

In this chapter, we've investigated various skills of forensic document examiners, including exposure of hidden writing, document dating, and detection of forgery. Consider bringing a document examiner into your story if any of the following questions arise:

- Did the person who allegedly wrote a document do so?
- Did the machine that supposedly created a questioned document do so?
- When was a document created?
- Has a document been altered?
- Who among a group wrote an anonymous note?
- Is a signature genuine? If not, can the forger be identified?

When it comes to forgery, reality can be stranger than fiction. Remember the forged Hitler diaries? When experts examined the handwriting in the books, they used several writing samples forged by Konrad Kujau, the man who had also forged the diaries. Mark Hofmann's forged handwriting has also passed forensic scrutiny. But Hofmann took forgery several steps beyond those used to create the Hitler diaries; he faked paper and ink compositions as well.

Considered one of the most skilled forgers, Hofmann counterfeited the work of over 129 people, including Abraham Lincoln, George Washington, and Mark Twain. In addition to recreating handwriting and printing that appear genuine, he produced documents that passed forensic dating tests. Hofmann achieved this by obtaining paper produced in the appropriate time period, making his own ink according to an authentic formula used during the relevant time, and by using period-appropriate, handmade writing instruments, such as quill pens. To age documents, he applied an old vacuum cleaner to the back of a page and sprayed the front with hydrogen peroxide. This process brought portions of ink to the back side of the paper. But the process also introduced minute cracks in the ink (alligatoring), a sign that inspired forensic document examiners to duplicate the artificial aging process. During the early 1980s, Hofmann also forged hundreds of Mormon documents, which, if authentic, would have required serious revisions of Mormon beliefs. This project undoubtedly inspired the *Law and Order: Criminal Intent* episode, "The Saint" (2004).

In the next chapter, we'll turn our attention back to biological evidence. We'll investigate clues gleaned from the corpse of a murder victim, methods for determining time of death, the difference between a coroner and a medical examiner, and the types of experts who aid in the investigation of a corpse.

A Few FAQ from the Course

Are there any databases of handwriting samples or computer techniques for analyzing handwriting?

Yes to both questions. The Forensic Services Division of the U.S. Secret Service offers its Forensic Information System for Handwriting, or FISH, to federal, state, and local law enforcement agencies, who investigate threats against public officials and cases involving missing and sexually exploited children. A document examiner uses the system to scan and digitize text and writings. The examiner can search that material against previously recorded writings. California-based Topaz Systems, Inc. produces SigAnalyze™ for forensic document examiners. This software reconstructs the sequence of movements made by a writer while executing a signature and aids in the detection of forgeries.

Have any developments made handwriting examination more difficult?

One technical development that affected examiners was the change from the fountain pen as the writing instrument of choice to the ballpoint pen. This occurred around 1945. Ballpoint pens use viscous ink and a nonflexing tip. Consequently, ballpoint pens produce a writing line with little shading, compared with the writing produced from the nib of a fountain pen. More recently, the popularity of word processing software, email, and texting has assured that cursive writing is a dying skill. This means the loss of handwriting characteristics.

Aren't there many types of ink?

Modern ink can be found in four common forms. Black inks typically contain dye material and iron salts in a suspension of gallic or tannic acid. India ink (carbon black ink) is produced from a suspension of carbon particles in gum arabic. Colored inks are made using synthetic dyes with polymers and acids. Ballpoint pens use ink made with synthetic dyes or insoluble pigments with various solvents and additives.

CHAPTER 12

Remains to be Seen

"The next person to arrive was Dottor Ettore Rizzaradi, *medico legale* for the city of Venice and thus officially responsible for declaring the victim dead and for making the first speculation as to the time of that event."
— Donna Leon's *Doctored Evidence* (2004).

When confronted with a corpse, investigators want to know the identity of the deceased, when that person died, and how that person died. In this chapter, we'll survey the techniques used to obtain this information from human remains.

The organization of a medicolegal death investigative system varies throughout the United States; it may be a medical examiner-based system, a coroner-based system, or an amalgam of medical examiner and coroner systems. These systems can be structured so that investigations originate from one state-level office (a centralized system), or investigations can be performed in more than one regional-, county-, or city-based office (a decentralized system). Medical examiner or coroner offices also vary in their official affiliations. They can be a part of a public health department, a public safety department, or independent of government agencies.

According to a 2002 survey performed by the Centers for Disease Control and Prevention, 22 states had medical examiner systems, 18 states had mixed medical examiner and coroner systems, while 11 had coroner systems. In those states with a mixed system, some counties were served by coroners, others by medical examiners, and still others relied on a referral system in which a coroner submitted cases to a medical examiner for autopsy. Regardless of the organization, officials ran most death investigations at the county level.

A coroner is an appointed or elected public official who makes inquiries into certain types of deaths. Depending upon the jurisdiction, an individual may meet the requirements for a coroner by reaching a minimum age (often 18), avoiding any felony convictions, graduating from high school, and residing in the relevant county or district. The coroner must investigate a death, assign a cause and manner of death, and list the information on a certificate of death. To fulfill these duties, a coroner may employ physicians, pathologists, or forensic pathologists to perform autopsies.

Typically, a medical examiner is a licensed physician who is usually appointed and who may have state, district, or county jurisdiction. The medical examiner must investigate and examine persons who died a sudden, unexpected, or violent death. A medical examiner's duties may include conducting inquests about the cause of death, performing autopsies and microscopic examinations, and ordering additional forensic tests. A particular jurisdiction may not require a physician medical examiner to be a specialist in death investigation or pathology. But some do demand these qualifications. To qualify as a pathologist—a physician trained to determine a cause of death—an individual must acquire at least four years of specialized training after graduation from an approved medical school.

If the person in charge of a death investigation is a coroner or a medical examiner who has not specialized in pathology, then a forensic pathologist may be brought into the case. A forensic pathologist can be called upon to perform an autopsy, to determine the manner of death, to estimate the time of death, to determine the type of weapon used, to reconstruct how a person received injuries, and to establish the identity of the deceased. To become a forensic pathologist in the United States, a medical school graduate either spends five years training in anatomic and clinical pathology and one year training in forensic pathology, or trains for four years in anatomic pathology and one year in forensic pathology. To become certified, a candidate must then pass an American Board of Pathology examination that endorses special competence in forensic pathology.

The Corpse at the Crime Scene

"Now, years later, most crime scene techs knew to collect the largest maggots they could find on a body, as those would probably have hatched from the earliest flies to find the body. By collecting and preserving those maggots and sending them to a forensic entomologist, the crime scene techs could get a pretty good idea how long ago the murder had occurred."
—*Flesh and Bone* by Jefferson Bass (2007).

Let's say that the first responder finds a corpse. Typically, the medical examiner's office or coroner's office has jurisdiction over that body. After that jurisdiction is in effect, the body should not be touched, moved, or searched without consent from the person who must certify the death. After a preliminary examination at the scene, the body is placed in a clean plastic sheet or body bag and transported for autopsy.

The mechanics of a death investigation vary from state to state. In Alabama, for example, a death investigation team looks into unlawful, unnatural, and suspicious deaths. The death investigation team includes a state medical examiner, who is a forensic pathologist; a forensic investigator, who is a law enforcement officer trained in death investigation; and forensic autopsy technicians, who obtain and correlate scene information, background history, and postmortem examination findings.

Death investigation team members investigate crime scenes and backgrounds of those involved, conduct examinations in the laboratory, obtain evidence, and may testify in court. Typically, the state medical examiner relies on information about the crime scene gathered by the forensic investigators. However, the state medical examiner may conduct the investigation at the crime scene if the case involves a complicated industrial or aircraft accident, or a capital murder, such as a murder committed during a kidnapping.

The thoroughness of a death investigation varies from case to case. A postmortem examination may be limited to an external examination of the body. The record of a complete death investigation, however, may include an initial report of the death—provided by a police officer, an attending physician, or a family member—to the medical examiner or coroner, a determination of circumstances surrounding the death, findings from the investigation of the place where the body was found, the results of a post-mortem exam or autopsy, the results of laboratory tests, and a certification of the cause and manner of death.

Sometimes investigators learn that a certain place may contain a buried body. This sparks a hunt for a clandestine grave. The area can be searched using ground-penetrating radar to create a high-resolution cross-sectional image of the ground, thermal infrared imagery to detect disturbances in soil, or by taking soil gas readings to detect methane and other gases produced by a decomposing body. Investigators may use cadaver dogs to locate decomposing and skeletal remains and search for areas with inconsistent vegetation or sunken ground. After investigators find a hidden grave, specialists carefully sift for evidence. Heavy digging machinery is avoided at least because it destroys spatial relationships between the remains and potential evidence.

An examination of a body may focus on estimating the time of death, uncovering the identity of the deceased, and determining a cause and manner of death. We'll look at each of these objectives in turn.

Estimating the Time of Death

"'What's that white stuff?' Racine asked.
'Adipocere.'
'Adipocere,' he repeated.
'Grave wax,' I said, not in the mood for a chemistry lesson. 'Fatty acids and calcium soaps from muscle or fat undergoing chemical changes, usually after long burial or immersion in water.'"
—Forensic anthropologist Dr. Temperance Brennan gives rookie crime scene recovery member René Racine a lesson in Kathy Reichs' *Monday Mourning* (2004).

"Sanchez told us the Columbia medical examiners had found confused lividity patterns on Brubaker's body that in their opinion meant he had been dead about three hours before being tossed in the alley. Lividity is what happens to a person's blood after death."
—Lee Child's *The Enemy* (2004).

Investigators have three indicators for estimating time of death that can be found up to about 48 hours after death. This time period is known as the early postmortem interval.

Livor mortis (hypostasis) occurs when the heart ceases function. Blood stops circulating and sinks to the lowest portions of the body. Consequently, the lower surfaces acquire a discoloration as the capillaries become engorged with blood, while the upper portions of the body pale as they are drained of blood. Livor mortis becomes noticeable 30 minutes to 3 hours after death. Lividity becomes fixed when pressure exerted on capillary walls causes them to burst. This may occur from 6 to 24 hours after death. If lividity has not become fixed when a body is moved, the blood will flow again and create new areas of lividity.

Rigor mortis is the stiffening of muscles that causes a rigidity of the body at the joints. This condition may be due to the breakdown of muscle glycogen to lactic acid, which increases acidity in muscle cells and causes contraction. Rigor mortis can occur about one to six hours after death. Rigor becomes fully established between 6 to 24 hours after death but can disappear between 12 to 36 hours postmortem. Heat accelerates the onset of rigor mortis, whereas cold delays it. Rigor mortis may occur sooner than expected if the victim had exerted muscles before death, such as in a struggle or in an electrocution.

Algor mortis refers to a decrease in body temperature following death. A clothed adult may reach ambient temperature in about 20 to 30 hours. A rough rule is that the body cools 1 degree Celsius per hour after death. An examiner measures a corpse's temperature in its brain, rectum, or beneath the liver.

In mild temperatures, decomposition of a body exposed to air begins soon after death and can be apparent 24 to 72 hours postmortem. Early signs include the development of a greenish discoloration in the skin of the flanks and abdomen. Higher temperatures speed the rate of decomposition. If a body has been buried, decomposition occurs at a much slower rate due to decreased insect activity, cooler temperature, and less oxygen. The deeper a body is buried, the slower the decay rate.

Saponification can occur if a body decomposes underwater or in wet soil. In this process, the body's fat decays into a waxy yellow-white substance called adipocere.

On the other hand, a body buried in a dry environment—especially in a hot sandy area—will become mummified. The soft tissues rapidly dehydrate, and this inhibits bacterial growth. The process preserves internal organs and identifying marks, such as scars and tattoos.

If a corpse is older than 72 hours, then the most accurate method of determining the time of death requires an identification of the species of maggots that have infested the body. Typically, the first insects to attack a body are flies that lay eggs in the eyes, nose, mouth, and open wounds. The common housefly becomes the predominant visitor of a body left indoors, while a body lying outdoors attracts blow files (blue and green bottle flies) and sheep maggot flies. A forensic entomologist examines maggots to determine species and may raise the maggots to adult flies for further verification. The presence of certain insect species can indicate the season of death, while the presence of nonindigenous insects may indicate that the body was dumped.

For bodies buried more than a year, investigators may request a forensic botanist to examine roots and stems of perennial plants to estimate the length of time since burial. If the killer damaged plant life when burying the body, then new growth began at this time. By counting the number of rings of new growth in a root, a botanist may determine an approximate amount of time since burial.

Forensic palynology can provide information about whether a body had been moved since death and, perhaps, indicate where the body has been. This subdiscipline of botany focuses on the identification of ubiquitous pollen and spores.

If only bones remain, then investigators may call upon a forensic anthropologist to estimate time clapsed since death. The examiner will consider the time necessary for soft tissue to decompose, taking into account factors such as environmental temperature, humidity, whether the body had been buried, access to insects and animals, rainfall, whether the body had been clothed, and the acidity of the soil. In general, bones from a person dead more than 50 years at the time of discovery are considered to be of archeological, not forensic, interest.

The Body Farm

More than 25 years ago, world-renowned forensic anthropologist Dr. William Bass started the Outdoor Anthropological Research Facility to study the processes and timing of postmortem decay. Covering a little over two acres behind the University of Tennessee Medical Center, the facility—popularly known as "the Body Farm"—contains corpses decomposing through a 12-month cycle under trees, submerged in water, or buried underground. Analyses of the decomposition process aid investigators to establish the time-since-death of human remains. Afterwards, researchers collect skeletons, measure the remains for a forensic database, and store the remains in the Anthropology Department's depository, one of the world's largest skeleton collections.

Expanding beyond its original purpose, researchers use the Body Farm to develop and test new forensic technologies, and the facility serves as a site to train cadaver dogs and their handlers. Students of the National Forensic Academy, typically law enforcement investigators and crime scene technicians, also train there. Several months before a new academy class arrives, faculty members scatter evidence. Students must carefully search the grounds, mark locations of evidence, photograph and bag their findings. They must also locate a clandestine grave.

The Search for Identity

"'I called up to Asheville and asked for a forensics team to be sent down, Doc; they don't want anything moved till they get here - probably tomorrow.'

'Why the hell did you do that?' Sully demanded.

Aggrieved, the sheriff said, 'Because I'm supposed to when unidentified bodies are found, dammit. With all these serial killers and whatnot around, you never know when some bone a dog dug up'll turn out to be Charlie Manson's third-grade teacher or Ted Bundy's left toe!'"

—Sheriff J.T Hamilton follows procedure in Kay Hooper's *Amanda* (1995).

A hunt for the deceased's identity can begin by searching pockets for identification cards. The outer clothing can be sent to a lab for examination of trace evidence and identifying marks, such as laundry marks, manufacturer's marks, and dry cleaning tags. A laundry may stamp clothes with dye that fluoresces under ultraviolet light and identifies the laundry and customer. Since these marks are durable, an examination of a piece of clothing may reveal a series of marks and illuminate its laundry history.

During an autopsy, a pathologist will note abnormalities that may lead to the victim's identity. Medical conditions such as ulcers, gallstones, arthritis, or cardiovascular disease can be checked against medical records. Tattoos, scars, and birthmarks may also help to identify the victim. Ultimately, positive identification of the deceased may require visual recognition by family or acquaintances. Investigators may also attempt to identify the deceased by fingerprint analysis, X-ray comparisons, DNA comparisons, or dental comparisons. Many states and the FBI use computerized dental identification systems to identify bodies. But what happens if the remains are bones?

A forensic anthropologist may provide a tentative identification by determining characteristics that can be checked against records of suspected missing persons. Preliminarily, a forensic anthropologist must decide if a specimen is truly bone. This may require microscopic examination if the specimen is a small fragment or has been extensively charred. If it is bone, then the examiner must determine if it is human bone. A positive determination is not always possible, however; human bone can resemble bone from other primates, bears, and cats. If the forensic anthropologist concludes that the remains are human, then the bones are examined to establish class characteristics, including the age of the person at time of death, gender, and ethnicity. The examiner then focuses on individual characteristics, such as height of the person (traditionally estimated by measuring arm and leg bones) and unusual features, including evidence of bone trauma during life.

If a skull is recovered and investigators have a photo of a potential victim, then an examiner can superimpose photos of the skull and that individual's photograph. Computer imaging aids this effort. Digital imaging can also create a sketch of a deceased's face based on calculated soft tissue depths at various points on a skull. In a more traditional approach, a forensic artist applies clay to a skull or a cast of a skull to produce a three-dimensional reconstruction of the deceased's face. Briefly, an artist drills a series of holes into the skull or cast at certain anatomical reference points. Rods are inserted into each hole and secured so that they protrude to heights consistent with data on the depth of soft tissue layers at each anatomical point. After placing artificial eyeballs into the sockets, the artist applies modeling clay to the skull surface to build up the muscular structure of the face. The artist then adds clay to cover the rods and smoothes contours of the cheeks and jaws.

Cause and Manner of Death

"'Right. Cause of death,' she said. 'Severe cerebral haemorrhage caused by savage and multiple blows to the top, back and side of the head. The killer wanted this one unambiguously dead.'"

—Inspector Zé Coelho consults a pathologist in Robert Wilson's *A Small Death in Lisbon* (1999).

In a medical examiner system, state law typically requires the medical examiner to determine manner of death. Under a coroner system, a pathologist usually gives the coroner a finding that establishes a cause of death, and the coroner combines this information with other investigative results to make a decision about the manner of death. In either system, the possibilities for manner of death are natural, homicide, accident, suicide, or undetermined.

The University of Iowa's Department of Pathology provides the following scenario to illustrate the manner of death concept. Suppose that Tom is shot with a rifle. If the wound was self-inflicted, then the manner of death would be accidental if Tom had been cleaning the rifle when it discharged, or suicide if Tom had deliberately inflicted the wound. If someone else shot Tom, the manner of death would be accidental if a stray hunting bullet hit Tom, or homicide if the wound was intentionally inflicted. If there is no information about how Tom was shot, then the manner of death would be undetermined.

The cause of death is the trauma, disease or combination of both that produced the termination of life. The proximate cause of death is the disease or injury that initiates an expected, foreseeable, and unbroken series of events that leads to death. The immediate cause of death is the factor that causes death at a particular time and place. The immediate and proximate causes may be the same, but this is not necessarily so. Let's consider two examples.

In one example, an elderly man with a history of arteriosclerosis suffers a fatal heart attack. The immediate cause of death is the heart attack, while the proximate cause of death is arteriosclerosis. The manner of death is natural.

In another example, Bernice seeks revenge and uses a butcher knife to stab Howard in the stomach. Although operations repair the physical damage, Howard develops septicemia due to an impaired immune system which he has had his entire life. Despite treatments, Howard dies from septicemia. The knife wound is the proximate cause of death and septicemia is the immediate cause of death. The manner of death is homicide, and the law does not give Bernice any benefit because she happened to pick someone with a poor immune system.

Autopsy Findings

"At the center of it all, by the pooling that marked the seat of the blaze, lay a blackened body, this one on its side, curled in a familiar pugilistic pose."
—Peter Robinson's *Playing with Fire* (2004).

"'Nobody can pin down the time of death any closer unless they saw it happen. He's been dead anywhere from a half hour to a couple of hours. I can do better on cause of death. I don't need an autopsy to figure this one. Blunt trauma to the head. Massive hemorrhaging.'"
—Dr. Burford in Carolyn Hart's *Engaged to Die* (2003).

Preliminary steps in an autopsy include an inspection of the body before removing clothing, collecting the clothing for further examination, observing the general condition of the body, and noting indications about time of death. An autopsy includes an evaluation of apparent age, height, weight, state of nutrition, scars, tattoos, eye and hair color, condition of teeth, muscular development, abnormalities, marks of medical procedures, and a detailed examination of injuries. Photos are taken to identify the deceased and to document injuries or presence of disease. X-rays may expose fragments of a weapon, and document bone fractures, deformities, and evidence of surgical procedures. An internal examination traces wound tracks in the body and reveals the conditions of the organs.

In Switzerland, the University of Berne's Institute of Forensic Medicine and its Institute of Diagnostic Radiology collaborated to produce virtual autopsy technology, or Virtopsy®. Dr. Michael Thali, Virtopsy® Project Manager, predicted that the virtual autopsy technique may eventually be deemed an acceptable alternative to current practice. The virtual autopsy combines computed tomography and magnetic resonance imaging to reveal information about the general pathology of a body, as well as details about tissues and trauma injuries. If a weapon caused a death, investigators can perform a three-dimensional surface scan of the wound. Using a computer-aided design program, they can then compare a virtual model of the injury with the three-dimensional image of a simulation created with a similar type of weapon.

Previously, we considered the types of damage and marks left by firearms. Here are some signs associated with other causes of death.

Asphyxia (anoxia) occurs when a body's tissues and organs are deprived of oxygen. Acute asphyxia can produce a blue discoloration of the lips and fingertips due to a reduction in oxygen-carrying hemoglobin (cyanosis). Small hemorrhages (petechiae) may also be present. These appear as dark red spots beneath the skin surface, especially on the face, conjunctiva of the eye and within the lungs. Asphyxia can come about in many ways, such as:

- a decrease in the ability of tissues to use oxygen (for example, cyanide poisoning),
- a reduction in the ability of hemoglobin to carry oxygen (for example, carbon monoxide poisoning), and
- mechanical interference with the passage of air into the respiratory tract (for example, drowning).

Smothering (suffocation) occurs when breathing becomes impossible despite the availability of adequate oxygen. A killer smothers the victim by closing the nostrils and mouth, and these actions can leave small lacerations on the inside of lips. On the other hand, the victim may have few visible signs of trauma if the killer used a soft object—such as a pillow—to obstruct air passages. During the nineteenth century, William Burke and William Hare sold corpses to the anatomy departments of teaching hospitals in Edinburgh, Scotland. When demand exceeded supply, they murdered victims by kneeling on the chest and using their hands to close off the nose and mouth. This smothering technique is now known as burking.

Strangulation may be due to homicide, suicide, or an accident. Homicide can be carried out by manual strangulation or strangulation with a ligature made of wire or rope. In manual strangulation, the assailant compresses the airway or blood vessels to render the victim unconscious. This creates fingernail marks and neck bruises from the killer's fingers and thumbs. Strangulation by ligature leaves horizontal grooves around the neck. A person may use a ligature to commit suicide, but suicide by manual strangulation is not possible; manual pressure to one's own neck stops after reaching unconsciousness. Accidental strangulation is often associated with sexual asphyxia.

A person drowns by inhaling water into the air passages, which causes choking and results in the formation of mucus in the throat and windpipe. The foamy mucus passes into the lungs and further disrupts air passages. Findings consistent with drowning include swollen lungs, foam in and around the mouth and nostrils, large quantities of water in the stomach, and hemorrhages in the middle ear. However, tests cannot prove that a person drowned; drowning is typically determined by excluding other causes.

About twenty percent of drowning cases are dry drowning. Here, the victim dies of asphyxia due to submersion without inhaling much water beyond the larynx. The inhalation of a small amount of liquid can cause a spasm of the larynx and obstruction of air into the lungs. Consequently, the victim of dry drowning lacks large amounts of fluid in the lungs and stomach.

Typical signs of drowning are also missing in cases of reflex cardiac arrest. In this situation, a person enters very cold water and dies from a heart attack.

A pathologist may be asked to determine if cutting or stabbing wounds were the result of homicide or suicide. Hesitation marks (or trial attempts) indicate suicide. These are superficial cuts in the area of the fatal wound that the person inflicted to work up determination and to test the weapon before making the fatal wound. Other factors include the direction of cut, and the left- or right-handedness of the deceased. In suicides, cuts are usually found on the throat, wrists, or thighs and are usually regular and parallel.

Knives, scissors, or daggers can produce stab wounds. Stab wounds are inflicted by pushing a weapon into a body, damaging vital organs and causing internal bleeding. The corners of a stab wound can provide clues about the weapon. If the instrument had a single cutting edge, then the dull side probably created a squared-off wound or two small tears. A two-edged weapon, such as a stiletto, produces a wound in which both ends are sharply incised. A technique may be used to produce a cast of a stab wound. An examiner carefully dissects the part of the body that contains the wound, layer by layer, to enable the creation of a three-dimensional representation of the wound. Once again, note that the technique of injecting caulk into a knife wound to make a cast—pioneered by TV's *CSI* team—simply does not work.

A puncture wound is produced with an instrument that has a sharp point but lacks sharp edges. Puncturing weapons include an ice pick and screwdriver.

Incised wounds (cuts) are inflicted by an attacker who makes a series of slashes. An incised wound is longer than deep, which is the opposite of a stab wound. The victim of such an attack may have defensive wounds.

A chopping wound is produced by an edged tool, such as an ax. Although similar to a cutting wound, a chopping wound has a ring of contusion injury and signs of crushing.

The types of injuries associated with blunt force trauma include abrasions, bruises (contusions), lacerations (tears), and fractures. An abrasion is denuded skin caused by friction. An abrasion's pattern may indicate the type of weapon used. Bruises are caused by the breaking of small blood vessels and the transfer of blood into surrounding tissue. Lacerations occur when force is applied to soft tissue and stretches the skin beyond the point of elasticity. The result is a tear. An examination of a blunt force wound may indicate the direction of force that caused the laceration.

Blunt force can crack and break bones. Fatal blows are typically delivered to the head, which may show depression fractures where the bones were driven into the brain. Clues about the shape of a weapon may be gleaned from the shape of the fractured area. The fracture may also suggest the relative height and strength of the attacker. Military Police investigator Jack Reacher benefited from these types of clues in Lee Child's *The Enemy* (2004).

A person may be burned by heat, chemicals or electricity. Investigators may find a fire victim lying in a pugilistic position: clenched fists or bent arms due to contraction of muscles from heat. Generally, a victim of a fire dies from suffocation from smoke or by carbon monoxide poisoning before the fire starts to burn the body. If a pathologist does not find high levels of carbon monoxide in the victim's blood or soot in airways, then death probably took place before the fire started.

Summary

"'When he was out of the room, I poured the chloral hydrate into his glass and then, after he had drunk it, I waited for it to take effect. I bound up his hands because I was frightened he would wake up. I shot him, turned up the heating to conceal the time of death, just in case I had been seen.'"

—A killer explains how he attempted to fool the authorities in M.C. Beaton's *Death of a Macho Man* (1996).

"'The lividity indicates she was killed and left on her back for a while,' I said, 'long enough for it to set, and after that she was turned onto her stomach.'

'So someone came back,' Eddie suggested.'"

—Gregg O. McCrary describes one of his cases in *The Unknown Darkness: Profiling the Predators Among Us* (2003).

In this chapter, we've surveyed the tasks of death investigators: seeking the identity of the deceased, estimating a time of death, and uncovering clues about the cause and manner of death. The biological clues that we considered can only provide estimates for a time of death. The best way to pin down the time is to find a reliable person who witnessed the death. In a mystery or crime story, an estimate of the time of death impacts the alibi of a suspect. Introducing a time of death estimate in the middle of a story, or changing the estimated time, can stir the pool of suspects and place your various players' actions into a new perspective. Speaking of bodies, the ever-reliable Michael Connelly very effectively uses forensic medical evidence clues in *The Fifth Witness* (2011).

We briefly considered how a forensic artist can reconstruct facial features from a skull. This technique played a role in Martin Cruz Smith's *Gorky Park* (1981), Sue Grafton's *Q Is for Quarry* (2002), Ian Rankin's *The Falls* (2001), Beverly Connor's *Airtight Case* (2000), the *Wire in the Blood* episode "Shadows Rising" (2002), and *Prime Suspect 2* (1992) among other novels and films. Dr. Nikki Alexander in the series *Silent Witness* (1996—?) routinely performs facial reconstruction. An advantage of including this technique in a story is that it takes time to perform. Consequently, the results can be inserted at any point and, perhaps, alter the path of the investigation. A different type of facial reconstruction—digital enhancement of a photo—injected suspense into the Kevin Costner movie, *No Way Out* (1987), a remake of the 1948 film *The Big Clock*, which was based on Kenneth Fearing's classic crime novel.

By the way, we've seen that a forensic pathologist has invested almost a decade in arduous and expensive education. Bear this in mind before you decide to write about a forensic pathologist who risks a career by charging around the countryside like an amateur detective.

We wrap things up in the next chapter, where we'll look at the analysis of language and behavior, identification based on scent, and potential role models for fictional investigators.

A Few FAQ from the Course

Is it possible to apply facial reconstruction techniques to ancient remains?

Yes. The June 2005 issue of *National Geographic Magazine* features an analysis of King Tutankhamun's remains with a high-resolution computed tomography scanner. Forensic artists and physical anthropologists used the data to show how King Tut looked the day that he died, about 3,300 years ago.

What causes a floater to float?

A body submerged in water for a length of time rises because bacteria produce gas during decomposition.

What is meant by "coup/contre-coup effect"?

When the head is propelled forward, the brain travels with the skull, and when the head hits a surface and stops moving, the brain strikes the inside of the skull, causing a coup injury. When the head bounces away from the surface, the brain bounces away as well, striking the opposite end of the skull and causing the contre-coup injury.

What is a "psychological autopsy"?

A psychological autopsy is a technique that helps to clarify the manner of death. The objective is to understand the circumstances and state of mind of the victim at the time of death. A psychological autopsy is performed by reconstructing the lifestyle and circumstances of the victim and by investigating the behavior and events that led to death.

After a body is in the morgue, is it up to the lead investigator to decide if an autopsy should be performed?

Details about requirements for performing a forensic autopsy vary from one jurisdiction to another. In general, a decision to perform a forensic autopsy depends upon the circumstances surrounding a death, where a person dies, the next of kin, and, sometimes, even the deceased's insurance policy. A forensic examination may be performed if death was violent, sudden and unexpected, occurred under suspicious circumstances, or was employment-related. The death of a person whose body will be cremated or otherwise unavailable for later examination, or a death that may present a threat to public health can also demand an autopsy. Ultimately, a decision about performing a forensic autopsy may depend upon a budget.

CHAPTER 13

Coup de Grâce

We'll bring our forensic science survey to a close by taking bird's-eye views of real and fictional forensic science expert role models. But, first, we'll briefly explore several more types of analyses that aid criminal investigations: the analyses of language, behavior, and scent.

Forensic Linguistics

"One thing was certain. It was the same voice on both messages.
A man's voice. American. Southern accent. Speaking slowly, deliberately.
Fairfax pushed his glasses up onto his nose, started typing on his keyboard.
He brought up a voice analysis program.
Then he compared the taped voice's digital signature – or 'voiceprint' – with the signatures of every other voice in the DIA's mainframe, every voice the Agency had ever secretly recorded."
—Defense Intelligence Agency mathematician Dave Fairfax in Matthew Reilly's *Area 7* (2001).

Linguistics is the study of language and its use. In the forensic arena, investigators call upon linguistics specialists to identify voices, interpret the intended meaning in oral and written statements (such as confessions), translate foreign languages, and identify authors of documents. We'll look at three areas of linguistics that have forensic applications; two focus on speech, and the third focuses on written communication.

Auditory phonetics (also called practical phonetics). This area of forensic linguistics focuses on how a person hears and interprets spoken language. An examiner skilled in auditory phonetics aims to identify witnesses and victims with cues, such as:

- perceived pitch,
- quality of the language,
- speed of speech,
- mannerisms (such as a frequent use of the word "like" or turning every sentence into a question by ending with an upward inflection),
- volume level of speech,
- breath patterns,
- the way that words are put together, and
- dialect or accent.

In criminal investigations, auditory phonetics plays a role in "earwitness" line-ups (also called voice parades) and telephone speaker recognition. A recorded voice may require audio enhancement, a preliminary processing by a computer or external filtering device to remove as much noise as possible.

Acoustic phonetics (also called instrumental phonetics). Here, the examiner analyzes speech using acoustic methods to detect physical characteristics of speech with the objective of speaker identification and discrimination. In brief, voice characteristics are recorded and transferred to a sound spectrograph, which produces voice spectrograms. A spectrogram—a graphic representation of time, energy, and frequency—provides the following cues: bandwidth, mean frequency, gaps between words, transitions between words, and nasal patterns. Voice identification with a sound spectrograph requires a comparison between a recording of a questioned voice and a recording of known origin.

Sometimes, a spectrogram is called a voiceprint, suggesting that an examiner can match two spectrograms from different recordings. This is not the case. A perfect match is unfeasible because any speaker's voice has very few invariable characteristics. Instead, examiners decide about the probability of identity based on voice characteristics and spectrogram data.

Stylistics. Forensic stylistics focuses on individual or group characteristics found in written language. Characteristics of style include document format, spelling, capitalization, abbreviations, punctuation, word choice, content, and syntax (phrasing and grammar). In the case of questioned authorship, an examiner may want to determine if one person authored all writings of a set or if a questioned writing was written by one of a number of possible authors. Forensic stylistics may also be used to examine transcripts of conversations.

Crime and mystery writers have taken advantage of linguists in their stories. For example, a forensic linguist studies a tape recording and offers opinions on the speaker's educational level and geographic origin in James Lee Burke's *Purple Cane Road* (2000) and in *Autley House* (2003) by Brett F. Woods. Linguists determine whether the same person wrote threatening notes in *Shooting Chant* (2000) by Aimee Thurlo, and analyze the nature of symbols written over victims' beds in Harker Moore's *A Cruel Season for Dying* (2003). In the *Law and Order* episode "Benevolence" (1993), a linguist performs a forensic stylistics analysis of telephone conversation transcripts to help police narrow the search for a killer.

Forensic Psychology

Forensic psychologists apply the science of psychology to questions relating to law. Specific activities of forensic psychologists include:

- evaluate and treat victims or witnesses of crime,
- train victim service providers,
- conduct psychological assessments in litigation matters,
- train police officers to deal with the mentally ill,
- provide services to police officers after a shooting,
- establish screening procedures for law enforcement employees,
- assist police investigations by developing psychological profiles of criminals,

- consult with police during a hostage-taking incident,
- advise investigators on tactics for interrogating a suspect,
- reconstruct the personality of a deceased individual (psychological autopsy),
- evaluate the effectiveness of programs for offenders,
- establish screening procedures for correctional officer positions,
- evaluate a defendant's competency to stand trial,
- conduct child custody evaluations,
- evaluate school policies aimed at preventing violent behavior,
- consult with government agencies about methods to prevent criminal activity,
- assist attorneys in jury selection, and
- consult with school personnel on identifying potentially dangerous students.

The Federal Bureau of Investigation considers psychological criminal investigative analysis to cover crime analysis, crime scene analysis, profiling, investigation strategy, interviewing techniques, threat assessment, and trial strategy. Fictional psychologists often engage in these activities, particularly in the development of a profile.

One type of profile is a sketch of psychological and demographic features that suggest the kind of person who may commit a particular sort of crime. This prospective approach forms the basis of the Computer Assisted Passenger Prescreening System. Implemented by the Federal Aviation Administration in 1998, CAPPS analyzes information from a passenger's itinerary to search for behavioral characteristics associated with a high security risk. In the wake of the September 11, 2001, terrorist attacks, Congress authorized the development of CAPPS II, designed to authenticate identity and perform a risk assessment on every airline passenger.

In a criminal investigation, profiling involves the identification of personality traits, behavioral tendencies, geographic location and demographic features of a criminal based on the characteristics of a crime. A criminal profiler aids investigators by narrowing the field of possible suspects. Profilers may also try to predict when and where the criminal will strike again.

Ex-FBI profiler Gregg O. McCrary offers a concise description of the profiling process in his book, *The Unknown Darkness: Profiling the Predators Among Us* (2003):

> For us, this was a classic profiling case. I assessed an offender's behavior across a series of crimes. We analyzed verbal, physical, and sexual behaviors that the offender exhibited with the victim. We looked for patterns, evidence of a signature, and any changes over time, and then made logical inferences from the information we had.

McCrary also offers a warning about fictional profilers: Any resemblance between the work of fictional profilers and real profilers is usually coincidental. Fictional profilers often rely upon instinct and deductive skills, whereas real profilers use their comprehensive training in psychology and criminal investigations. Without specialized training, a profiler can steer an investigation onto the wrong track.

Of course, misdirection has its uses in fiction. For example, an academic psychologist tried to help police in "To Be a Somebody" (1994), an episode of the British TV series *Cracker*. Due to a lack of training, the psychologist unwittingly gave the police a wrong profile of a serial killer, which derailed the investigation until forensic psychologist Dr. Eddie Fitzgerald put things back on track.

Another point to consider about profilers is that they draft a rough psychological sketch of a criminal based on evidence found at a crime scene. The accuracy of a profile suffers when law enforcement personnel incorrectly or incompletely describe a crime scene and evidence to a profiler. A criminal who stages a crime scene may also lead a profiler astray.

Detecting Lies

In 1921, August Vollmer, Berkeley, California's progressive chief of police, read an article by Harvard University researcher William Moulton Marston, who thought that he could detect verbal deception with a machine that measured an increase in blood pressure. Vollmer discussed lie-detecting machines with Sergeant John A. Larson. The sergeant built a variation of the inflatable rubber tube apparatus that doctors used for blood pressure measurements. Although Larson called his machine the cardio-pneumo-psychogram, it soon became known as the lie detector. Leonard Keeler, another recruit to the Berkeley police force, redesigned Larson's detector by adding a respiration-checking device and a galvanometer component to measure changes in skin resistance caused by perspiration. The polygraph was born. Modern computer-assisted polygraphs measure variations in blood pressure, heartbeat, pulse, skin resistance and breathing. In North America, law enforcement agencies primarily use the polygraph as an investigative tool, not for collecting evidence to be presented during a trial.

For years, scientists have studied an alternative to the polygraph: a brain scanning technique called functional magnetic resonance imaging (fMRI). The utterance of a truthful or a deceptive reply to a question can affect the activity of different parts of the brain, and fMRI detects changes in blood flow that indicate changes in brain activity. One day, the technique may become part of the criminal investigator's toolbox.

Skilled investigators can also detect lies by observing the behavior of a suspect during an interview. You can find tips for recognizing the red flags of deception in "Lie Detectors" by Dan Gordon in *UCLA Magazine* (October 1, 2011), which is available online (magazine. ucla.edu).

Making Sense of Scents

"'Human scent,' said Chad, 'has historically been defined as a biological component of decomposing dead skin cells, the skin raft theory.'

'I know,' said Danny with exaggerated patience.

'Current research suggests human body odor is much more complex,' said Chad. 'Like Latin.'

'Latin?'

'Well, it was complex for me,' said Chad."

—Detective Danny Messer and lab technician Chad Willingham discuss human scent evidence in Stuart M. Kaminsky's *CSI:NY: Blood on the Sun* (2006).

For more than a century, scent-discriminating dogs have supported European criminal investigations. Traditionally, canines aided police by doggedly trailing a suspect's scent. During the latter part of the twentieth century, investigators found a new way to employ the canine's olfactory skills: perform a scent lineup to connect a person with a crime via scent evidence. Tomasz Bednarek, Head of the Warsaw Metropolitan Forensic Laboratory, says that dogs trained for scent identification are "specialist, biological devices." The canine nose, reputed to have a sense of smell 1,000 to 10,000 times more superior than that of humans, does offer a sensitive forensic analysis device.

Scent identification rests upon an assumption that humans have unique odor profiles that remain constant over time, and that dogs can be trained to recognize that unique scent in a mixture of other odors. Studies suggest that various factors contribute to the distinctiveness of a person's scent. The most important factor appears to be genetics, followed by diet, hygiene, and state of health.

G.A.A. Schoon (Netherlands National Police Agency and Leiden University) investigated how the age of odor trace evidence affects the performance of Dutch and German scent identification dogs (*Forensic Science International* 147:43 (2005)). Although the dogs performed faultlessly in matching odors collected on the same day, their performance level dropped when presented with scent evidence stored for two weeks. Schoon suggested that the initial drop was due to the volatile nature of scent.

Allison Curran, Scott Rabin and Kenneth Furton (International Forensic Research Institute, Florida International University) used gas chromatography-mass spectroscopy to analyze the volatile components of human odor signatures. Their results show that variation in human scent can be due to the presence of certain compounds that vary among individuals and a combination of common compounds that differ in ratio from person to person. The group could detect measurable amounts of human scent compounds months after transfer to sterile gauze.

Under laboratory conditions, human scent may persist for even longer periods. Vladimir Martynov, the head of the criminology expert center at the Russian Interior Ministry, created a store of criminals' smells. Martynov preserves scents for up to two years by storing items worn by criminals in hermetically sealed containers at a low temperature.

Human scent endures outside the laboratory as well. In 2003, the Federal Bureau of Investigation tested the feasibility of detecting aged human scent in a heavily populated residential area. Researchers selected a test subject who had lived in a Stafford, Virginia house for seven years before moving to Albuquerque, New Mexico. Six months after the subject had moved to New Mexico, researchers placed a bloodhound team at a Stafford intersection several houses away from the old residence. After sniffing a letter that the subject had mailed from New Mexico, the dog trailed to and identified the correct house. The study showed that human scent resists the deteriorating effects of weather.

In 2001, the FBI and Southern California Bloodhound Handlers Coalition showed that human scent can survive an explosion and fire. The researchers prepared four pipe bombs and two containers of gasoline. Six test subjects handled a bomb or gas can for one to two minutes. After detonating or burning the devices, researchers collected debris and transferred scents from the debris to gauze pads. On the day of the experiment, the test subjects and six decoys walked along trails in a public park. After placing 20 bloodhound teams at the start of a trail, the handlers gave their dogs a sniff of a scent pad. The dogs trailed and identified the target person in 53 of 80 bomb debris experiments and in 31 of 40 arson debris experiments with no false identifications.

Police investigations benefit from human scent-detecting dogs that track or trail an individual, or that connect a suspect with evidence in a scent lineup. Dogs can track a person without a scent sample of their quarry. They achieve this by following the odor of crushed vegetation and disturbed ground, indicators of a fresh track. Tracking dogs may also use traces of fresh generic human scent to aid their pursuit.

Trailing and scent lineups require a scent sample. Traditional scent collection techniques include direct scenting, swiping, and absorption. In the direct scenting method, a handler allows a dog to smell an article of evidence. In the swiping method, a sterile gauze pad is wiped across the surface of evidence, and the pad is used as the scent source. The absorption approach relies upon the ability of a sterile gauze pad to absorb scent from an item of evidence. These traditional methods have a drawback: collection of scent can remove or contaminate DNA, fingerprints, fibers, and other trace evidence.

The FBI and many police departments have turned to the Scent Transfer Unit (STU) to create scent pads. The STU-100® is a portable vacuum that uses airflow to convey the components of human scent onto sterile gauze pads. The scent pads can be stored in zip-lock or heat-sealable bags until needed.

The Europeans have taken the lead in developing the latest canine contribution to police investigations: a scent identification lineup to link a suspect with crime scene evidence. The Dutch National Police, for example, devised a scent lineup system that withstands the scrutiny of the country's courts. The bare-bones procedure goes like this. A scent identification dog and its handler enter a test room that contains 10-centimeter stainless steel scent carrier tubes clamped to platforms. After passing several quality assurance tests, the suspect identification stage begins with the dog sniffing a scent evidence object collected from the scene of the crime. The dog then smells the scent carrier tubes, which had been handled by a suspect or by adults not associated with the suspect. If the dog picks the scent carrier tube handled by the suspect, then police conclude that the scent evidence object and the suspect share an odor similarity. In this procedure, the dog's handler does not know who touched the scent carriers. The handler's ignorance avoids the so-called Rosenthal effect, a nonverbal, or even unconscious, suggestion to a dog working in a lineup.

Scent identification also aids U.S. investigations, but the results usually can't justify an arrest. Police typically seek corroborating evidence to develop probable cause that a person committed a crime. Can a prosecutor introduce scent lineup evidence in a U.S. court? That depends. U.S. judges arrive at differing conclusions about whether scent lineup evidence should be deemed admissible in court.

Here's an important caveat at the tail end of this brief look at scent evidence: human scent can be transferred from one person or object to another. Consequently, a scent relationship can establish a direct or indirect link between a person and an article of a crime, but can't prove that an individual participated in a crime.

A Hitchhiker's Guide to Real Forensic Scientists

"Finch: 'Last night I injected my blood into this rabbit. Next I'll extract his blood into a syringe . . .'

Federal Marshal Jared Stone: 'What will that prove?'

Finch: 'It's a protein test. Hopefully I can use it to determine whether the blood on Luci's dress is human.'"

—1880s Pinkerton Agent Larimer Finch explains a technique invented more than a decade later and on the other side of the world in "No Excuse" (2003), an episode of the TV show *Peacemakers*.

We've covered many topics in forensic science. The following list of contributors provides historical highlights on the development of basic forensic science techniques. If you plan to write a historical mystery story, you'll want to have an idea about the development timeline. And you may find a role model or two for your characters.

Mathieu Orfila (father of forensic toxicology): Spanish chemistry instructor who taught in Paris and published *Traite de Poisons or Toxicologie Generale* (1813), the first scientific study of poison detection.

James Marsh: English chemist who devised a method to detect arsenic in 1836, which became the first analytical method in toxicology introduced during a criminal trial.

Jean Servais Stas: Belgian chemist who devised a method for detecting vegetable alkaloids in 1850.

Alexandre Lacassagne: During the 1870s–1890s, this French surgeon's contributions to forensic science include descriptions of gunshot wounds, the use of tattoos for identification, methods for estimating time of death, correlations between striations on a bullet and rifling patterns of firearm barrels, identification based on bone and dental examination, and crime scene blood spatter analysis.

Alphonse Bertillon: French criminologist who developed anthropometry, a system of bodily measurements for identification purposes. Police forces around the world adopted Bertillonage, which premiered in Paris during the 1880s.

Francis Galton: English scientist who described rules for a fingerprint classification system in his book, *Finger Prints* (1892).

Juan Vucetich: Born in an area today known as Croatia, Vucetich moved to Argentina, where he joined the Buenos Aires police force and devised a fingerprint classification system in the 1890s.

Edward Henry: British civil servant who formulated a fingerprint classification system, introduced in India around 1897.

Hans Gross (father of criminalistics): Austrian judge who promoted the application of science to criminal investigation, as described in his book, *System der Kriminalistik* (1893).

Paul Uhlenhuth: Assistant professor at the University of Greifswald who invented a method in 1900 for distinguishing human blood and animal blood. He used his new test to aid a murder investigation one year later.

Karl Landsteiner: Austrian-American pathologist who developed the modern classification of the four primary blood types in 1900.

Edmond Locard: French scientist who established the world's first dedicated medicolegal lab in 1910, emphasized the value of pore marks found in fingerprints, and devised the principle that "every contact leaves a trace."

Leone Lattes: Italian physician who first applied blood typing to civil and criminal investigations, beginning with a 1915 marital dispute.

Albert S. Osborn: American pioneer in the field of questioned document examination, whose books, *Questioned Documents* (1910) and *The Problem of Proof* (1922), became the seminal texts of the discipline.

Saburo Sirai: Japanese scientist who discovered the phenomenon of secretors in 1925. That is, a person may secrete proteins characteristic of his or her blood into other bodily fluids.

Calvin H. Goddard (father of forensic ballistics): American criminologist, physician, and military historian who joined New York City's Bureau of Forensic Ballistics in 1925 and pioneered techniques for identifying a weapon that fired a particular bullet.

Masato Soba: Japanese fingerprint examiner who developed the superglue fuming method for visualizing latent prints in 1977.

David Ashbaugh: a Royal Canadian Mounted Police constable who wrote *Ridgeology* (1983), emphasizing the method of individualization through an examination of friction ridges and consideration of ridge detail in its totality.

Alec Jeffries: English scientist who developed DNA typing and applied his technique in the 1986 Colin Pitchfork case.

Kary Mullis: American scientist who invented—during the mid-1980s—the polymerase chain reaction, the method for rapidly duplicating DNA fragments.

Peter Gill: In the early 1990s, this researcher at Britain's Forensic Science Service devised the polymerase chain reaction-short tandem repeat (PCR-STR) method, which is the standard technique for analyzing DNA.

Are you considering a character who is a scientist and a detective like Sherlock Holmes? Let's look at cases solved by two real scientific detectives: Luke S. May and Edward Oscar Heinrich.

Around 1917 in the early morning of an Idaho mining town, the wife of a mine official awoke to an odd sound: somebody breathing in the dark room. She screamed for help when she felt hot breath on her face. Panicking, the intruder mistook a tall window for a door, and fumbled for a minute, looking for a doorknob. The burglar lit a match to get bearings and then fled from the room. Days later, the sheriff lacked any leads for the burglar's identity. The county prosecuting attorney suggested that they call Luke S. May, a private detective and head of the Revelare International Secret Service (Pocatello, ID).

Luke May, a youthful, slender, tall sleuth, who spoke with a soft voice and dressed immaculately in a dark suit, interviewed the official's wife. He stopped her when she mentioned that the burglar had struck a match.

"Where did he drop the match?" May asked.

The woman pointed to an area by the window.

"We've left everything in the room just as it was," the mine official said.

The detective searched the floor and found 13 matches. Twelve had grooves in the shafts, whereas the last match was round and crimped at the end.

"This one with a crimp is the one we want," May told the sheriff.

"Say, I can get you a million just like that," the sheriff remarked.

"Maybe a million similar to it," May said, "but not one just like it. There are no two things in the world exactly alike, under the microscope."

May's microscopic examination of the match exposed a fiber dissimilar in texture and color from hundreds of fibers in his collection. He concluded that the intruder had worn clothes of foreign manufacture. The match also had a metallic crystal and a greasy stain with a speck of coal dust.

Microchemical analysis of the crystal revealed a composition of brass and iron, a combination that suggested brazing to repair a machine.

The sheriff and May investigated seven nearby mines. A repairman at one of the mines had recently completed a brazing job to fix a hoisting engine. The private detective questioned the repairman, who wore a European-cut suit with an unusual texture. In the man's pocket, May found matches identical to the one that the burglar had dropped. The pocket also contained threads like the fiber found on the burglar's match, grease stains and coal dust. Dirt under the man's fingernails included filings of brass and iron. Faced with the evidence, the repairman confessed to the burglary. His many successes as a scientific detective earned Luke May the title, "America's Sherlock Holmes."

On the rainy, chilly morning of October 11, 1923, Southern Pacific's Express Train No. 13 departed the Oregon town of Ashland, nestled in the Klamath Range of the Siskiyou Mountains. The train slowly climbed to Siskiyou summit and then entered a 3,000 foot long tunnel. Three armed men dropped from the top of the tunnel, and clambered toward the locomotive cab. Before the train exited the tunnel, two men armed with sawed off shotguns swung into the cab and ordered engineer Sidney Bates and fireman Marvin Seng to halt the train as soon as the railway post office car cleared the tunnel. A third gang member hammered on the mail car with his fist, but mail clerk Edwin Daugherty refused to open the door. The outlaw attached dynamite to the door of the mail car—too much dynamite. The car blew apart, killing Daugherty and incinerating $40,000. The holdup men shot Bates, Seng, and brakeman Charles Johnson, escaping empty-handed.

Under the lead of Southern Pacific Chief Special Agent Dan O'Connell, a large posse pursued the bandits. They only found items that the culprits had discarded: empty sacks, a DuPont blasting machine, a .45 caliber Colt revolver, a pair of greasy blue denim overalls and a knapsack with shoe covers soaked in creosote, intended to throw bloodhounds off the trail. Weeks later, investigators arrested a garage mechanic, who wore dungarees that appeared to be stained with the same greasy material as the evidence overalls.

O'Connell sent the overalls to scientific detective Edward Oscar Heinrich for a closer examination. From his lab on the ground floor of his home that overlooked the San Francisco Bay, Heinrich informed law enforcement officials that they had the wrong man; the stains were pitch from a fir tree, not auto grease. Heinrich added that the overalls had been worn by a left-handed lumberjack accustomed to working around fir trees in the Pacific Northwest. Moreover, the man had light brown hair, stood about five feet ten, weighed about 165 pounds, and was a Caucasian in his early twenties. Later, Heinrich explained that microscopic examination of the overalls and pocket debris revealed the presence of pitch from fir trees and particles of Douglas fir needles, common in the forests of the Pacific Northwest. Heavier wear on the left side pockets, compared with those on right, and the fact that the garment buttoned from the left indicated a left-handed person. By measuring the overalls, Heinrich estimated height and build. Microscopic analysis of a single strand of light brown hair that clung to one button provided an approximate age of the culprit and indicated that the fugitive was Caucasian.

Heinrich discovered a paper fragment with faded writing buried in the bottom of a deep, narrow pencil pocket. Treatment with iodine vapor showed that the paper was a registered mail receipt numbered 236-L. Further investigation revealed that the receipt had been issued in Eugene, Oregon to Roy d'Autremont, who had sent $50 to a brother in Lakewood, New Mexico. Investigators traveled to Eugene, where they talked with the father of Roy, Ray and Hugh d'Autremont. Heinrich's portrayal of a bandit matched the description of Roy.

The recovered Colt pistol also pointed to Roy d'Autremont. Although someone had obliterated the pistol's exterior serial number, Heinrich knew that the manufacturer started to duplicate serial numbers inside the guns. Heinrich dismantled the pistol and reported the second serial number. This led police to a Seattle store where the gun's purchaser had signed the name of William Elliot. Heinrich compared Elliot's signature with a sample of Roy's handwriting and found them indistinguishable.

The U.S. government launched a worldwide manhunt that lasted for years. Hugh d'Autremont was finally captured in Manila in 1927. News about the widely-publicized arrest traveled to Ohio where an elderly and partially blind man named Albert Collingsworth saw a newspaper photo of Hugh's brothers. Roy and Ray closely resembled two men that he knew. Collingsworth alerted the police, and FBI agents arrested the two d'Autremont brothers in Steubenville, Ohio. The case earned Heinrich the nickname: "Wizard of Berkeley."

A Hitchhiker's Guide to Fictional Forensic Scientists

If you think that you might like to feature a forensic science expert in your story, then you may wish to study specialists who inhabit the fictional world. The following list of characters will help you on your way. Each entry includes the character's creator and the date of the character's first appearance in print.

The Generalists

Sherlock Holmes: the most famous fictional detective who solved crimes by combining a scientific approach with a healthy dose of intuition (Sir Arthur Conan Doyle, 1887).

John Evelyn Thorndyke: considered to be fiction's first scientific detective (R. Austin Freeman, 1907).

Craig Kennedy: Columbia University chemistry professor who solved crimes using scientific techniques (Arthur B. Reeve, 1911).

Lincoln Rhyme: criminalist and former head of a New York City police department forensic team (Jeffery Deaver, 1997).

Examiners of Human Remains

Daniel Webster Coffee: forensic pathologist-sleuth based in the U.S. Midwest (Lawrence Blochman, 1950).

Kay Scarpetta: chief medical examiner for the Commonwealth of Virginia (Patricia Cornwell, 1990).

Jessica Coran: an FBI medical examiner (Robert W. Walker, 1992).

Joanna Blalock: forensic pathologist (Leonard Goldberg, 1994).

Lindsay Chamberlain: forensic anthropologist based at the University of Georgia (Beverly Connor, 1996).

Temperance Brennan: forensic anthropologist who splits her time between Montreal's Laboratoire de Médicine Légale and North Carolina (Kathy Reichs, 1997).

Dr. Bill Brockton: forensic anthropologist at the University of Tennessee's Anthropology Research Facility (Jefferson Bass (a pseudonym for Dr. Bill Bass and Jon Jefferson), 2006).

David Hunter: forensic anthropologist (Simon Beckett, 2006).

Forensic Behavior Experts

Jack Crawford: section chief of the FBI's Behavioral Science section (Thomas Harris, 1981).

Will Graham: an FBI agent who hunts serial killers (Thomas Harris, 1981).

Clarice M. Starling: protégé of Jack Crawford (Thomas Harris, 1988).

Alex Cross: Washington, D.C. police detective and forensic psychologist (James Patterson, 1992).

Tony Hill: clinical psychologist/criminal profiler based in Northern England (Val McDermid, 1995).

Frank Clevenger: consulting forensic psychiatrist to the Massachusetts police (Keith Ablow, 1997).

Kathryn Dance: kinesics expert and interrogator with the California Bureau of Investigation (Jeffery Deaver, 2006).

Other Forensic Specialists

Gideon Oliver: Washington State forensic anthropologist (Aaron Elkins, 1982).

Emily Hansen: forensic geologist (Sarah Andrews, 1994).

Eve Duncan: forensic sculptor based near Atlanta, Georgia (Iris Johansen, 1998).

Patrick Kincaid: forensic document examiner (Jeffery Deaver, 1999).

Carol Starkey: L.A. bomb squad veteran (Robert Crais, 2000).

Nick Polchak: forensic entomologist (Tim Downs, 2003).

Dexter Morgan: blood spatter analyst for the Miami police department (Jeff Lindsay, 2004).

Summary

"Members of crime scene recovery units are typically not scientists. They are technicians. They collect hairs, fibers, glass fragments, paint chips, blood, semen, saliva, and other physical evidence. They dust for prints. They shoot pics. When the goodies are tagged and logged, the crime scene unit's involvement is over. No high-tech magic. No heart rush surveillance. No hot lead shootouts. Specialists with advanced degrees do the science. Cops chase the bad guys.

But Tinsel Town has done another tap dance; the public has been conned into believing crime scene techs are scientists and detectives . . ."
—Kathy Reichs' *Monday Mourning* (2004).

In this chapter, we've briefly toured methods for analyzing language, behavior, and human scent. We've also surveyed real and fictional forensic scientist role models. Throughout this book, you've seen that real forensic analyses take time. While this fact may be inconvenient for a 60-minute TV show, a person who writes fiction destined for publication benefits from delayed information; delays create plot twists by forcing your investigator and readers to adopt a new perspective. These delays can be caused by a late discovery of evidence, a deferred examination of the evidence by a backed-up lab, and by the amount of time required to analyze the evidence. If pressed, your evidence expert may offer a faulty preliminary opinion about the evidence, and this can set your investigator along the wrong path as well.

Our perusal of the many methods for analyzing evidence provides a foundation for you to formulate stories that include forensic science. You can find instructive examples of approaches for blending traditional police work with a periodic infusion of forensic analysis discoveries in Jeffery Deaver's Lincoln Rhyme series and Paul Robinson's Detective Chief Inspector Alan Banks stories. It's up to you to decide the degree to which your story reflects bona fide forensic science. Reread the criticism quoted above from Kathy Reichs' *Monday Mourning* (2004). Despite this condemnation of the

Hollywood view of forensic science, the story's forensic anthropologist soon sets off on her own sleuthing adventure, presumably because the local police are busy working on a big project. Technical accuracy need not get in the way of a good story.

I hope that this forensic science survey satisfied your curiosity about the basic techniques that you see on film or read about. If you do plan to enhance your own fiction with forensic science, then I wish you good luck on walking the grid of your imagination.

A Few FAQ from the Course

What's the difference between a forensic psychologist and a forensic psychiatrist?

The basic difference between a psychiatrist and psychologist is that a psychiatrist has earned a medical degree. Traditionally, only the psychiatrist could prescribe drugs. However, states have enacted laws that create prescription privileges for psychologists. Another difference is that judges may have a bias toward a psychiatrist when it comes to court testimony because psychiatrists approach mental disorders from the viewpoint of medicine.

What are some examples of forensic behavior experts on film?

Forensic behavior experts are very popular in mystery movies and TV shows. Movie examples include *Silence of the Lambs* (1991) with FBI Behavioral Science Chief Jack Crawford and his protégé, Clarice M. Starling; *Manhunter* (1986) and *Red Dragon* (2002) with Jack Crawford and serial killer hunter Will Graham; *Kiss the Girls* (1997) and *Along Came a Spider* (2001) with police detective and forensic psychologist Alex Cross; and *Taking Lives* (2004) with FBI profiler Illeana Scott. Examples from TV shows include forensic psychologist Eddie "Fitz" Fitzgerald in *Cracker* (1993–1996), clinical psychologist and profiler Tony Hill in *Wire in the Blood* (2002 2003), psychologists Elizabeth Olivet and Emil Skoda in *Law & Order* (1990–2010), profiler Frank Black in *Millennium* (1996–1999), forensic psychiatrist George Huang in *Law & Order: Special Victims Unit* (1999–?), criminal psychology-savvy Detective Robert Goren in *Law & Order: Criminal Intent* (2001–2011), forensic psychologist Samantha Waters and profiler Rachel Burke in *Profiler* (1996–2000), forensic psychiatrist Jane Halifax in *Halifax, f.p.* (1994–2002), criminal profiler Helen Clyde in the *Inspector Lynley Mysteries* (2001–2007), profiler Grace Foley in *Waking the Dead* (2000–2011), human lie detector psychologist Cal Lightman in *Lie to Me* (2009–2011), the profiling team of *Criminal Minds* (2005–?), and human behavior expert Patrick Jane in *The Mentalist* (2008–?).

Suggested Resources

General References on Forensic Science and Crime Scene Investigation

Dutelle, Aric W. *An Introduction to Crime Scene Investigation* (2011).

Eliopulos, Louis, N. *Death Investigator's Handbook, Volumes 1-3* (2003).

Fisher, Barry A.J., William J. Tilstone, and Catherine Woytowicz. *Introduction to Criminalistics: The Foundation of Forensic Science* (2009).

Geberth, Vernon J. *Practical Homicide Investigation: Tactics, Procedures, and Forensic Techniques* (2006).

Horswell, John (ed.). *The Practice of Crime Scene Investigation* (2004).

Houck, Max M. and Jay A. Siegel. *Fundamentals of Forensic Science, Second Edition* (2010).

Newburn, Tim, Tom Williamson, and Alan Wright (eds.). *Handbook of Criminal Investigation* (2007).

Saferstein, Richard. *Criminalistics: An Introduction to Forensic Science, Tenth Edition* (2010).

Thorwald, Jürgen. *Crime and Science* (1967).

Wecht, Cyril H. *Crime Scene Investigation* (2004).

White, P.C. (ed.). *Crime Scene to Court: The Essentials of Forensic Science, Third Edition* (2010).

Wilson, Colin. *Written in Blood: A History of Forensic Detection* (2003).

Worrall, John L. and Craig Hemmens. *Criminal Evidence: An Introduction* (2005).

The FBI's *Handbook of Forensic Services* (www.fbi.gov) offers information about searching the crime scene, collecting evidence, and crime scene safety.

The U.S. Department of Justice and the National Institute of Justice published their guidance for processing a crime scene in *Crime Scene Investigation: A Guide for Law Enforcement* (www.nij.gov).

Three excellent resources for details about forensic science are *Evidence Technology Magazine* (evidencemagazine.com), *Forensic Science Magazine* (www.forensicmag.com), and the discontinued, but archived, *Forensic Science Communications* (www.fbi.gov).

How can you depict the best way to outfit your fictional crime scene team? Try browsing *Evident® Crime Scene Products* (www.evidentcrimescene.com), *Arrowhead Forensics* (www.crime-scene.com), or Crime Scene's CSI Shop (www.crimescene.com) websites.

The *Forensics.ca* website offers forensic science-related news—grist for the mystery mill.

Zeno's Forensic Site (forensic.to/forensic.html) is a one-stop shop for links on many aspects of forensic science.

In the June/July 2010 issue of *Forensic Magazine* (www.forensicmag.com), Jacob Dabrowski explains the benefits of documenting a crime scene with a high definition laser in "High Definition Laser Scanning Takes Forensic Geosciences to a New Level."

Blood Analysis

Bevel, Tom and Ross M. Gardner. *Bloodstain Pattern Analysis: With an Introduction to Crime Scene Reconstruction, Third Edition* (2008).

James, Stuart H. and William G. Eckert. *Interpretation of Bloodstain Evidence at Crime Scenes, Second Edition* (1998).

James, Stuart H., Paul E. Kish, and T. Paulette Sutton. *Principles of Bloodstain Pattern Analysis: Theory and Practice* (2005).

Wonder, Anita Y. *Bloodstain Pattern Evidence: Objective Approaches and Case Applications* (2007).

The Brazoria County Sheriff's Department Criminal Identification Division offers an overview on blood spatter interpretation (www.brazoria-county.com/sheriff/id/index.htm).

On his website, *J. Slemko Forensic Consulting* (www.bloodspatter.com), Mr. Slemko provides an illustrated tutorial on bloodstain pattern analysis.

DNA Analysis

Butler, John. *Forensic DNA Typing: Biology, Technology, and Genetics Behind STR Markers, Second Edition* (2005).

Butler, John. *Fundamentals of Forensic DNA Typing* (2010).

Rudin, Norah and Keith Inman. *An Introduction to Forensic DNA Analysis, Second Edition* (2002).

The National Academies Press provides an online copy of its 1996 book, *The Evaluation of Forensic DNA Evidence* (books.nap.edu), which includes an overview on DNA typing and the use of DNA evidence.

John M. Butler's *Short Tandem Repeat DNA* website (www.cstl.nist.gov/biotech/strbase) offers an overview and details on STR analysis.

The website of the Denver District Attorney's Office (www.denverda.org) provides information about legal decisions concerning various forms of forensic DNA analysis.

Issue 249 of the *National Institute of Justice Journal* includes the feature "DNA Evidence: What Law Enforcement Officers Should Know," which offers tips on collecting evidence for DNA analysis (www.nij.gov/nij/journals/welcome.htm).

Trace Evidence

Caddy, Brian (ed.). *Forensic Examination of Glass & Paint: Analysis & Interpretation* (2001).

Curran, James M., Tacha Natalie Hicks, and John S. Buckleton. *Forensic Interpretation of Glass Evidence* (2000).

Houck, Max (ed.). *Mute Witnesses: When Trace Evidence Makes the Case* (2001).

Houck, Max (ed.). *Trace Evidence Analysis: More Cases in Mute Witnesses* (2004).

You can find facts about fibers on the American Fiber Manufacturers Association, Inc.'s *Fibersource* website (www.fibersource.com).

The November-December 2010 issue of *Evidence Technology Magazine* (www.evidencemagazine.com) includes "Forensic Interpretation of Glass Fragments" by Mukesh Sharma, Shailendra Jha and V.N. Mathur.

Arson, Explosives, and Poisons

DeHaan, John D. and David J. Icove. *Kirk's Fire Investigation, Seventh Edition* (2012).

Emsley, John. *Elements of Murder: A History of Poison* (2005).

Icove, David J. and John D. DeHaan. *Forensic Fire Scene Reconstruction, Second Edition* (2008).

Macinnis, Peter. *Poisons: From Hemlock to Botox to the Killer Bean Calabar* (2011).

Marshall, Maurice and Jimmie Oxley. *Aspects of Explosives Detection* (2009).

Stevens, Serita D. *Deadly Doses: A Writer's Guide to Poisons* (1990).

Thurman, James T. *Practical Bomb Scene Investigation, Second Edition* (2011).

Trestrail, III, John H. *Criminal Poisoning, Second Edition* (2007).

The *InterFire Online* website (www.interfire.org) offers many resources about arson investigation, from preliminary inspection of a fire scene to lab analysis.

On the *T.C. Forensic* website (www.tcforensic.com.au), you'll find articles on arson investigation, such as "The Basics of Fire Investigation" and "The Science and 'Art' of Fire Investigation."

The National Institute of Justice publication, *Fire and Arson Scene Evidence: A Guide for Public Safety Personnel*, describes basic procedures for fire scene documentation and evidence collection (www.nij.gov/pubs-sum/181584.htm).

The March-April 2012 issue of *Evidence Technology Magazine* features two relevant articles: "An Introduction to Fire-Related Death Investigation" by Matthew M. Lunn and "Collecting Trace Evidence Explosive Residues at Post-Blast Scenes" by Max M. Houck.

In *A Guide for Explosion and Bombing Scene Investigation* (www.nij.gov/pubs-sum/181869.htm), the National Institute of Justice describes procedures for the identification, collection, and preservation of evidence at an explosion scene.

In their 1998 book, *Black and Smokeless Powders*, the National Academies Press describes techniques for finding bombs and those who make the bombs (books.nap.edu). The Academies' *Existing and Potential Standoff Explosives Detection Techniques* (2004) describes chemical characteristics of bombs and methods of detecting explosives.

In Court TV's Crime Library article "Forensic Toxicology," Katherine Ramsland offers historical and current perspectives about forensic toxicology (www.crimelibrary.com).

Firearms

Di Maio, Vincent J.M. *Gunshot Wounds: Practical Aspects of Firearms, Ballistics, and Forensic Techniques, Second Edition* (1999).

Heard, Brian J. *Handbook of Firearms and Ballistics: Examining and Interpreting Forensic Evidence, Second Edition* (2008).

Schwoeble, A.J. and David Exline. *Current Methods in Forensic Gunshot Residue Analysis* (2000).

Warlow, Tom. *Firearms, the Law and Forensic Ballistics, Third Edition* (2012).

The *Firearms Id.com* website offers photos and illustrations of firearms and ammunition, case descriptions, articles on firearm identification, and the virtual comparison microscope (www.firearmsid.com).

On the *Forensic Medicine for Medical Students* website (www.forensicmed. co.uk) you'll find a tutorial on firearms, firearms identification, and descriptions of firearm injuries. (Hint: Look for the gun icon.).

The Bureau of Alcohol, Tobacco, Firearms, and Explosives provides basic information on the National Integrated Ballistic Information Network on its NIBIN website (www.nibin.gov).

In the December 2010/January 2011 issue of *Forensic Magazine* (www. forensicmag.com), Mike Barrett makes his case for 3D forensic ballistics systems. Dale Garrison's "Recent Advances in Forensic Ballistics" in the March-April 2011 issue of *Evidence Technology Magazine* (www.evidencemagazine.com) also explores the advantages of the technology.

Fingerprint Analysis

Ashbaugh, David R. *Quantitative-Qualitative Friction Ridge Analysis: An Introduction to Basic and Advanced Ridgeology* (1999).

Beavan, Colin. *Fingerprints: The Origins of Crime Detection and the Murder Case That Launched Forensic Science* (2001).

Cole, Simon. *Suspect Identities: A History of Fingerprinting and Criminal Identification* (2002).

Jones, Gary W. *Introduction to Fingerprint Comparison* (2000).

Lee, Henry C. and R. E. Gaensslen. *Advances in Fingerprint Technology, Second Edition* (2001).

On its website, the Chesapeake Bay Division of the International Association for Identification (www.chdiai.org) offers a tutorial on the ACE-V method and guidelines for selecting latent fingerprint processing techniques.

The FBI provides background information on the Integrated Automated Fingerprint Identification System, including services provided (www.fbi. gov).

The *Latent Print Examination* website (onin.com/fp) offers a wealth of information about fingerprint evidence, including the latest *Daubert* court challenges.

The *Ridges and Furrows* website (www.ridgesandfurrows.homestead. com/index.html) provides information on the biological basis of fingerprints, methods for developing friction ridge impressions, and an overview of the ACE-V process.

The National Institute of Justice claims that its publication, *The Fingerprint Sourcebook* (2011), "aims to be the definitive resource on the science of fingerprint identification" (www.nij.gov/pubs-sum/225320.htm).

The May-June 2008 issue of *Evidence Technology Magazine* (www.evidencemagazine.com) includes John Louis Larsen's "Prints from Skin," which details methods for obtaining latent impressions from a corpse.

Other Impression Evidence

Bodziak, William J. *Footwear Impression Evidence: Detection, Recovery and Examination, Second Edition* (2000).

Bodziak, William J. *Tire Tread and Tire Track Evidence: Recovery and Forensic Examination* (2008).

Bowers, C. Michael. *Forensic Dental Evidence: An Investigator's Handbook* (2004).

Hilderbrand, Dwane S. *Footwear, The Missed Evidence, Second Edition* (2007).

Johansen, Raymond J. and C.M. Bowers. *Digital Analysis of Bite Mark Evidence* (2000).

McDonald, Peter. *Tire Imprint Evidence* (1992).

The website of the American Board of Forensic Odontology (www.abfo. org) provides definitions and standards for bitemark analysis.

Forensic Dentistry Online (www.forensicdentistryonline.org) offers information on scientific and legal aspects of bite mark analysis.

Foster and Freeman's website (www.fosterfreeman.com) provides background information and illustrations on the shoeprint image capture and retrieval system.

Professor Doug Linder's *Famous Trials* website (law2.umkc.edu/faculty/projects/ftrials/ftrials.htm) includes information on the Bruno Hauptmann trial, such as photos of the homemade ladder and Arthur Koehler's testimony on toolmarks.

Forensic scientists are not the only professionals who analyze tracks. On the *Beartracker's Animal Tracks Den* website (www.bear-tracker.com), Kim A. Cabrera offers information about clues that trackers use to trace humans and animals.

Issue 258 of the *National Institute of Justice Journal* includes the feature "Forensic Databases: Paint, Shoe Prints, and Beyond" (www.nij.gov/nij/journals/welcome.htm).

The November-December 2010 issue of *Evidence Technology Magazine* (www.evidencemagazine.com) includes Tom Adair's "Footwear Impression Evidence."

Computer Forensics and Forensic Accounting

Brown, Christopher L. T. *Computer Evidence: Collection & Preservation, Second Edition* (2010).

Casey, Eoghan (ed.). *Digital Evidence and Computer Crime, Third Edition* (2010).

Marcella Jr., Albert and Robert S. Greenfield (eds.). *Cyber Forensics: A Field Manual for Collecting, Examining, and Preserving Evidence of Computer Crimes, Second Edition* (2008).

Silverstone, Howard and Michael Sheetz. *Forensic Accounting and Fraud Investigation for Non-Experts, Second Edition* (2007).

Taparia, Jay. *Understanding Financial Statements: A Journalist's Guide* (2003).

InvestorWords.com provides glossaries on various financial topics. You might recall a quote from Sarah Graves' *The Dead Cat Bounce*. At *InvestorWords.com*, you'll learn that a "dead cat bounce" is a "quick, moderate rise in the price of a stock following a precipitous decline."

The National Institute of Justice's views on the best way to seize electronic evidence can be found in *Electronic Crime Scene Investigation: A Guide for First Responders, Second Edition* (www.nij.gov/pubs-sum/219941.htm).

Forensic accountant Alan Zysman's article, "Forensic Accounting Demystified," (www.forensicaccounting.com) offers an overview of his area of expertise.

The U.S. Department of Justice provides information on legal aspects of cybercrime on its *Cybercrime.gov* website, as well as a copy of the agency's manual, *Searching and Seizing Computers and Obtaining Electronic Evidence in Criminal Investigations.*

A project of the FBI and the National White Collar Crime Center, the *Internet Crime Complaint Center* (www.ic3.gov) website offers tips on ways to avoid Internet auction fraud, credit card fraud, investment fraud, business fraud, and Nigerian letter scams.

Do you want to know more about "419" fraud, telemarketing fraud, letter of credit fraud, or Ponzi schemes? The FBI's *Be Crime Smart* website (www.fbi.gov/scams-safety) is a good place to start.

The *DFI News* website (www.dfinews.com) provides information about computer forensics, network forensics, analysis of mobile devices, and background on the legal processes that support computer forensic evidence.

The January 2012 issue of *DFI News* includes an article on the application of the Locard Exchange Principle to computer forensics: "The Digital Forensics Cyber Exchange Principle" by Ken Zatyko and John Bay (www.dfinews.com).

Will your investigators examine mobile communication devices? In the August/September 2009 issue of *Forensic Magazine* (www.forensicmag.com), you'll find Don L. Lewis' "Examining Cellular Phones and Handheld Devices." Douglas Page explores mobile device forensics in the December 2011/January 2012 *Forensic Magazine* article "CSI Cell Phone." In the September-October 2011 *Evidence Technology Magazine* (www.evidencemagazine.com) article "Best Practices in Mobile Phone Investigations," Evan Dixon offers an overview on phone examinations.

Forensic Document Analysis

Brunelle, Richard L. and Kenneth R. Crawford. *Advances in the Forensic Analysis and Dating of Writing Ink* (2003).

Hamilton, Charles. *Great Forgers and Famous Fakes: The Manuscript Forgers of America and How They Duped the Experts* (1996).

Kelly, Jan Seaman and Brian S. Lindblom. *Scientific Examination of Questioned Documents, Second Edition* (2006).

Levinson, Jay. *Questioned Documents: A Lawyer's Handbook* (2000).

Morris, Ron N. *Forensic Handwriting Identification: Fundamental Concepts and Principles* (2000).

Foster and Freeman's website (www.fosterfreeman.com) provides information about their electrostatic imaging system and the video spectral comparator, equipment that your forensic document examiner would want in the lab.

The Georgia Bureau of Investigation offers an illustrated overview of the type of analyses performed by the agency's Questioned Documents Section (dofs.gbi.georgia.gov).

On his *Norwitch Document Laboratory* website (www.questioneddocuments.com), document examiner F. Harley Norwitch provides many overviews on topics relating to his craft, including handwriting theory, signatures, forgery, indented writing retrieval, photocopier and typewriter examinations, and paper examinations. You'll also find questioned document brain teasers that test your skill as an examiner.

Emily J. Will offers information on the theory of handwriting identification, document examination applications, cases, and a tour of her forensic document examination laboratory on the *Emily J. Will–Forensic Document Examiner* website (qdewill.com).

The Forensic Document Examination Services, Inc. website (www.fde-services.com) provides overviews on handwriting identification, altered documents, indented writing and office equipment impressions, hints about handwriting specimens, ink analysis, and methods for dating documents.

On its website (www.envisagesystems.co.uk), Envisage Systems describes its Ribbon Analysis Workstation for examining typewriter ribbons. Even the company acknowledges the "surprising continuing widespread use of single-strike carbon typewriter ribbons."

The May-June 2010 issue of *Evidence Technology Magazine* (www.evidencemagazine.com) includes E'lyn Bryan's "Questioned Document Examination: An Overview of the Basic Techniques and Technology."

Corpse Examinations

Baden, Michael and Marion Roach. *Dead Reckoning: The New Science of Catching Killers* (2002).

Bass, William H. and Jon Jefferson. *Death's Acre* (2003).

Byrd, Jason H. and James L. Castner (eds.). *Forensic Entomology: The Utility of Arthropods in Legal Investigations* (2000).

Dix, Jay and Robert Calaluce. *Guide to Forensic Pathology* (1998).

Erzinçlioğlu, Zakaria. *Maggots, Murder, and Men: Memories and Reflections of a Forensic Entomologist* (2002).

Goff, M. Lee. *A Fly for the Prosecution: How Insect Evidence Helps Solve Crimes* (2001).

Greenberg, Bernard and John Charles Kunich. *Entomology and the Law: Flies as Forensic Indicators* (2002).

Iserson, Kenneth V. *Death to Dust: What Happens to Dead Bodies?* (2001).

Rebmann, Andrew and Edward David. *Cadaver Dog Handbook: Forensic Training and Tactics for the Recovery of Human Remains* (2000).

Sachs, Jessica Snyder. *Corpse: Nature, Forensics, and the Struggle to Pinpoint Time of Death* (2002).

Taylor, Karen T. *Forensic Art and Illustration* (2000).

In his article, "The Routine Autopsy," Dr. Edward O. Uthman provides a narrative account of an autopsy for the benefit of fiction writers (web2.airmail.net/uthman/Autop.html).

In "Autopsy," Dr. Ed Friedlander offers his description of the medical examination process (www.pathguy.com/autopsy.htm).

The *Forensic Art* website (www.forensicartist.com) provides an overview on the field of forensic art, including its history and services provided by forensic artists.

On his *Forensic Entomology* website (www.forensicentomology.com), Dr. J. H. Byrd offers an illustrated guide to forensically important insects.

Will handheld odor-sniffing technology replace sniffer dogs? Douglas Page's "LABRADOR: New Alpha Dog in Human Remains Detection?" in the June/July 2010 issue of *Forensic Magazine* (www.forensicmag.com) describes a new device that detects odors emanating from decaying, buried human remains.

The October-November 2011 issue of *Forensic Magazine* (www.forensicmag.com) includes James S. Mellett's article "Clandestine Graves: Geophysical Methods Used in Their Discovery and Subsequent Exposure," which provides an overview on noninvasive techniques for locating hidden graves.

In the February-March 2012 issue of *Forensic Magazine* (www.forensicmag.com), Ernie Allen's "Computerized Skull Reconstructions" explains the advantages of computed tomography scans and computerized modeling for facial reconstructions.

Analyzing Behavior, Language, and Human Scent

Bartol, Curt and Anne M. Bartol. *Introduction to Forensic Psychology: Research and Application, Third Edition* (2012).

Gerritsen, Resi and Ruud Haak. *K9 Professional Tracking* (2001).

Kaldenbach, Jan. *Human Scent Detection and Identification: K9 Scent Detection* (1998).

Keppel, Robert D. and William J. Birnes. *The Psychology of Serial Killer Investigations: The Grisly Business Unit* (2003).

McCrary, Gregg O. *The Unknown Darkness: Profiling the Predators Among Us* (2003).

McMenamin, Gerald R. *Forensic Linguistics: Advances in Forensic Stylistics* (2002).

Petherick, Wayne. *Criminal Profile: Into the Mind of the Killer* (2005).

Ramsland, Katherine. *The Forensic Psychology of Criminal Minds* (2010).

Rose, Philip. *Forensic Speaker Identification* (2002).

Schoon, Adee and Ruud Haack. *K9 Suspect Discrimination: Training and Practicing Scent Identification Line-Ups* (2003).

Syrotuck, William G. *Scent and the Scenting Dog* (2000).

Turvey, Brent E. (ed.). *Criminal Profiling: An Introduction to Behavioral Evidence Analysis, Fourth Edition* (2012).

Waters, Stan B. *Principles of Kinesic Interview and Interrogation* (2002).

The August-September 2011 issue of *Forensic Magazine* (www.forensic-mag.com) includes Douglas Page's "The Truth about Deception," which explores behavioral identification techniques for detecting lies.